IMAGES
of America

AROUND MARCELLUS

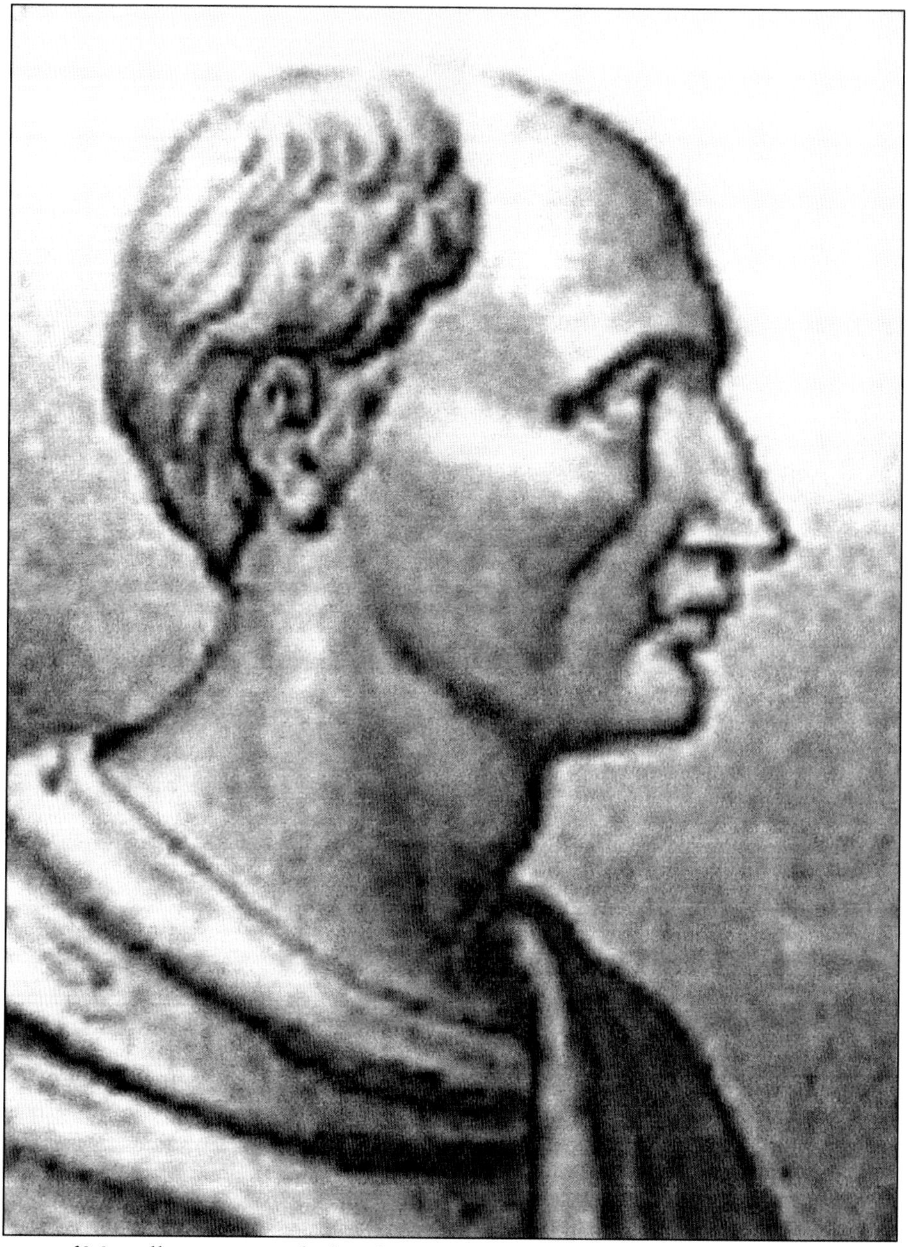

The town of Marcellus was named after the Roman general Marcus Claudius Marcellus (around 268–208 BC). He was consul five times, and in his first consulship he fought against the Insubrian Gauls and killed their king in single combat. In his third consulship he was a colleague of Fabius Maximus, and he went into South Italy and Sicily to begin the Second Punic War. He besieged Syracuse and took the city, in spite of the ingenious defenses made by Archimedes. He died as he lived, being ambushed by his enemies. He fell in a skirmish with Hannibal's men near Venusia. His legacy has lived on, embellished at times, but even so, he will always be known as "the Sword of Rome."

On the cover: Please see page 34. (Courtesy of Mercellus Historical Society.)

IMAGES
of America

AROUND MARCELLUS

Leslie Church Kraus

ARCADIA
PUBLISHING

ISBN 978-0-7365-4546-2

Published by Arcadia Publishing
Charleston, South Carolina

Printed in the United States of America

Library of Congress Catalog Card Number: 2006924315

For all general information contact Arcadia Publishing at:
Telephone 843-853-2070
Fax 843-853-0044
E-mail sales@arcadiapublishing.com
For customer service and orders:
Toll-Free 1-888-313-2665

Visit us on the Internet at www.arcadiapublishing.com

To the wonderful people of Marcellus, may you find as much joy in reading this book as I did in putting it together.

Contents

ACKNOWLEDGMENTS

I want to thank the Marcellus Historical Society for supplying the photographs used in this book. Since its beginning in 1960, the Marcellus Historical Society has procured, protected, and shared a wealth of pictures, belongings, and priceless artifacts of our wonderful history. The society's dedication to preserving the history of Marcellus is endless, and I would like to thank all the volunteers who have made this book become possible. Through their efforts and the countless hours that they have carefully cataloged each and every artifact, I was able to choose from hundreds of well-documented photographs. I especially want to thank Hollis Abbott, treasurer of the Marcellus Historical Society, for all his time and effort scanning the original photographs for me. I also wish to thank John Curtin for his help and his expansive knowledge of Marcellus's history. Lastly I want to thank my husband, David, for his continued support and his unwavering belief in me.

INTRODUCTION

In September 1776, the Continental Congress of the United States passed legislation that each state should have its own militia and in return, those that enlisted would be paid with parcels of land. In July 1782, the New York State legislature set apart an area of land that would be used for these land grants.

When the boundaries for Marcellus were first laid out in 1794, as township number nine of the Military Tract, it comprised all of Onondaga County south of the Seneca River, west of Onondaga Lake and Creek, north of the southern end of Otisco Lake, and parts of what are now Cayuga and Cortland Counties. The original townships of this first Onondaga County were plotted out by the surveyor-general Simeon DeWitt, but the names of these townships were attributed to assistant secretary of state Robert Harper. Harper, a former classics teacher, gave the military township number nine the name Marcellus after the Roman general Marcus Claudius Marcellus. By 1840, the creation of Camillus, a part of Onondaga, Otisco, Spafford, Skaneateles, and part of Sempronius in Cayuga County, left Marcellus with about one-tenth of its original acreage. On June 4, 1853, an election was held in the home of John Carpenter, and by a 41 to 10 margin, the village of Marcellus was officially incorporated.

The landscape of the village, and its surrounding township, is of rolling hills and deep valleys. Cutting through the valley is Nine Mile Creek. The creek flows from its southern origin, Otisco Lake, in a northern direction to its outlet, Onondaga Lake. With its varied elevations, Nine Mile Creek hosts numerous waterfalls, which provided the generation of power to the early settlers. The soil was a mixture of rich top soil (from the decomposition of the shale that is wide spread throughout the area) and clay, making it perfect for the farmers to grow their crops.

Most of the early settlers of Marcellus were from the New England area. They came from Massachusetts, Connecticut, Vermont, and Rhode Island. Among the first settlers within the Marcellus Township were William Cobb, Joab and Rufus Lawrence, Cyrus Holcomb, Samuel Tyler, John Burtis, and the Cody and Bowen families. That next year the first permanent village settlers arrived. They were the Honorable Dan Bradley and Deacon Samuel Rice along with their wives, sisters Hannah Beach Rice and Eunice Beach Bradley. In the winter of 1795–1796, Dan and Samuel opened up the first mill in Marcellus. It was called the Rice-Bradley Sawmill. Their sawmill was located at the base of East Hill, south of Main Street on the west side of Nine Mile Creek. That same winter, Dr. Elnathan Beach (brother to Hannah Beach Rice and Eunice Beach Bradley) settled in the village and built the first frame house, where he sold dry goods, groceries, and medicines. Dr. Beach, a practicing physician, was born and educated in Connecticut. He was a very prominent citizen and public figure. In 1799, he became the village's first postmaster and was appointed sheriff of Onondaga County and held these positions until his death in 1801, at the age of 40. In 1800, Marcellus had its very own grinding mill built by Richard May and his father-in-law Thomas Sayles. Prior to this mill being built, settlers had to travel to either Manlius or as far as Seneca Falls to have their crops processed. A trip such as this would usually take two or three days to travel, taking them away from their home and chores that needed to be done. About this time, work was beginning on the building of Seneca Turnpike. The turnpike, once known as the Great Indian Trail, was laid out with one of the steepest grades along its entire route entering the village of Marcellus from the east. It proceeded through the village, straight up what is now Slocombe Avenue, and over the route now known as Old Seneca Turnpike. In 1800, the route was changed to reflect its present location on its way west from the village. This enabled travelers a more gradual route going east to west. This turnpike was constantly traveled adding to the merchant's coffers as well as the village's population, by those who chose to stay. The story that goes along with the building of Seneca Turnpike is that at first the surveyors were trying to decide whether or not to put the turnpike through Camillus or Marcellus. When they went to Camillus to survey the area, the townspeople practically ignored them. Feeling slighted, the surveyors then went to Marcellus where they were greeted warmly and were offered dinner and hospitality. It was because of their warm welcome that Marcellus was gifted with the building of the turnpike through its village.

Nine Mile Creek has always been utilized for its natural power source and Marcellus saw the building of numerous mills along its banks. In 1812, Robert and Thomas Dyer built the woolen mill (later known to be the site of the Upper Crown Mill) and Jeptha Cossit built a powder mill. This powder mill was rumored to have supplied gun powder to the soldiers in the War of 1812. In 1817, a combined bark mill, tannery, and shoe shop was then built. By 1823, there were 19 mills and one furnace operating along the creek. By 1832, the first paper manufacturing plant was started and soon, many others would follow. By 1885, the Crown Mills Company was prospering as woolen manufacturers at both their upper and lower Crown Mill sites. The two mills constituted much of the employment for the people of Marcellus. The control of the Crown Mills Company went through a number of proprietors until it eventually passed into the hands of Edward Moir and remained in the Moir family until the mills closed. Edward Moir, born in Galashiels, Scotland, in 1846, emigrated to Canada in 1856, received woolen industry experience there, and purchased and enlarged the Auburn Mills in Ontario. He was recognized as being an authority in the woolen industry, which brought him to the attention of S. W. Barker, who brought Moir to Marcellus to replace Robert Waugh as superintendent. Moir also was elected village president in 1892 to 1893 and from 1905 to 1908.

During the stagecoach days, the village was the center of life and the scene of constant activity. Two coaches or more were run each way on the turnpike every day. The fare was 5¢ per mile and the stages also carried the mail to post offices on their routes. Marcellus was also fortunate to have trains and trolleys pass through its boundaries to provide transportation for both its inhabitants and for the goods they produced. The trains also transported the U.S. mail, which made the connection with the far-reaching communities more efficient. The trolley was a connection from Syracuse to Auburn and the train from Marcellus Falls to Otisco.

Marcellus was home to many important people. Dr. Dan Beach Bradley was one such person. Among many others were Nathan Kelsey Hall; Obil Fellows, a Revolutionary War soldier who was held as a prisoner of war by the English; English-born Dr. Lake Tefft, a practicing physician who served as president of the village in 1855 and who built North Home on North Street; Ralph C. Roe, a brilliant electrical engineer and the recipient of a doctor of engineering degree from Stevens Institute of Technology, who was employed to develop the first electric power plant in Marcellus; Erminnie Platt Smith; Calvin Bingham Jr., who grew the area's first primate apple; the Honorable Reuben Humphrey, an Onondaga County court judge and state senator; Thomas Kennedy, a mayor of Syracuse who was also that city's first commissioner of finance; Patrick Kelly, who served as Marcellus town supervisor and a county assemblyman; Frank Knapp; Robert E. Baker; Sidney Slocombe; and Edmund Reed.

A township is only as good as its natural resources and the people who inhabit the area, and fortunately Marcellus has been gifted with both. It has always been a close-knit community, in a picturesque setting, but for those of us who have lived in Marcellus and have raised our families here, we know it simply as "a great place to live."

—Leslie Church Kraus
Genealogist and Historian

One

Mills, Businesses, and Stores

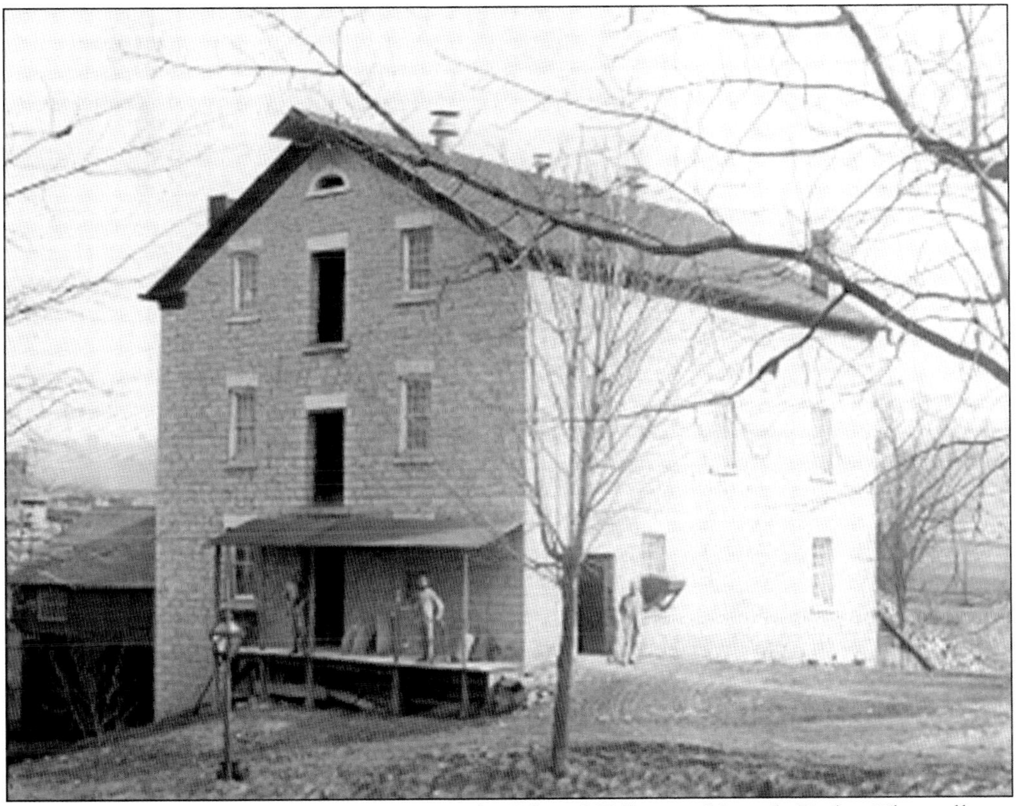

The Old Stone Mill was built in 1827–1828 by Edward Talbot and Joseph Taylor. The mill was used for grinding flour and feed. This mill, located on East Main Street, burned to the ground in 1888.

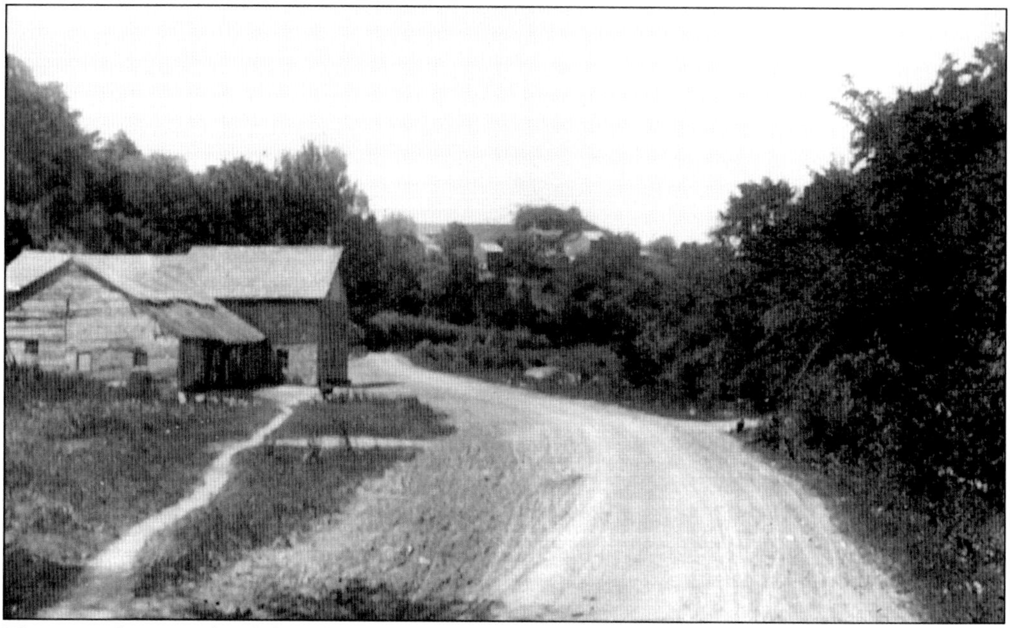

This is a photograph of the Plaster Mill in Marcellus Falls, taken in 1909, which was owned by Warren S. Walker. Walker built a dam and this plaster mill in 1856, procuring his gypsum mainly from Nose Hill and making from 10 to 15 tons of plaster a day.

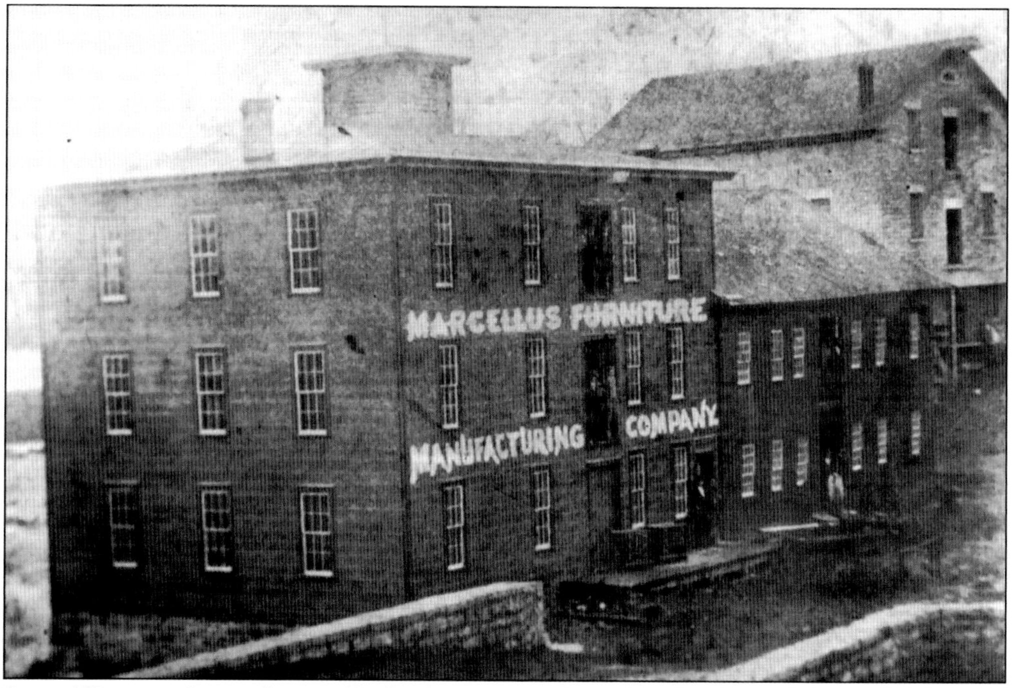

Samuel Hooper, who was born in England, came to Marcellus in 1848 and took over the furniture and undertaking business from N. C. Hoyt in about 1880. Hooper opened the Marcellus Furniture Manufacturing Company in partnership with William Gallup. The building burned down in the late 1890s. It is the present site of the McClurg Building and Marcellus Chocolate Pizza Company.

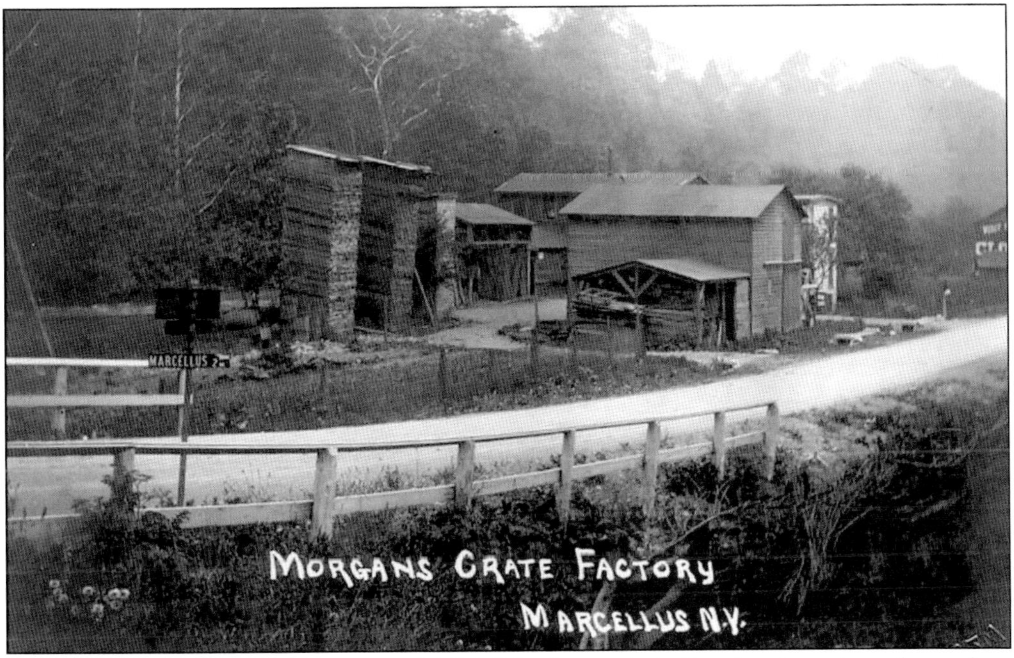

This is Morgan's Crate Factory around 1890. The factory is believed to have been located on Slate Hill Road and Seal Road. The factory was owned by Edward Morgan, who died in 1907.

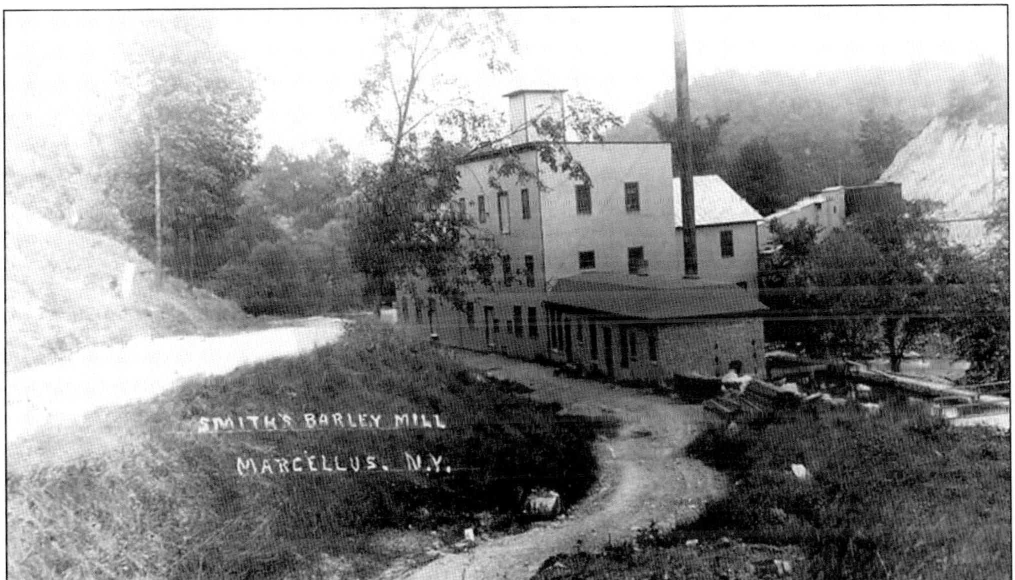

Allen V. Smith ran the Smith Barley Mill, and it was a great source of local employment until it moved to Wisconsin in 1959. The mill was later demolished to make way for Gorge Road when it was built in the 1960s.

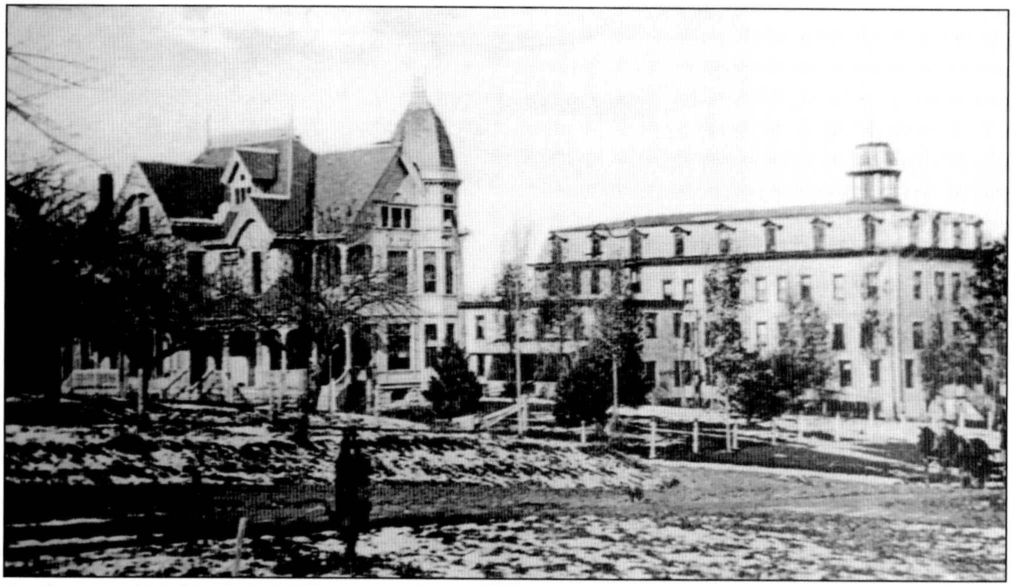

At the age of 21, Frank B. Mills acquired a small hand printing press and, in 1887, printed his first seed catalog. He set all the type himself, and mailed out 3,000 copies, securing about 118 customers. By 1895, he had over 400,000 customers from every part of the globe. He built a four-story building and named the facility the Rose Hill Seed House. The seed company closed its doors in 1953. This photograph shows the Mills family home on the left and the seed mill on the right.

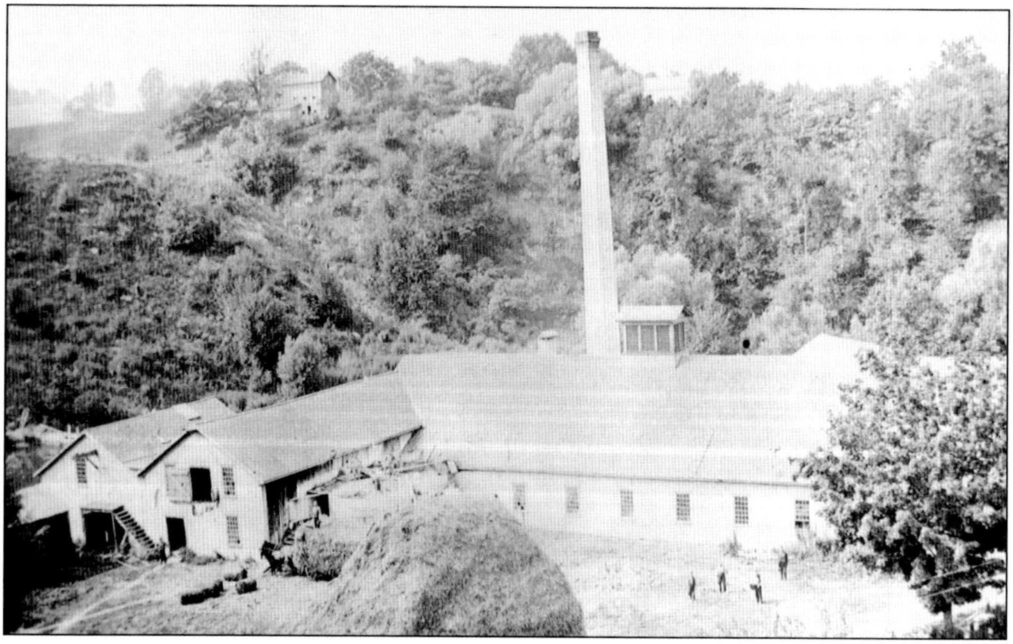

Lawless Paper Mill was located in Marcellus Falls. It primarily manufactured straw paper. This mill was also known as the Phoenix Mill because it burned down several times over the years but was always rebuilt. Another successful paper mill, located nearby, was the Sherman and Son Paper Mill, run by brothers Isaac and L. D. Sherman. The Shermans bought the mill from George Ryan in 1865. It was located on the former site of Jeptha Cossit's Powder Mill, which is said to have supplied gunpowder for the armies during the War of 1812.

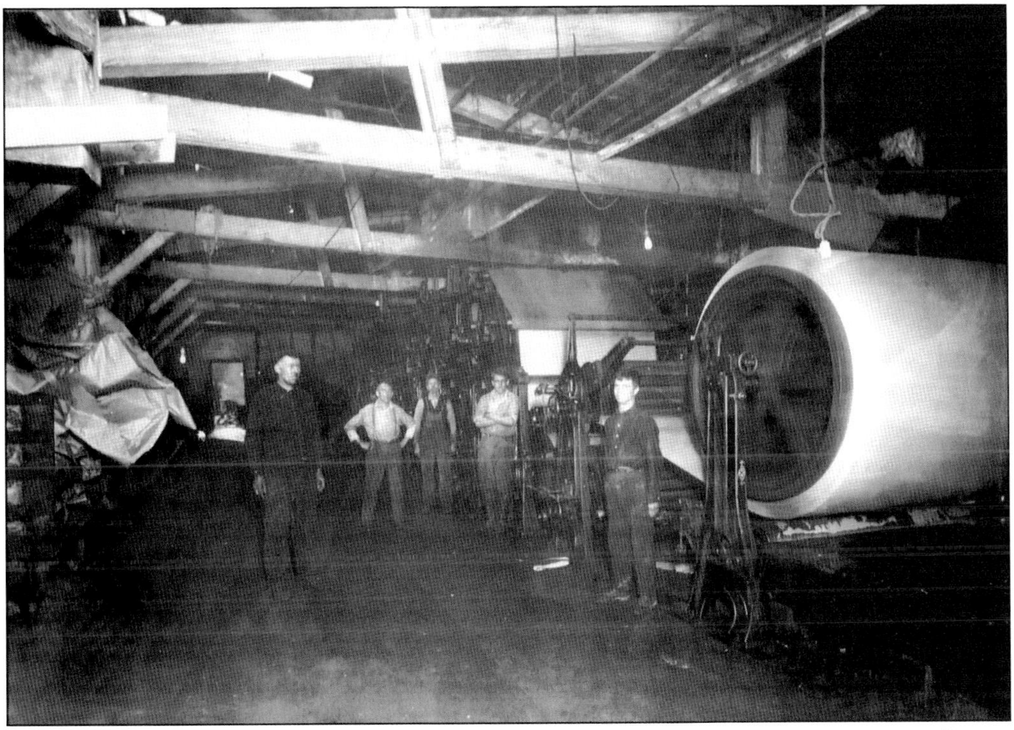

This photograph of the workers of the Martisco Paper Company mill in Marcellus Falls was taken in about 1930.

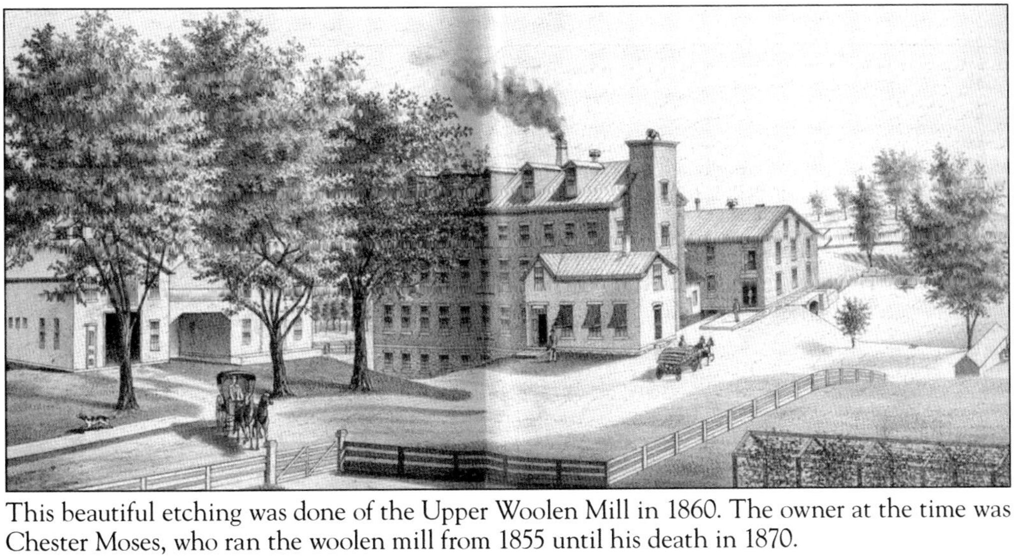

This beautiful etching was done of the Upper Woolen Mill in 1860. The owner at the time was Chester Moses, who ran the woolen mill from 1855 until his death in 1870.

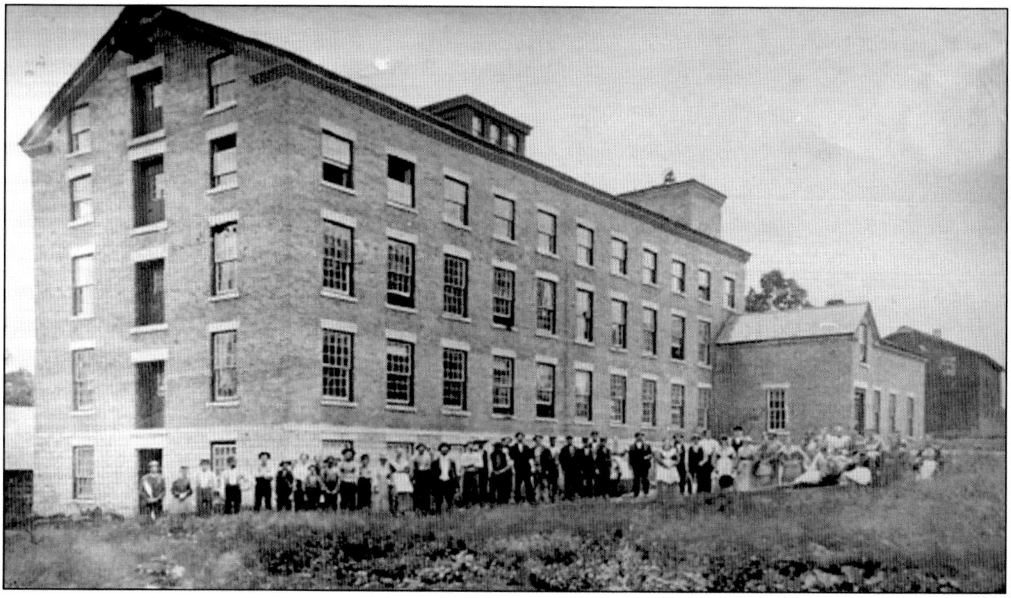

This photograph was taken of the workers standing outside of the Upper Crown Mill, located at the end of Maple Street (formally known as Factory Street). Originally called the Moses Mill, in 1886 it was taken over by a stock company under the name of the Marcellus Woolen Mills. Lucius Moses, son of the original owner, became president. Three years later, the company consolidated with the Crown Mill Company. In 1896, the upper mill was consuming 500,000 pounds of wool annually and the lower mill 400,000. Unfortunately, with the competition from imported fabrics and development of synthetics, the mills closed in 1955 and 1961 respectively.

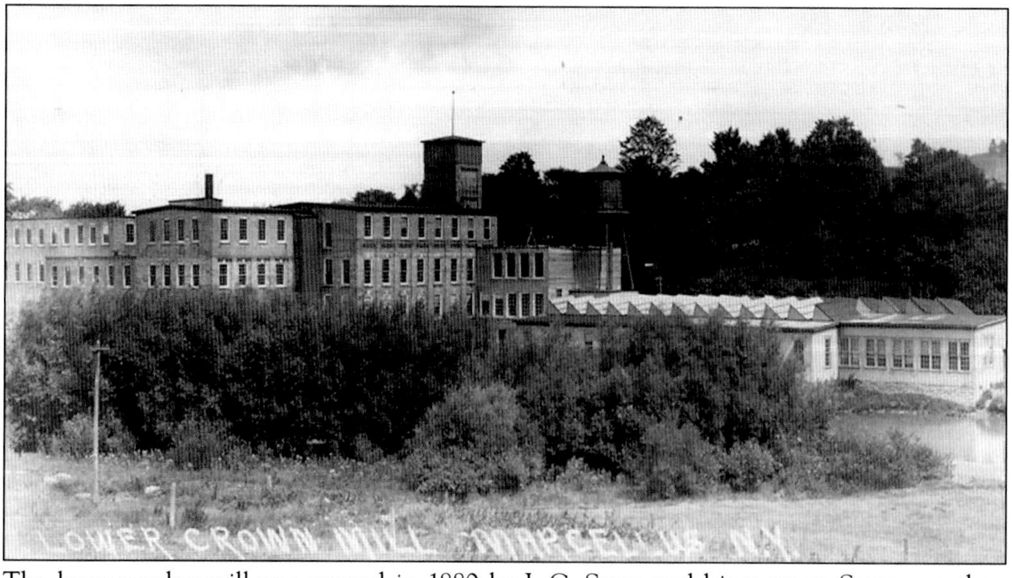

The lower woolen mill was opened in 1880 by J. C. Sayre and his partner. Sayre was then bought out by S. W. Barker and named Robert Waugh as its superintendent. Upon Waugh's death in 1883, Barker sought out Edward Moir, who had made a name for himself in the woolen mill business in Canada. Moir began working for the Crown Mills in January 1884. Under his direction, the mills flourished.

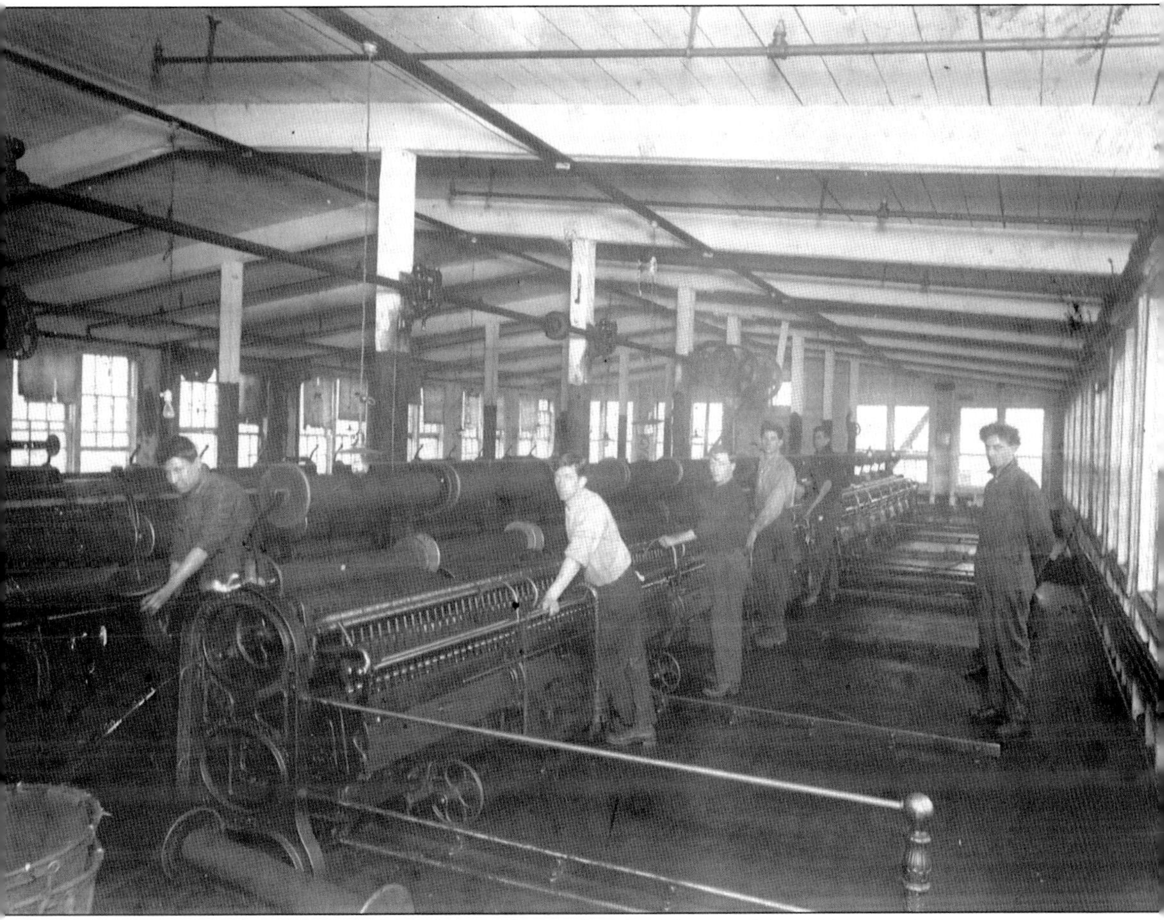

This photograph is of the inside of the woolen mill. In 1935, out of the 1,100 people living in the village, 300 of those residents worked at the mills.

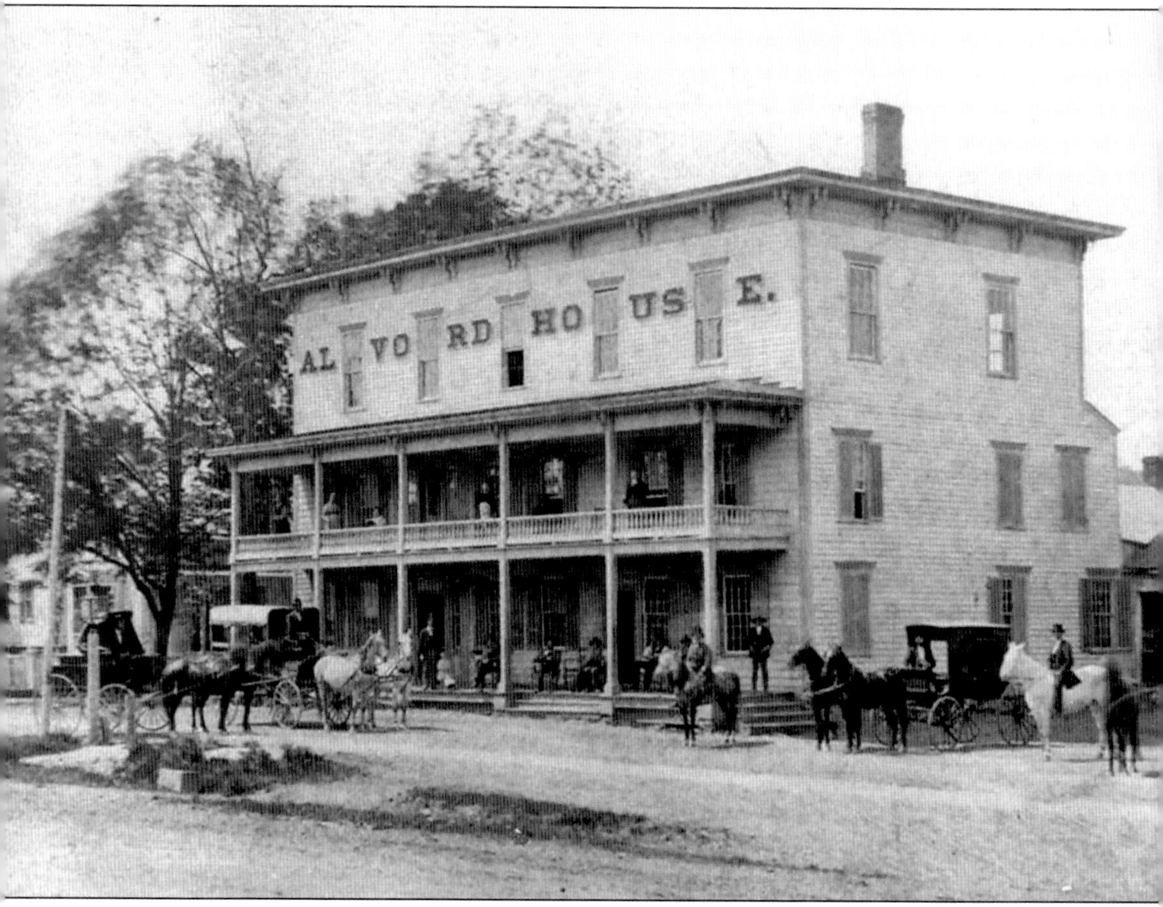

The Alvord House was built around 1815 by Dr. Bildab Beach, brother of the town's first postmaster, Dr. Elnathan Beach. Upon Elnathan's death in 1801, Bildab came and took over his practice. After serving in the War of 1812, Bildab returned to Marcellus and built the tavern. He devoted his time to running the tavern upon his retirement from his medical practice in 1820 until his death in 1856. The Alvord House advertised, "good rooms, kind attention, good board, good livery and omnibus to all trains." It was during this time that the Alvord House added the third-story ballroom. The dance floor was reported to be the best in the county.

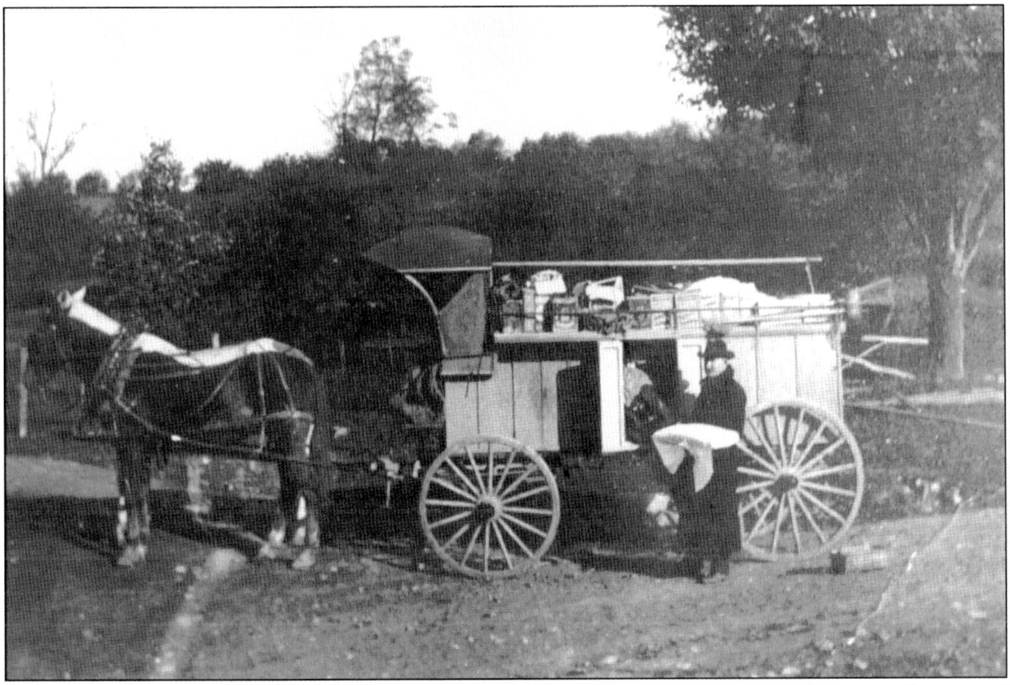

This merchandise wagon belonged to Aaron Waldron. He was known to have anything and everything on board his wagon. It was his version of a mercantile shop on wheels.

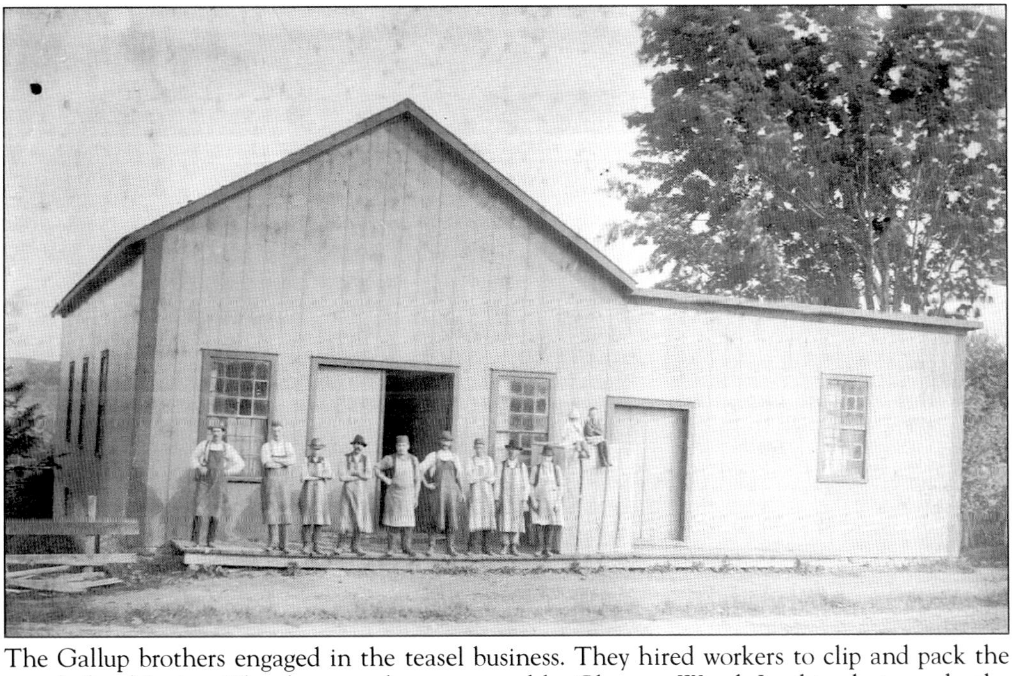

The Gallup brothers engaged in the teasel business. They hired workers to clip and pack the teasels for shipping. The shop was later operated by Clement Wood. In this photograph, the workers from left to right are Martin Dunn, John Keegan, Clement Wood, Will Higgins, Hoyt Wood, Harry Beachau, William Whitmore, ? Gaines, and ? Clarkson. Ruth Phillips, the future Mrs. Frank Griffing, and Buster Higgins are sitting on top of the box.

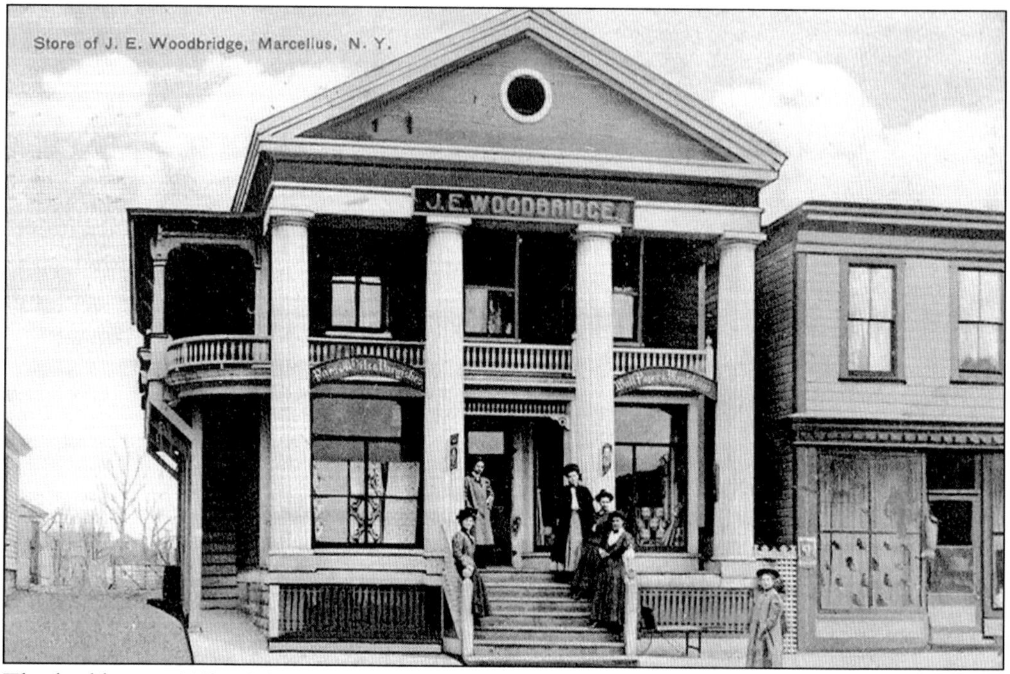

This building, at 14 East Main Street, was built in 1844 by Isaac Bradley to house his retail business. J. F. DeCourdres bought the building around 1900 and then sold out to J. E. Woodbridge. Around 1916, Woodbridge sold the building to Roy Smith, who sold paint, rugs, and linoleum. Prior to the 1950s, it was converted to a men's clothing store run by Arden Fisher. It then was rented to Joseph Miller, who installed the first laundromat. In 1955, the building sold to the Kershaw's for a lunchroom business. In 1964, the first floor of the building served as the Marcellus Rest Home, until 1977, when the entire building was finally converted into individual units.

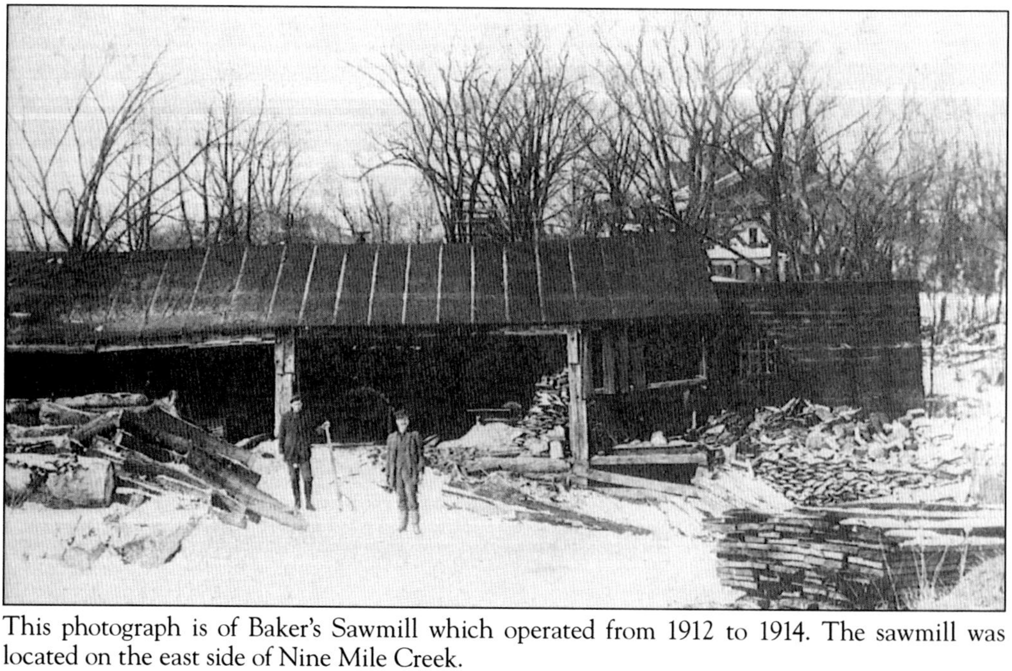

This photograph is of Baker's Sawmill which operated from 1912 to 1914. The sawmill was located on the east side of Nine Mile Creek.

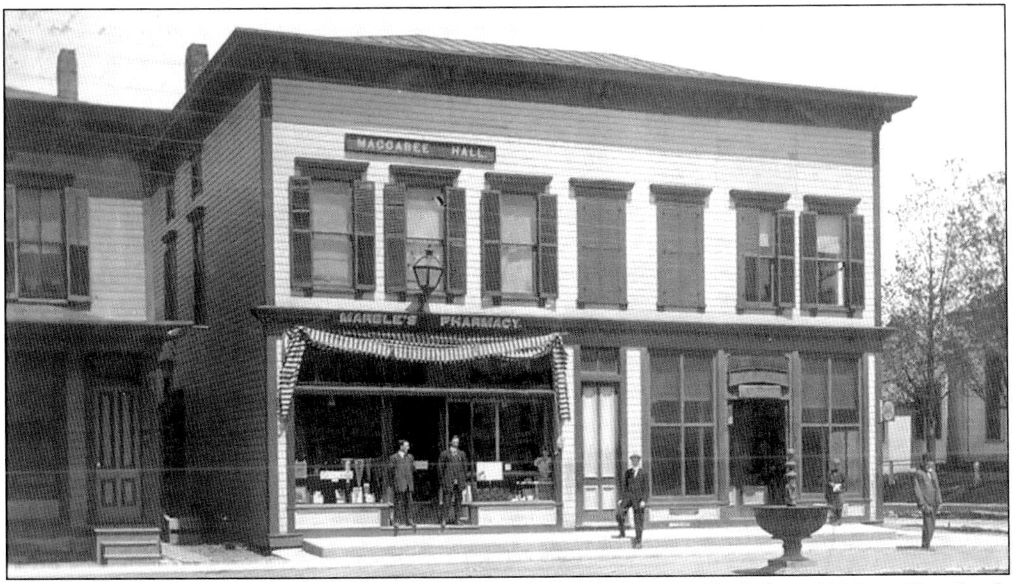

Austin Marble was the proprietor of Marble's Pharmacy in the Knapp Block from 1904 until his death in 1914. Thereafter, Ethel Marble carried on the business with the assistance of the pharmacist.

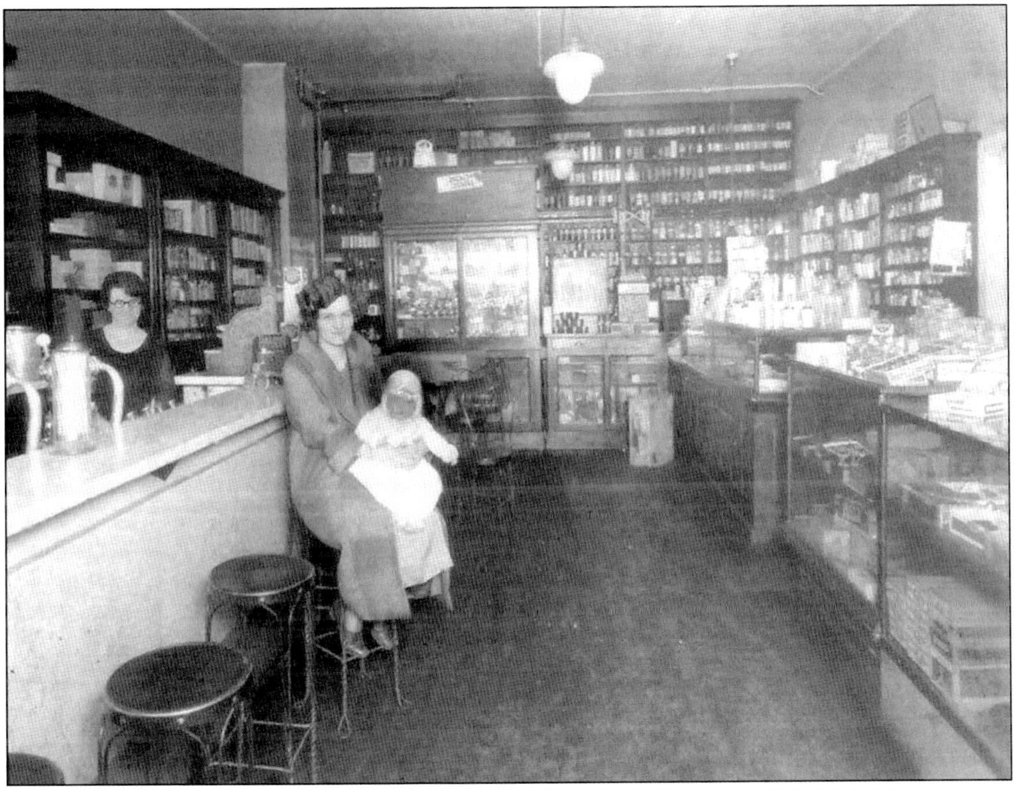

This photograph was taken in 1925 of the inside of Marble's Pharmacy. Ethel Marble, owner, is behind the soda fountain counter. Ethel's daughter, Dorothy Marble Woodford, is holding her son Emerson Woodford.

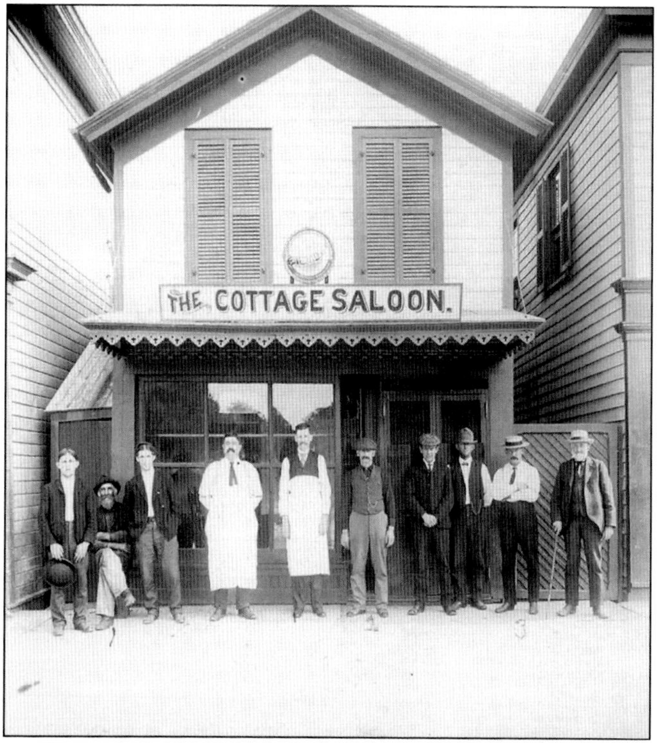

In 1910, the Cottage Saloon was owned by John Duggan. He continued to be open for business while a new three-story structure was being built around it. When the exterior was finished the interior was renovated. Upon Duggan's death, his son took over the business, which was advertised in 1914 as "C. B. Duggan's Hotel, and metropolitan barroom." This is the present site of the Village Tavern. Standing outside the saloon from left to right are Caron VanNasdall, Joseph Matteson, George Hellganz, Thomas Coyne, John Duggan, Jewett Dunlap, Charles Hellganz, Dr. Chase, Edward Rosser, and Monroe Woodford.

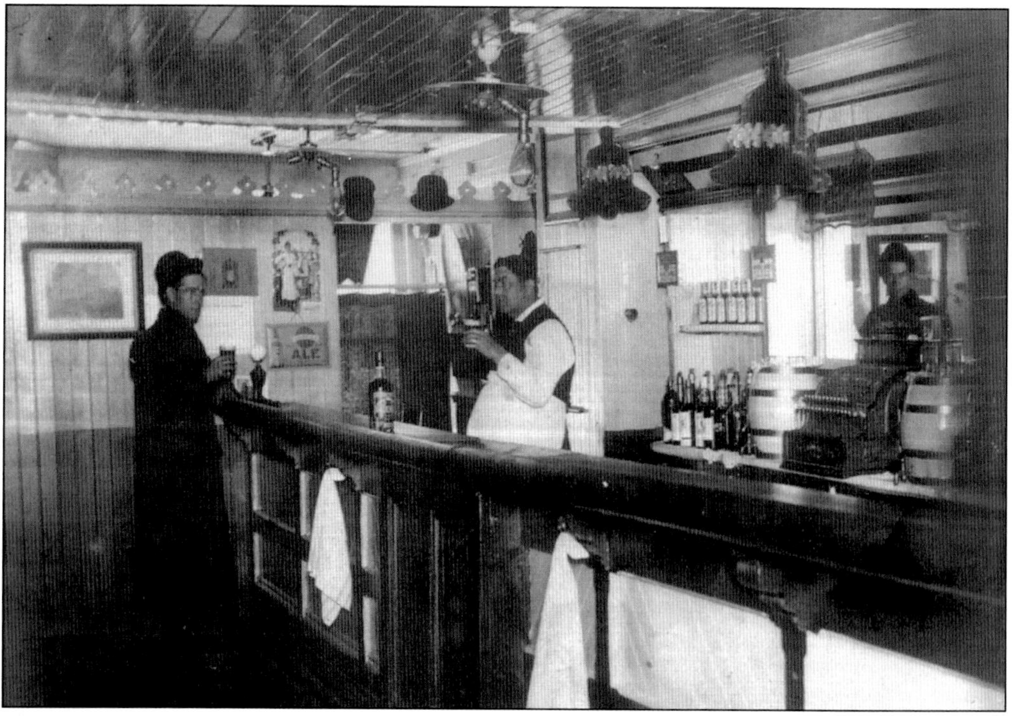

This 1905 picture is of the inside the Duggan's Cottage Saloon. He served fish fry and beer on Fridays for a nickel. "Cub" Arnold is standing at the bar while Thomas "Neg" Coyne is bartending. The use of nicknames was, and continues to be, a very common practice in Marcellus.

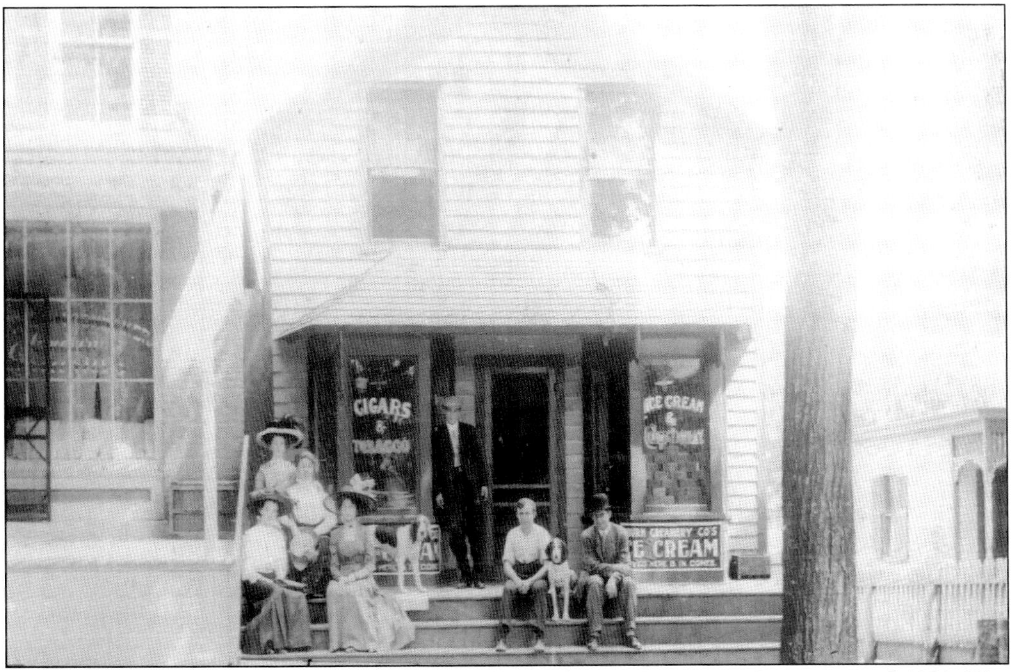

The Tobacco Store and Ice Cream Parlor was located at 21 East Main Street around 1890. The building was the site of the Video Store until it was destroyed in 1999.

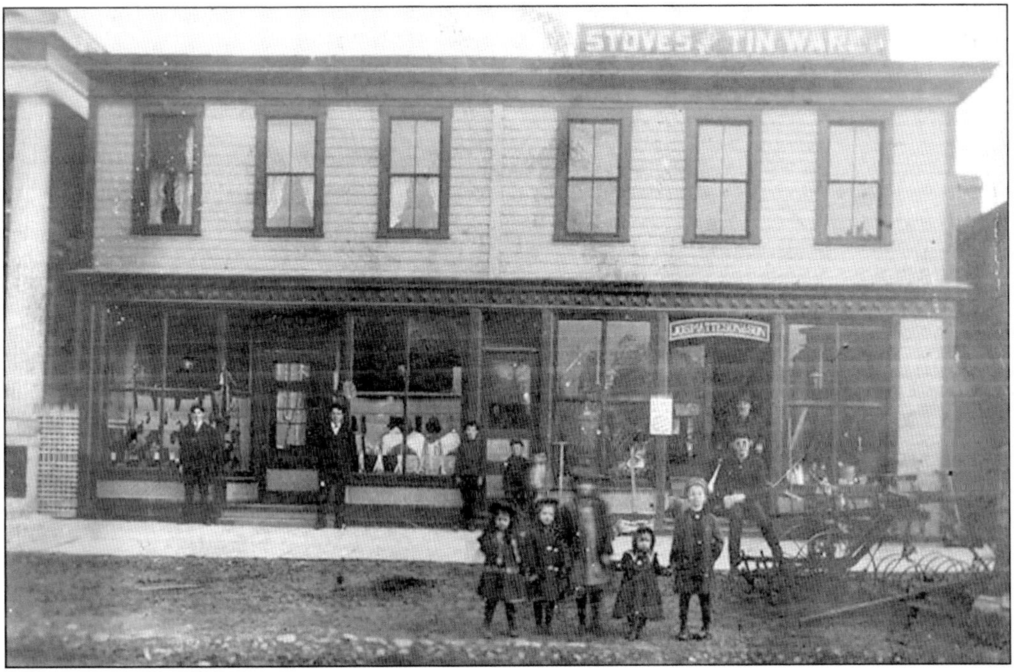

This photograph was taken in 1890 of the Stove and Tin Store, owned by William White and Joseph Matteson. The store opened for business around 1874. As the business flourished, it expanded into a hardware store. It is now the site of Reagan Insurance.

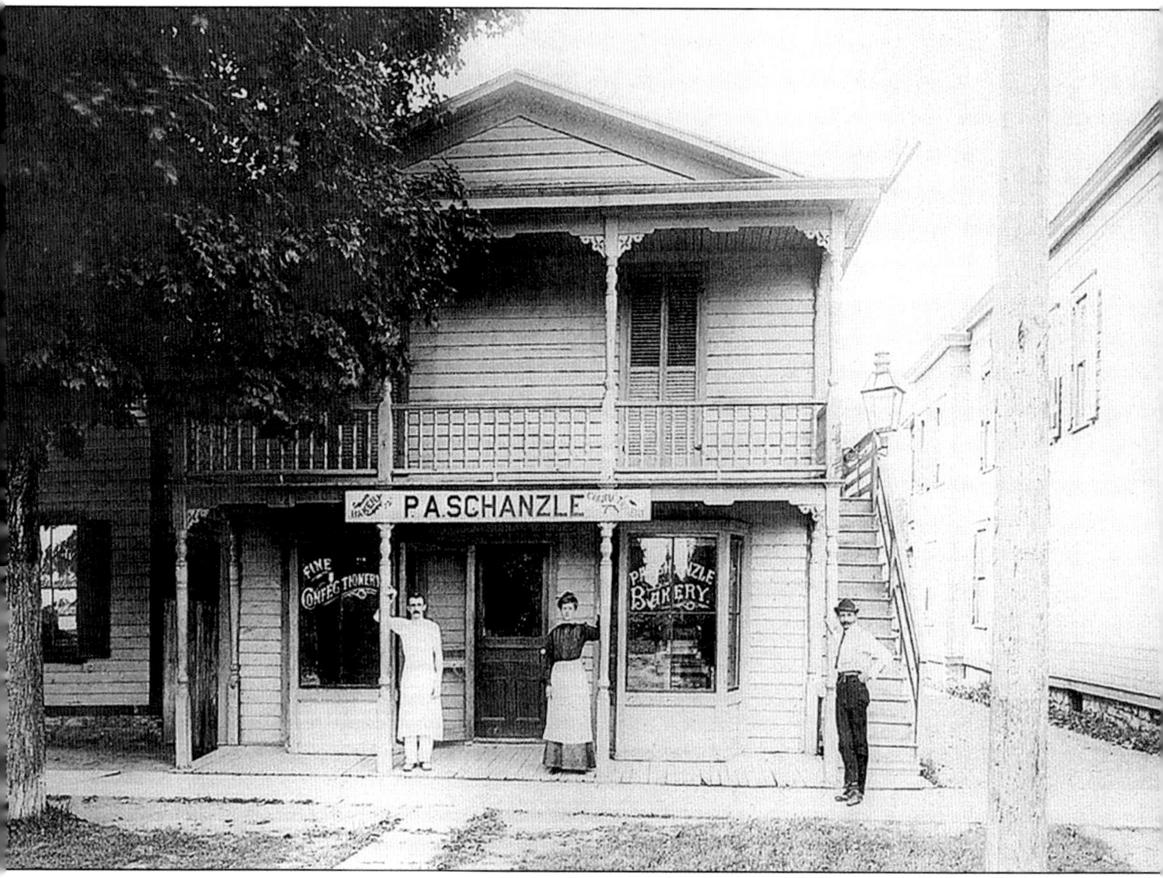

Schanzle's Bakery was known as the "neatest place of business in town." It was owned and operated by Phillip A. Schanzle and his wife. The family moved from Solvay in November 1903, so Schanzle could open his own bakery. In 1914, Levi Parsons III bought the building that housed Schanzle's Bakery and Schanzle moved his business next door. The bakery business grew to the point where he had to enlarge his building in 1918. He continued his business until his death in 1940.

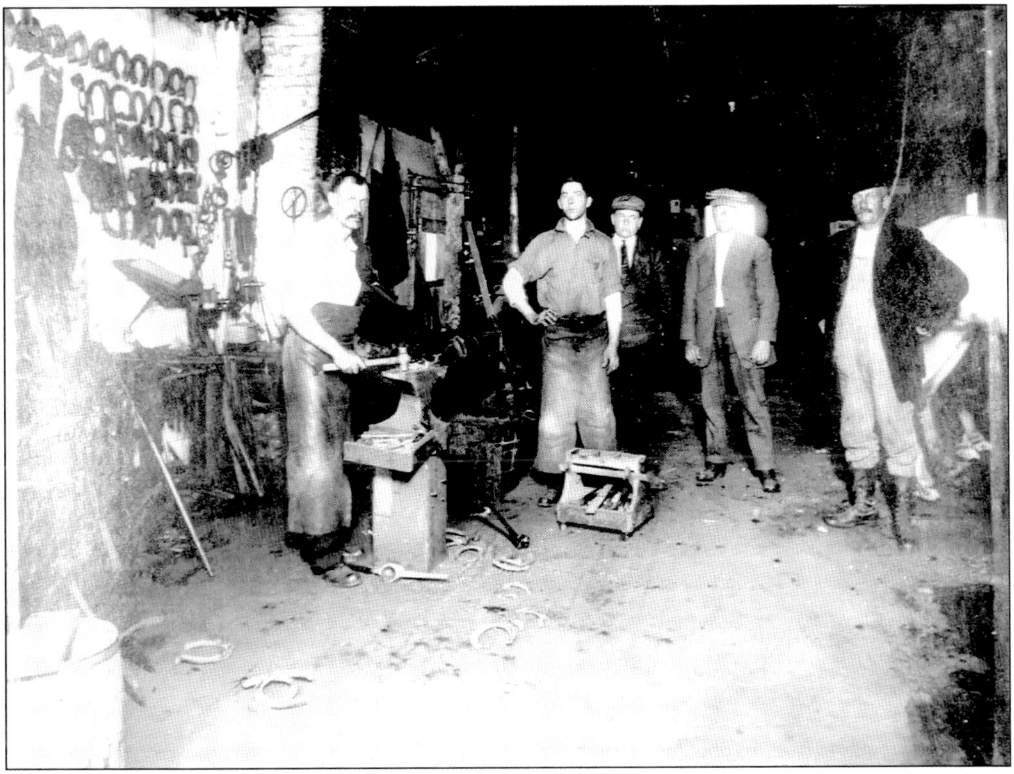

Samuel Pilot's blacksmith shop was located on North Street. This photograph was taken about 1915. From left to right are James Pilot, James Haster, Clayton Pilot, Horton Pilot, and George Hickman Sr..

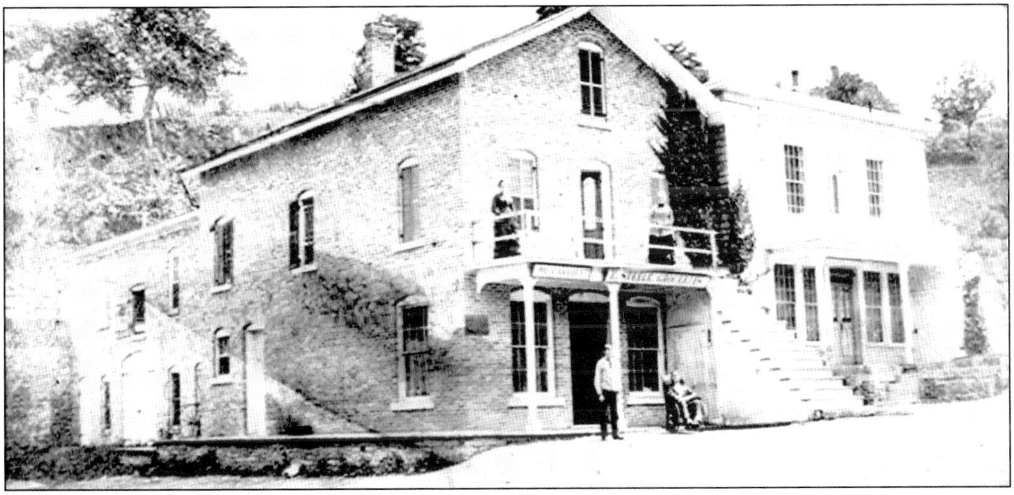

This is the site of the first Marcellus Falls Post Office and store. An old warranty deed found dates back to 1876, but it can be assumed that it was built a short time after the Auburn and Syracuse Railroad was built. The Marcellus Falls Post Office was officially closed in 1966.

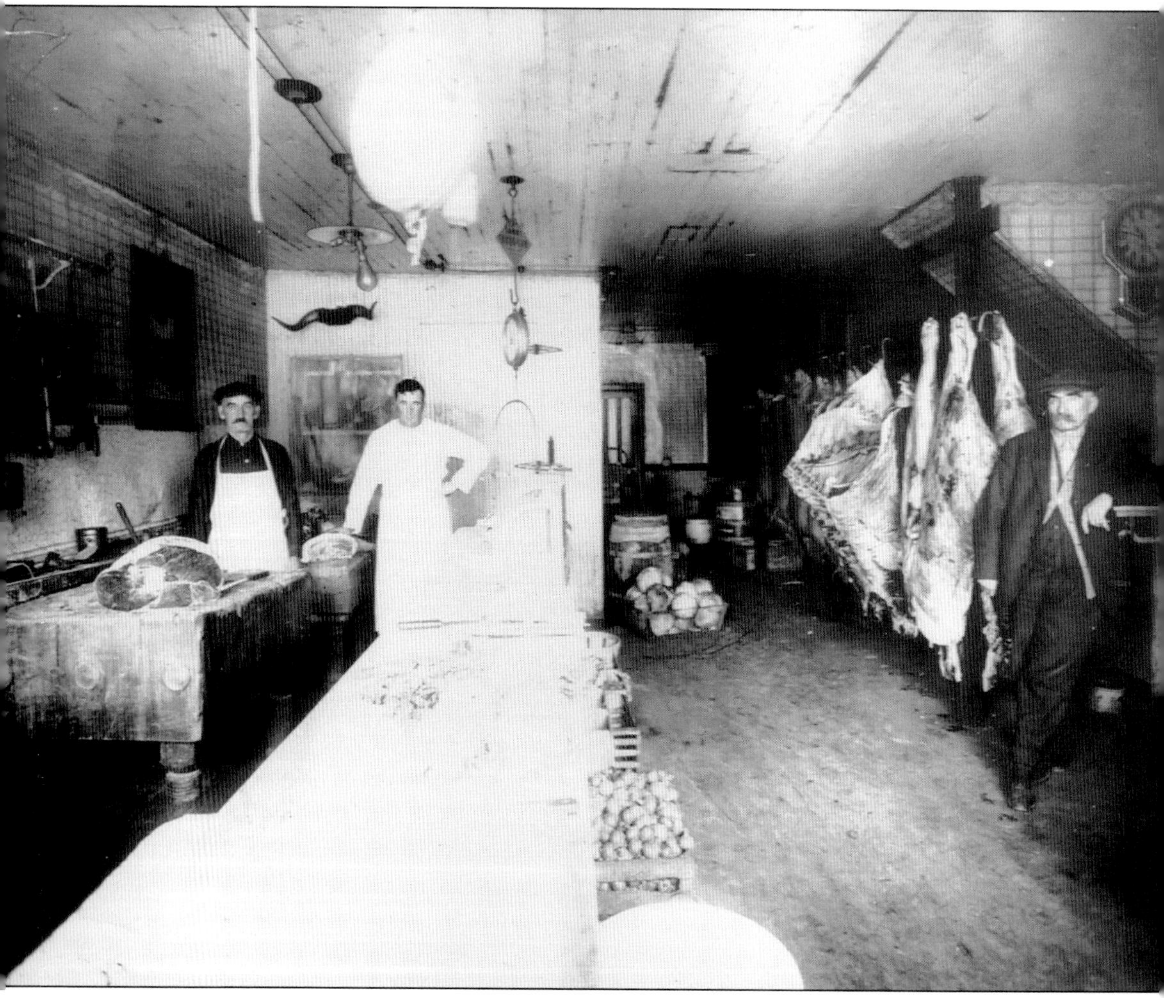

George Hickman's Meat Market was located at 4 East Main Street from before 1900 until 1934 when George Hickman II moved his meat market and grocery business to the barn behind his home on 10 First Street. The Hickman Meat Market stayed in business until the third generation owner Donald Hickman retired in 1970. Standing from left to right are George Hickman Jr., Dudley Hickman, and George Hickman Sr.

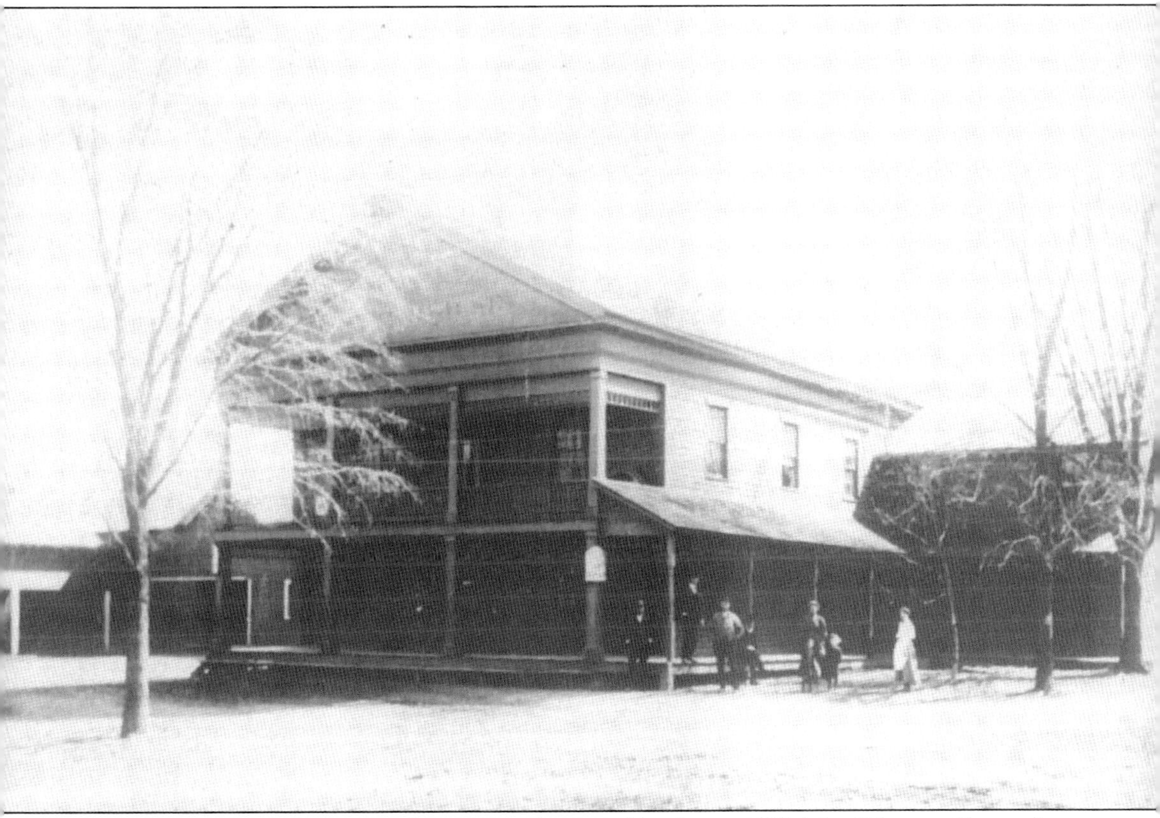

The old Marietta House, pictured here, was destroyed by fire in 1935. Mrs. Thomas Shea, who owned the Marietta House, then sold the existing barn and three acres to Donald and Ethel Dillon, who remodeled the barn into a restaurant and grill along with living quarters. Upon the death of Donald Dillon, Ethel carried on the business until 1969, when she sold the business to Thomas Donovan. The Donovan family is still running the Marietta House today as a restaurant and catering business.

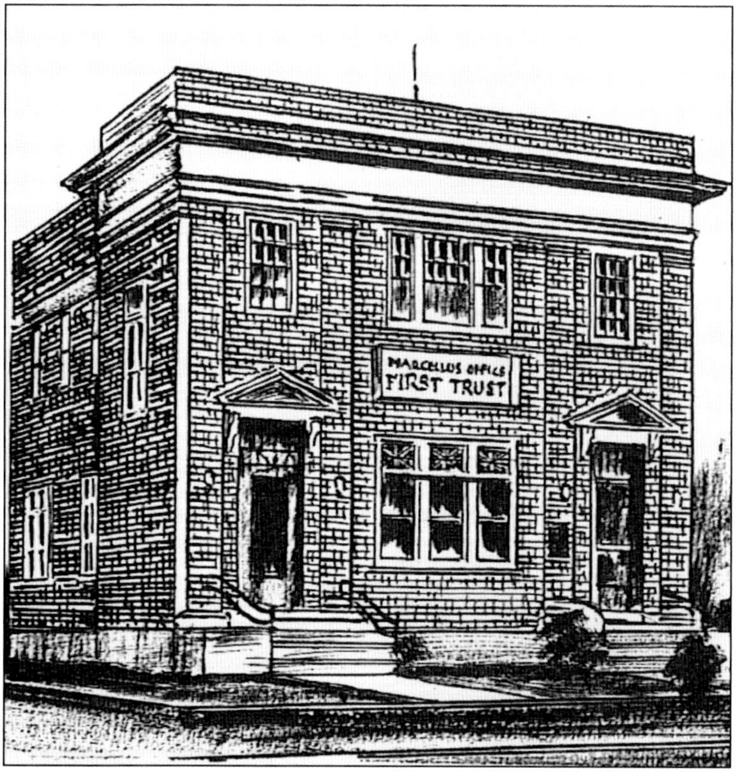

The First National Bank of Marcellus opened its doors for business in October 1910 in the small wood frame building that formally held the post office. The new brick building was built around 1915, and business was continued there until February 1956, when it merged with the First Trust and Deposit Company of Syracuse, with Marcellus serving as a branch office. Today it houses the offices of the Marcellus Town Hall.

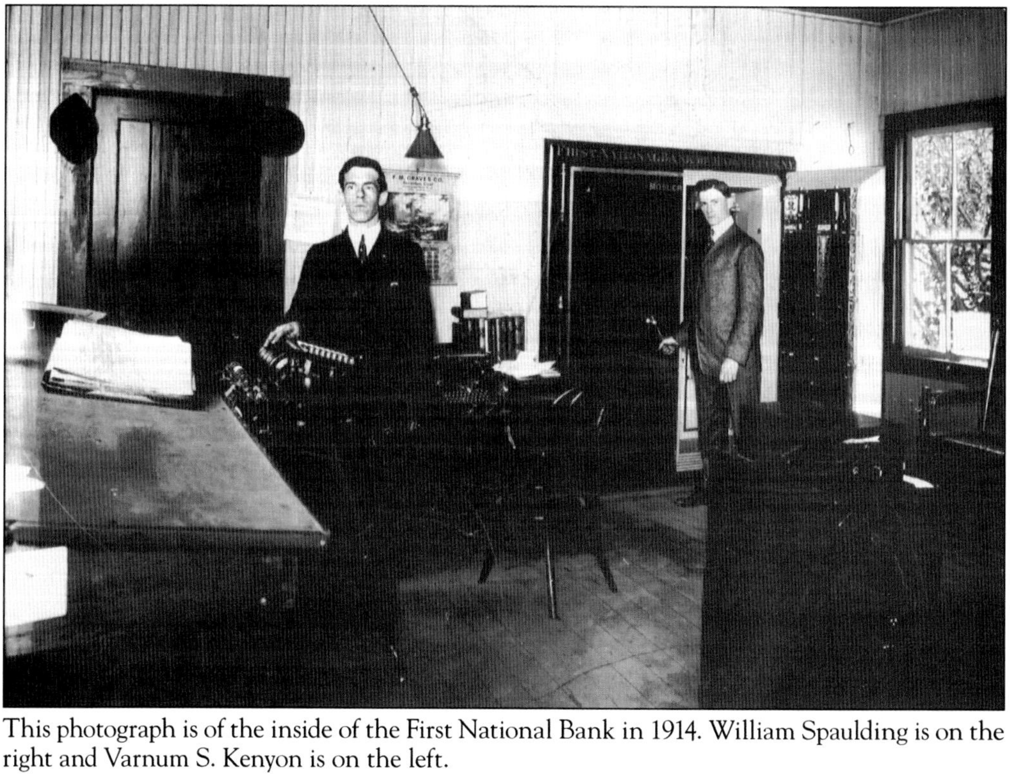

This photograph is of the inside of the First National Bank in 1914. William Spaulding is on the right and Varnum S. Kenyon is on the left.

Curtis Moses built the masonry store which stood at 19 East Main Street on the site that was previously a wagon shop. Steve Hunt later bought the building to run his grocery business. The building was destroyed in 1999.

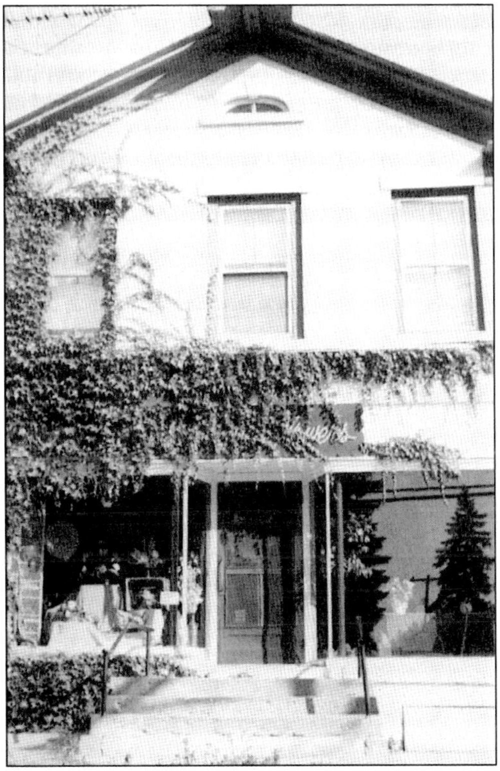

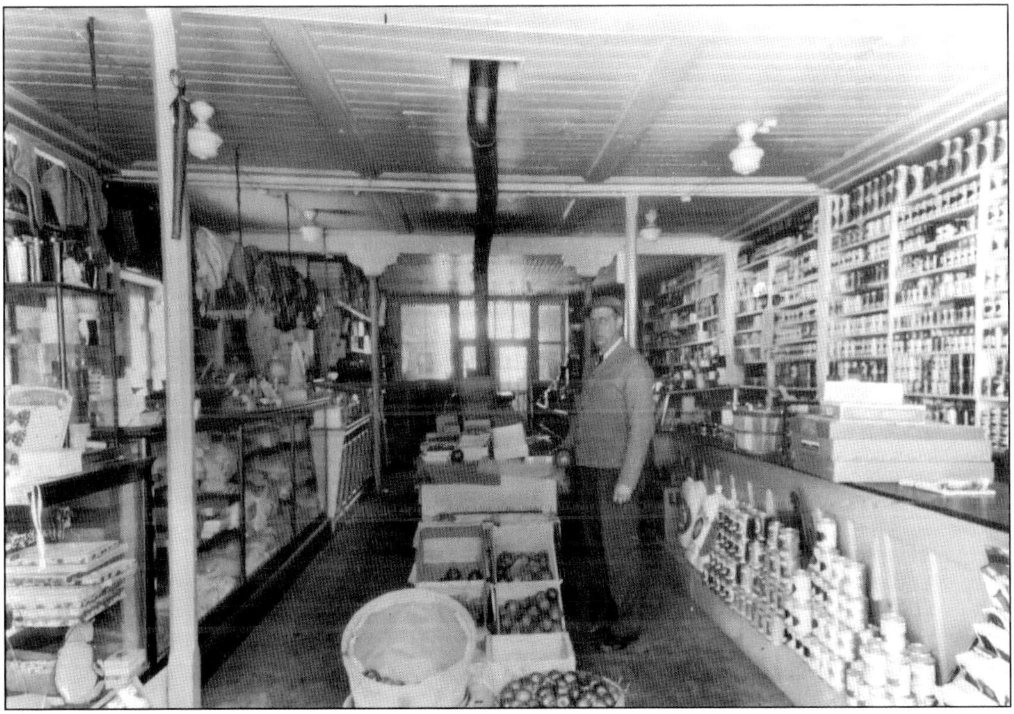

Steve Hunt is shown here standing in his store. Note the fresh produce and the canned goods lining the shelves.

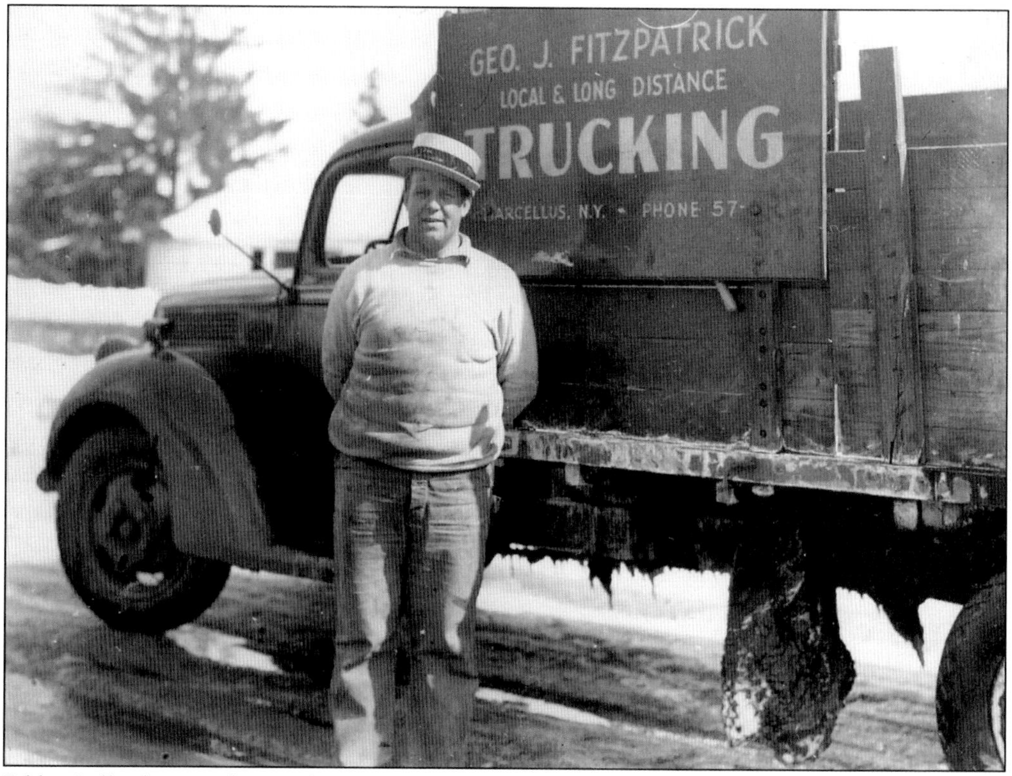

Eddie Collard is standing in front of the truck owned by George J. Fitzpatrick. The sign on the truck stated that the business did local and long-distance hauling.

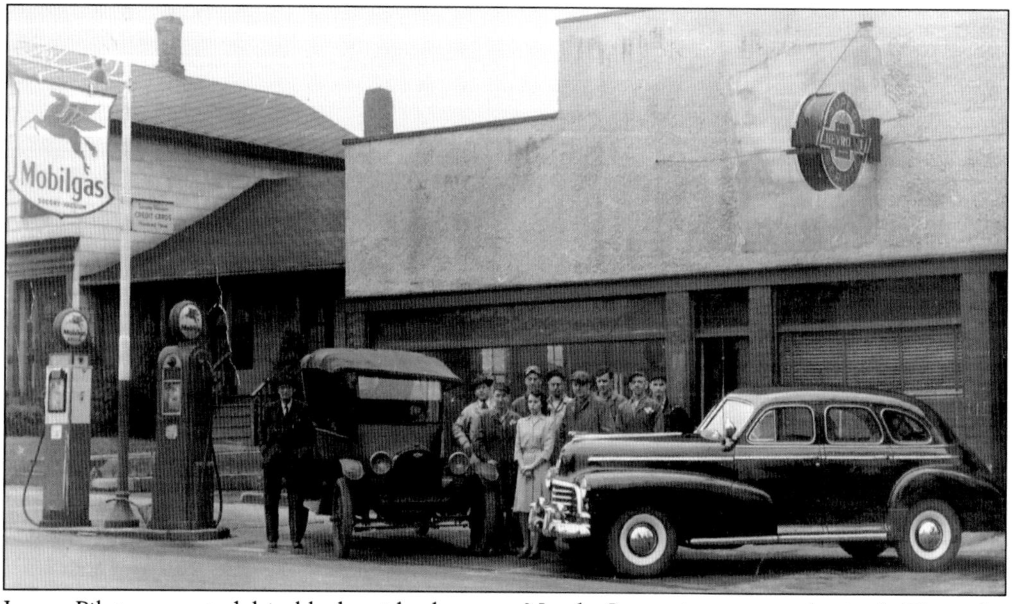

James Pilot converted his blacksmith shop on North Street into an authorized Chevrolet dealership. His two sons, Horton and Clayton, became active in the business. In 1930, Pilot Chevrolet advertised the new "Chevrolet Sixes." The standard sedan was priced at $635, the standard coupe at $575.

Two
Streets and Places

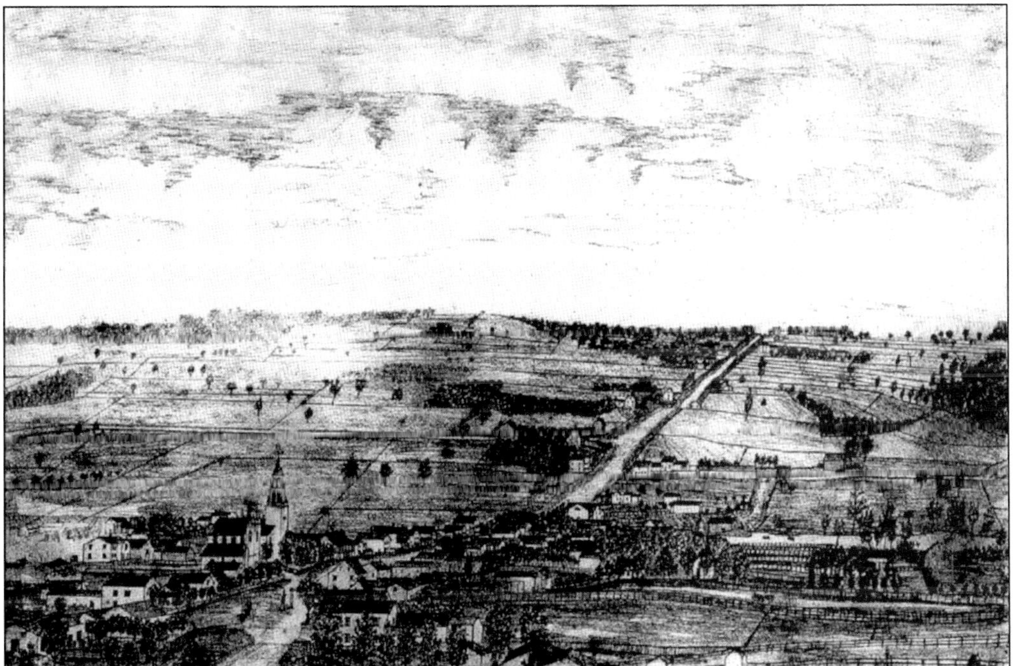

This etching is the oldest known illustration of the village of Marcellus. It was a pencil drawing done by Margaret F. Parsons in 1840, when she was 17 years old.

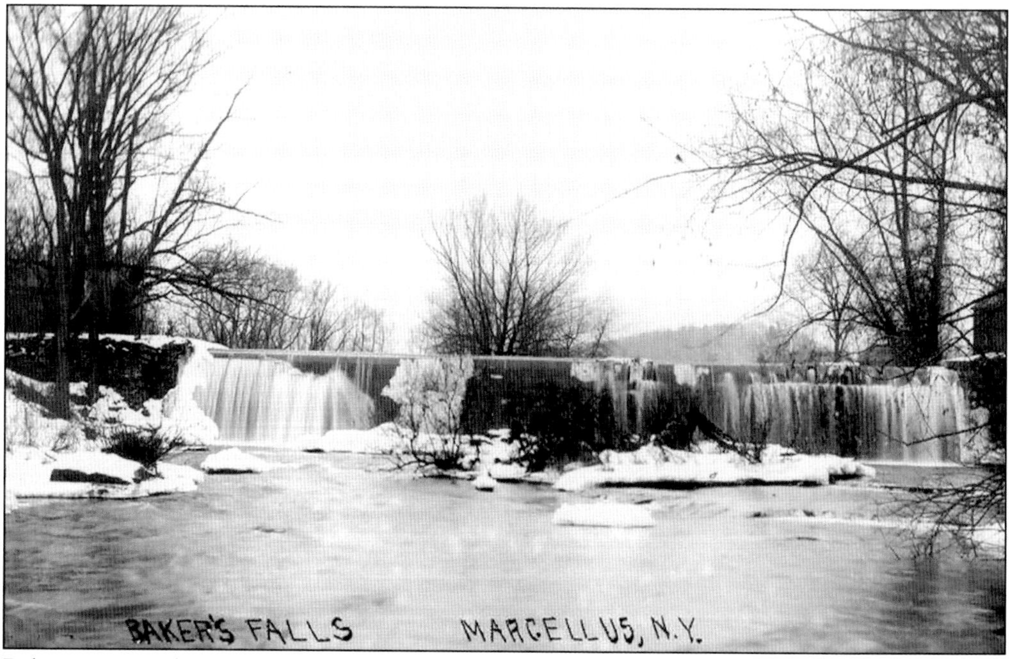

Baker's Dam and Mill were owned by Robert M. Baker. Baker's Dam was used to power the first telephone line that ran from the village to Marcellus Falls and served 16 customers. It also served as the power source for the first electric lights in the village. The dam is no longer in existence.

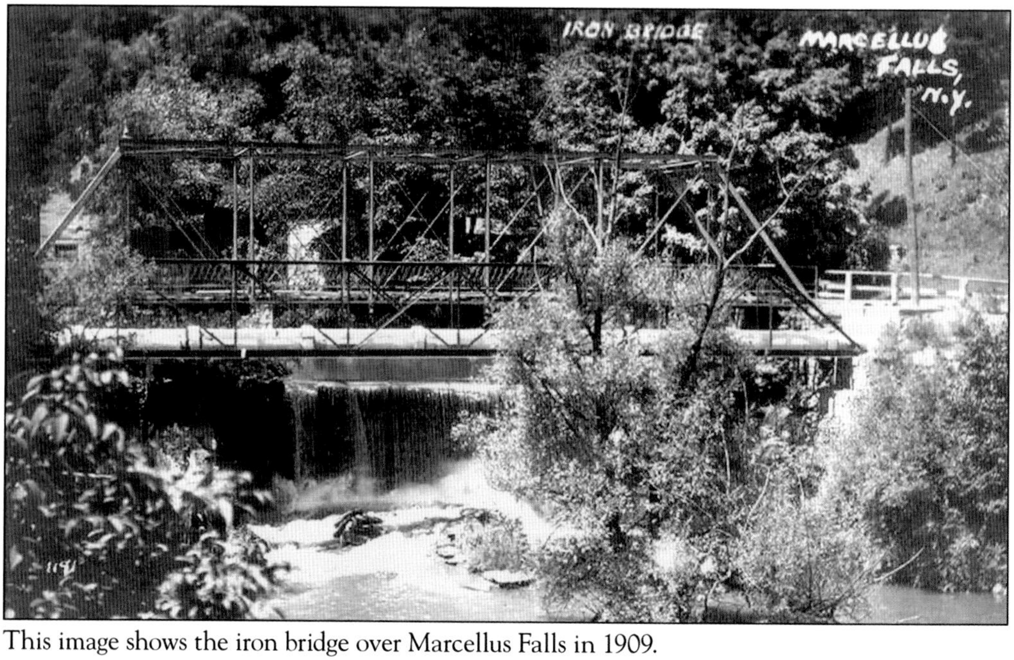

This image shows the iron bridge over Marcellus Falls in 1909.

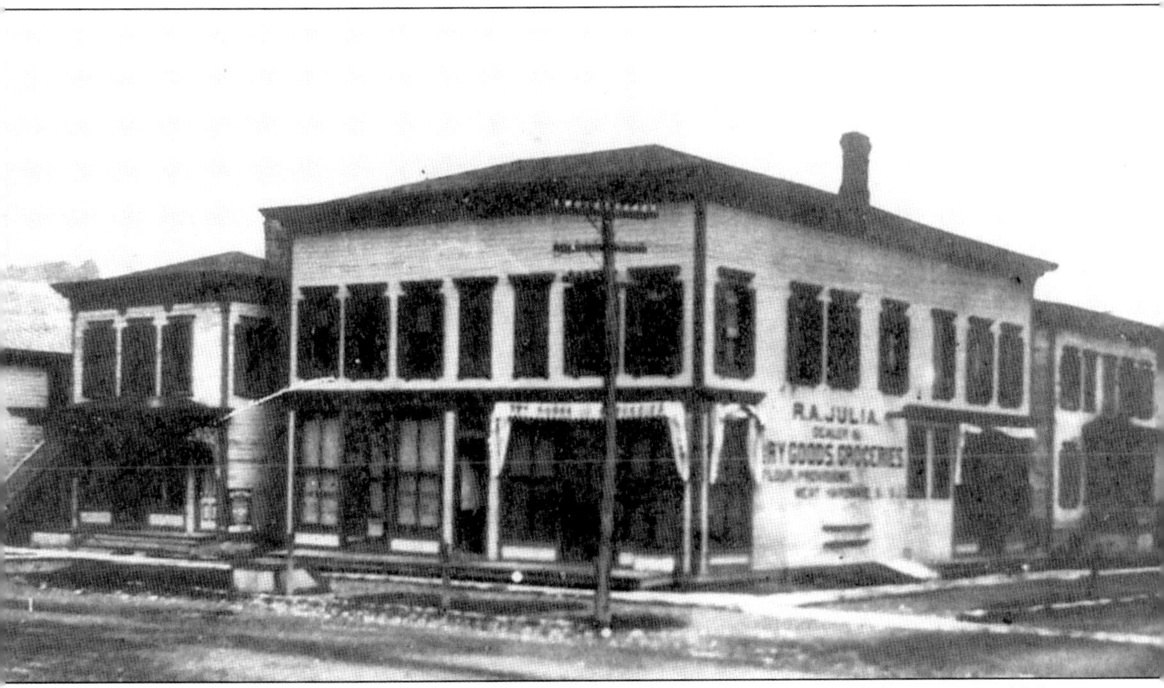

On July 3, 1879, one of the worst fires in the history of the village consumed the 10-year-old St. John's Episcopal Church, which sat on the west corner of North and Main Streets. Along with the church, two other stores to the west were also destroyed. A storekeeper named Michael Sheehan and lawyer William Gallup later rebuilt that section of Main Street.

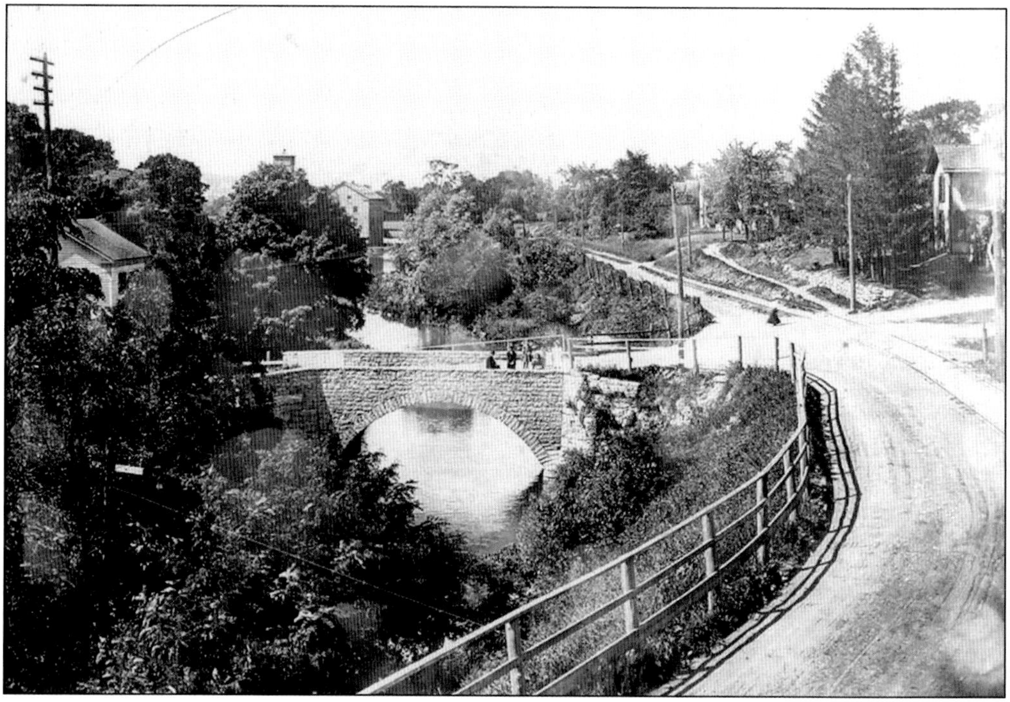

This photograph was taken looking north at the Main Street bridge around 1900.

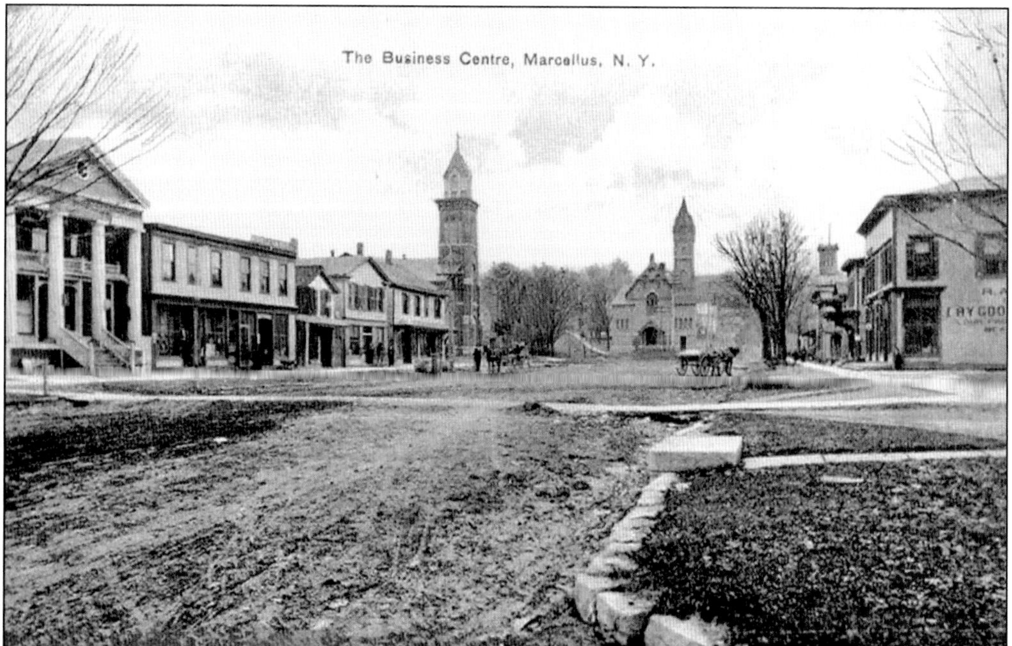

This is the business center of Marcellus in 1902. The business activity in the village proper comprised of two hotels, two barbers, three blacksmiths, four cigar makers, three physicians, one dentist, three saloons, one druggist, four meat markets, a millinery, a shoemaker, a laundry, a carpet weaver, a lawyer, and two insurance agents.

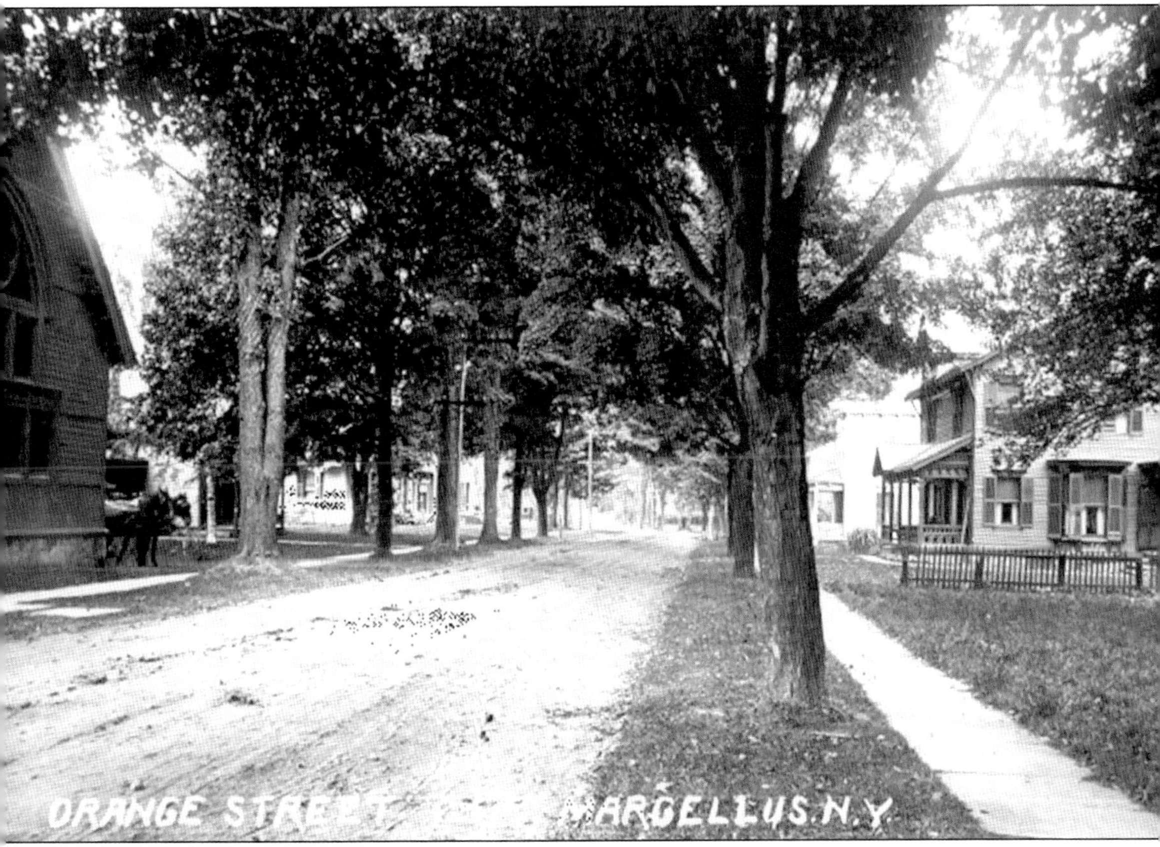

This photograph of Orange Street was taken in the early 1900s. On the far left is the Episcopal church before it was relocated to its present site on the corner of Orange and Maple Streets.

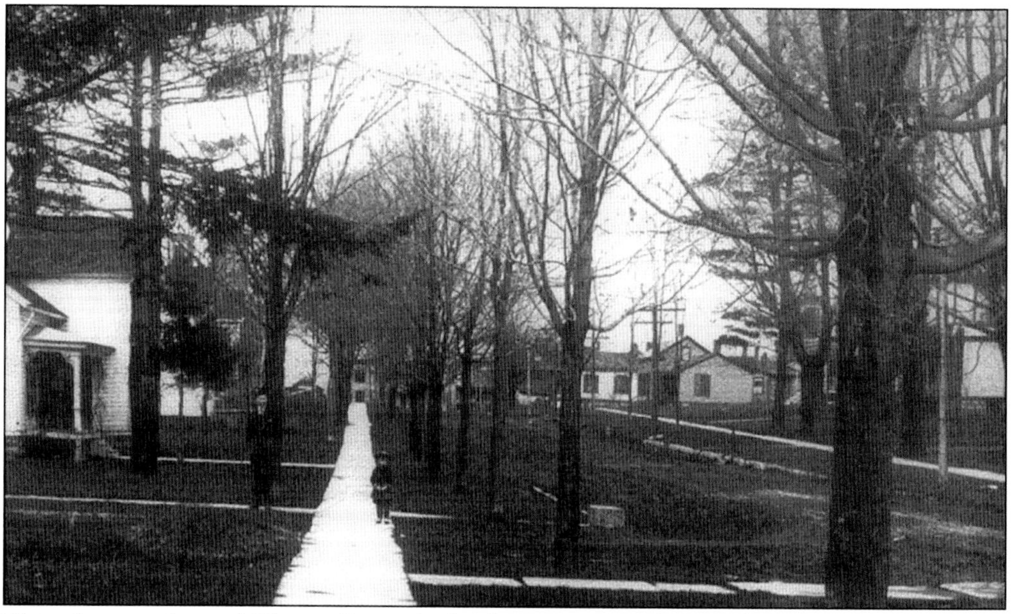

This photograph is of Cherry Street (today known as South Street), looking north. It was originally named for all the cherry trees that Amory Wilson, a nurseryman, planted along the street between what is now Flower Lane and Main Street.

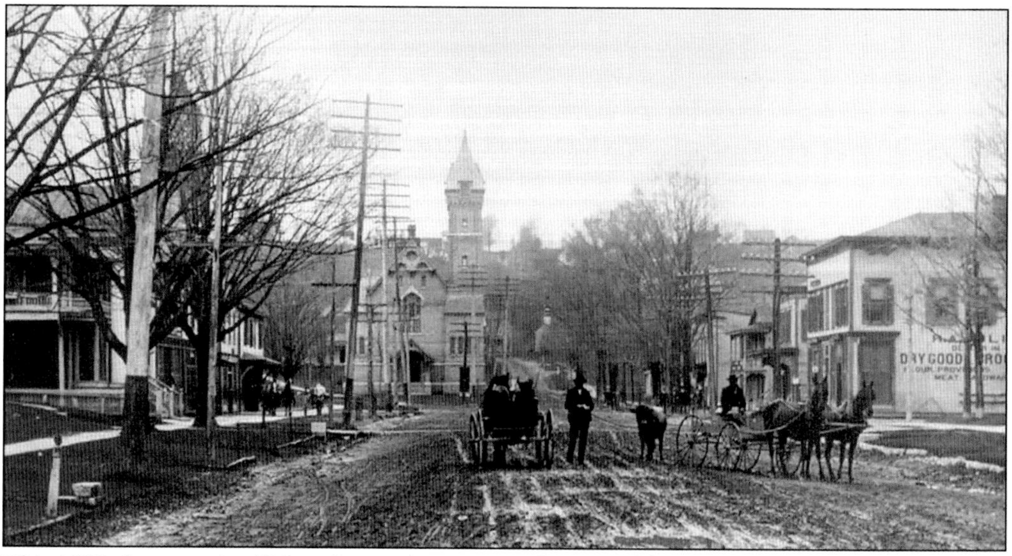

This 1907 photograph of Main Street shows not only its muddy ruts in its dirt street, but a close look reveals the new telephone poles that Frank W. Knapp was granted permission to erect. Knapp was the driving force in obtaining organized telephone service for Marcellus in 1903. He was village clerk in 1906. He commissioned the building on Nine Mile Creek, at the site of Robert Baker's sawmill, as a small electric generating plant. The plant made it possible to light 16 street lamps in the village plus some businesses and homes. Knapp called his enterprise the Marcellus Lighting Company. The lighting company eventually merged with Empire Gas and Electric, a holding company and predecessor of New York State Electric and Gas Company, which continues to provide electric power to the village today. Knapp also served as village clerk from 1894 to 1909.

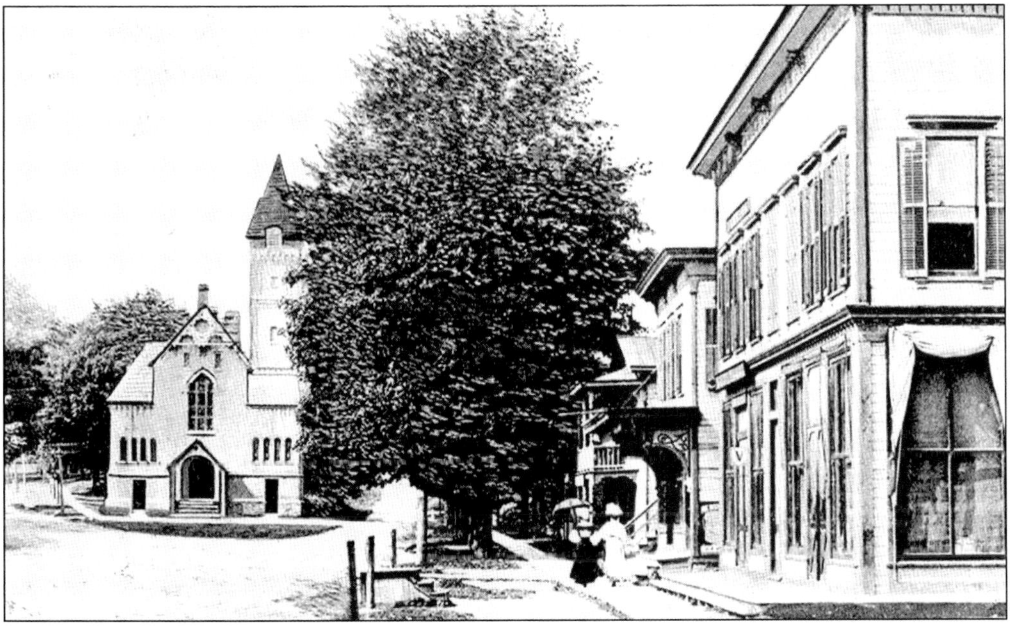

This view is of the north side of Main Street around 1910. When E. V. Baker Sr. became postmaster in 1909, the post office was moved into what was then the Knapp Block at the corner of North and Main Streets. The post office remained there until the current post office building was completed in 1962.

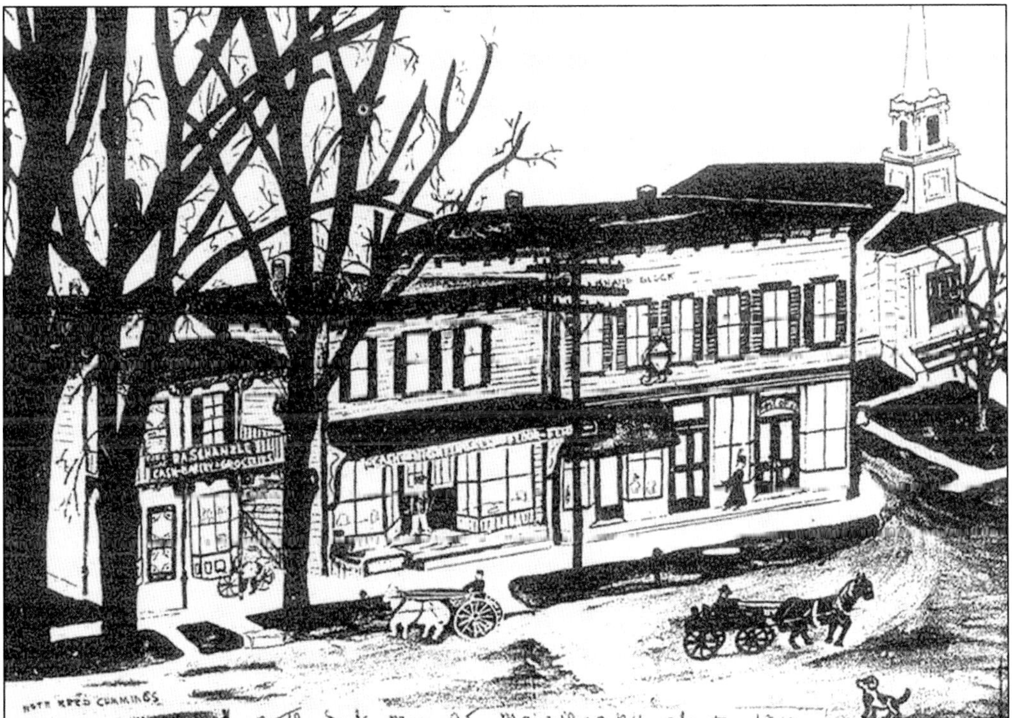

Seen here is an etching of what the north side of Main Street looked like in 1910. The etching was done by Ruth Reed Cummings.

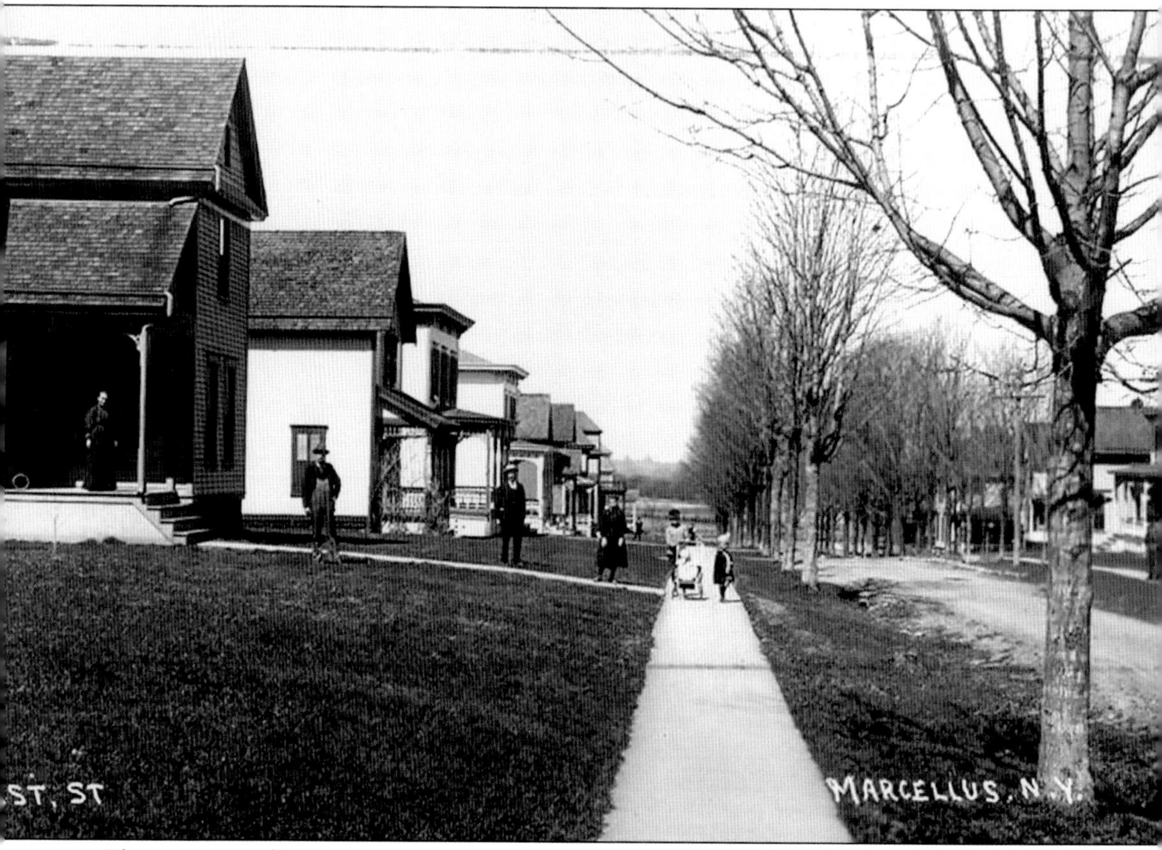

This is a view of First Street, looking north, in 1910.

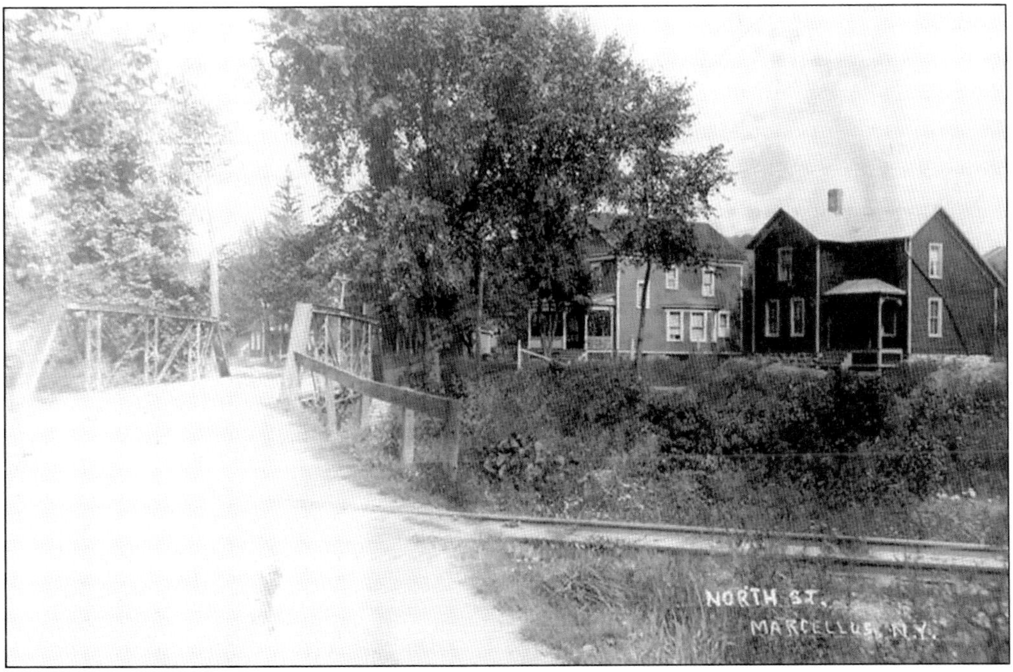

This view depicts North Street (across from the present high school) before the road was rerouted to its present state. This photograph was taken around 1910.

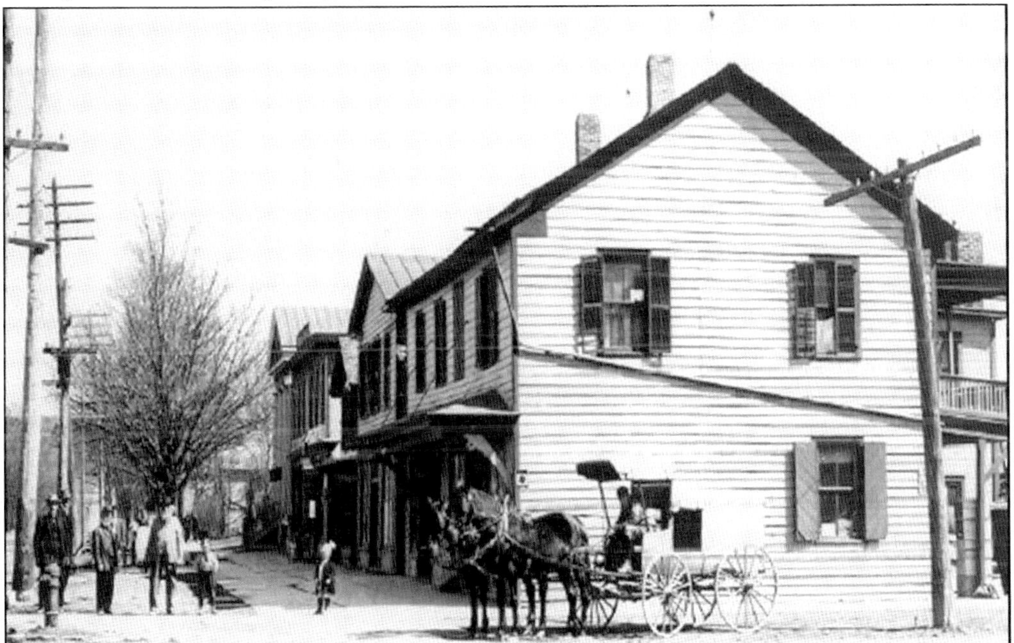

One of the early settlers, Thomas J. Field, built the corner building, at the corner of Cherry (now South) and Main Streets. Its original framing was done with rough timbers. In 1839, Isaac Bradley, son of the Honorable Dan Bradley, opened his own retail business. After Isaac Bradley moved his business to 14 East Main Street, the building lay vacant for many years until Fred Oakley, a wool buyer, rented it for a wool storehouse. This photograph was taken in 1914.

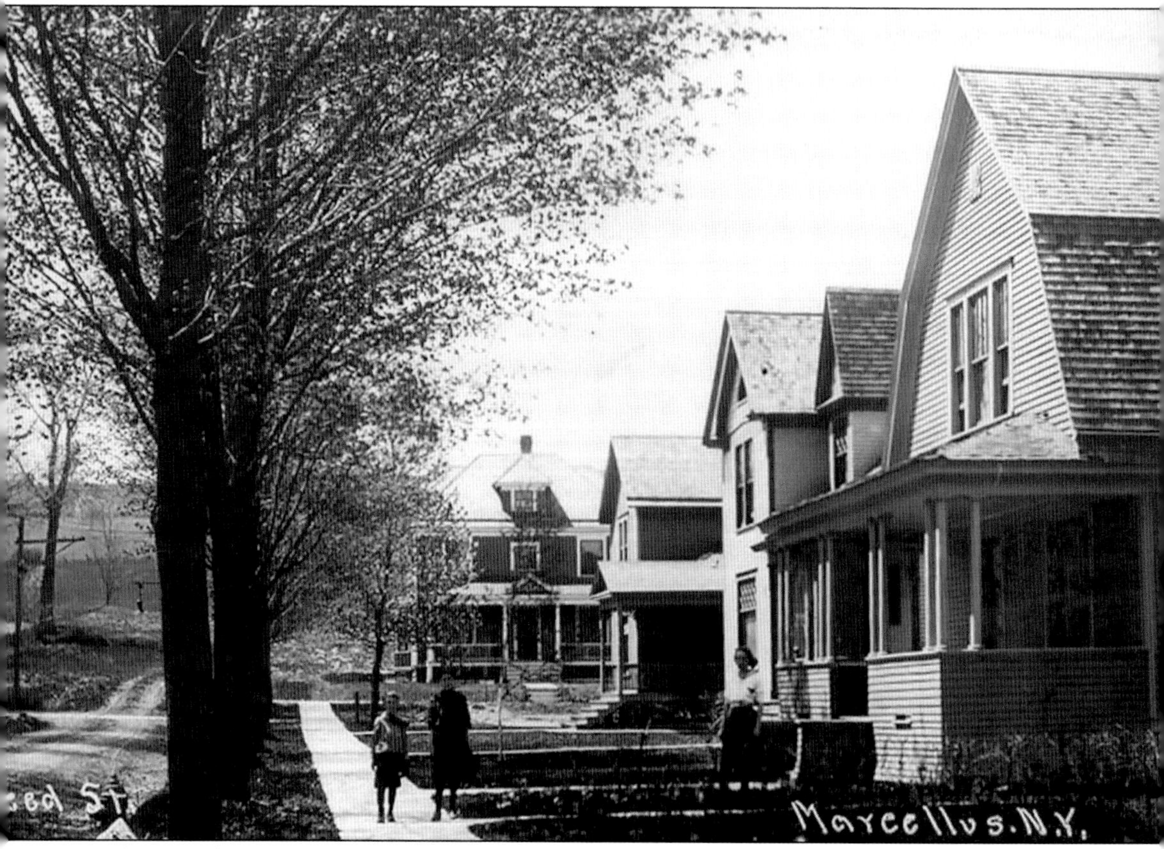

This is a photograph of lower Reed Street around 1914. Kasson Moak's home is directly to the right, and P. J. Kelley's home is next door, to the west.

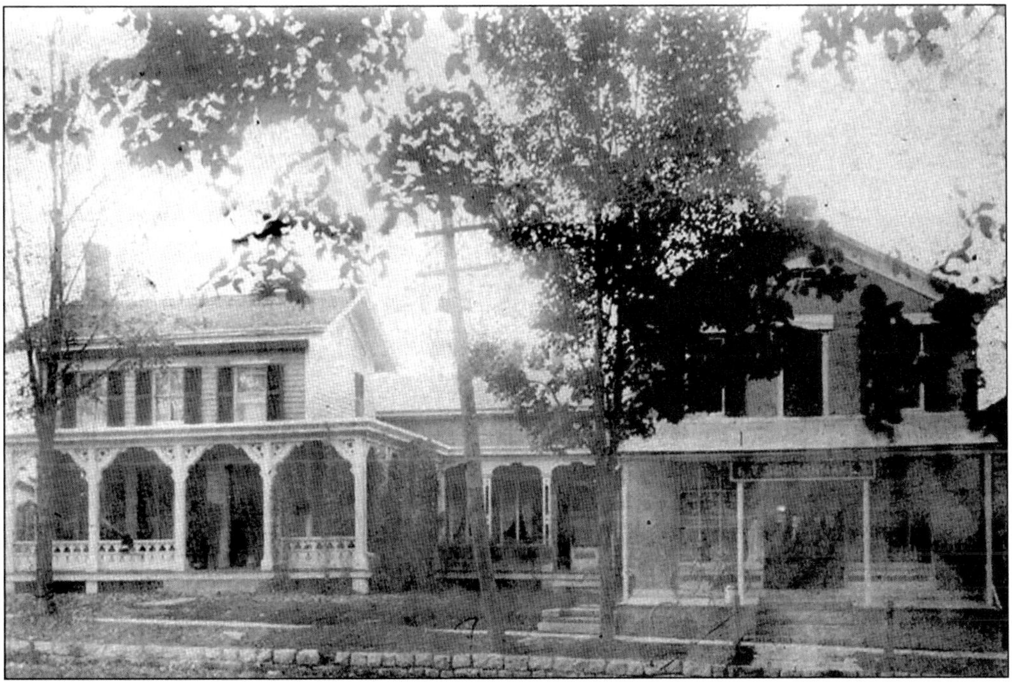

In the winter of 1795–1796, Dr. Elnathan Beach became the first physician in Marcellus and constructed the first wood frame house at what is now 17–21 East Main Street. He also opened the first general store. These buildings are no longer in existence.

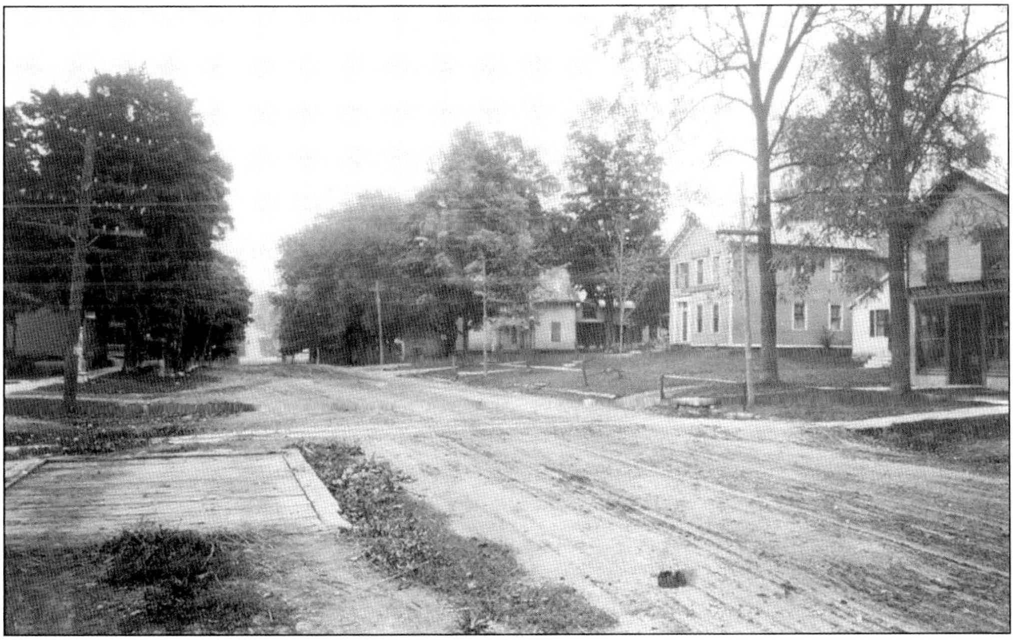

This *c.* 1912 photograph is of East Main Street. Note the village's first bank on the right.

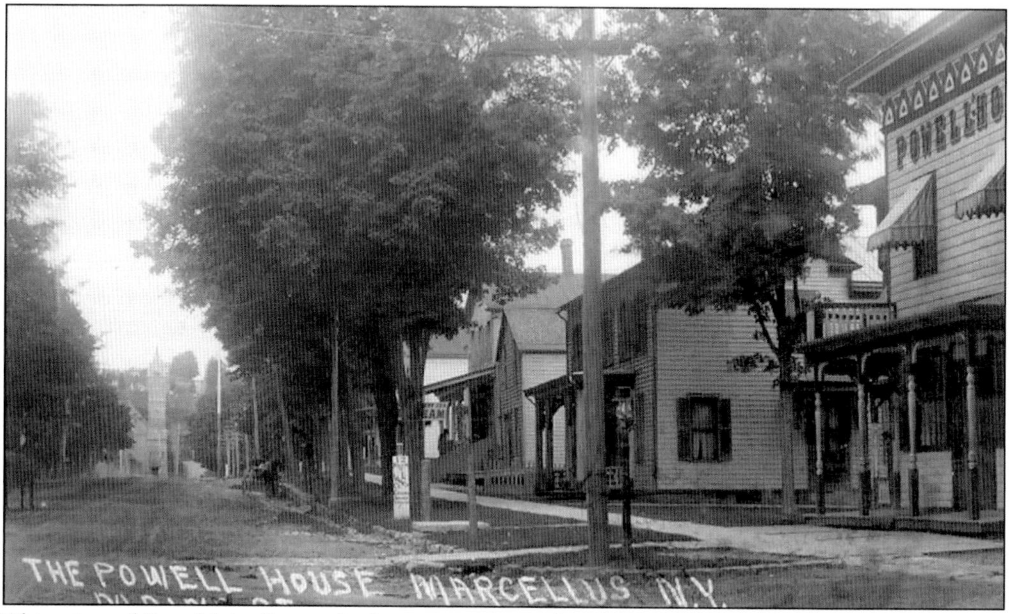

This view of East Main Street, looking west, was taken prior to 1910. The Powell House is to the right. It was built around 1828 by Harvey Rhodes, who used the building as a store until he sold to Bernard Powell. Powell purchased the old store and a half-building that stood on the northwest corner of Orange and Main Streets. He made additions to the original building of a second story, a new wing, and porches, and he turned the old store into a hotel, advertising the Powell House as "heated by steam with fine cuisine." The oil lantern, out front, was one of many purchased under the Daniel Coon administration in 1878 to provide lighting for the village. Michael Kennedy was the first lamplighter and was paid $3 a month to fill the oil and light the lamps each night. James Powell was the last village lamplighter when it was decided to light the streets with electric lamps in 1907.

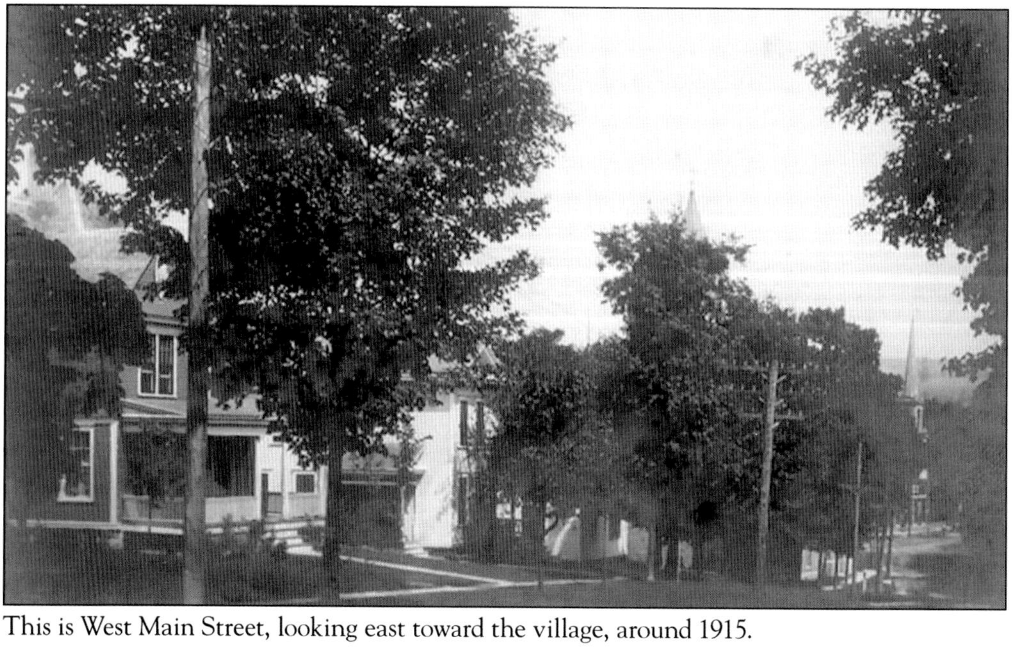

This is West Main Street, looking east toward the village, around 1915.

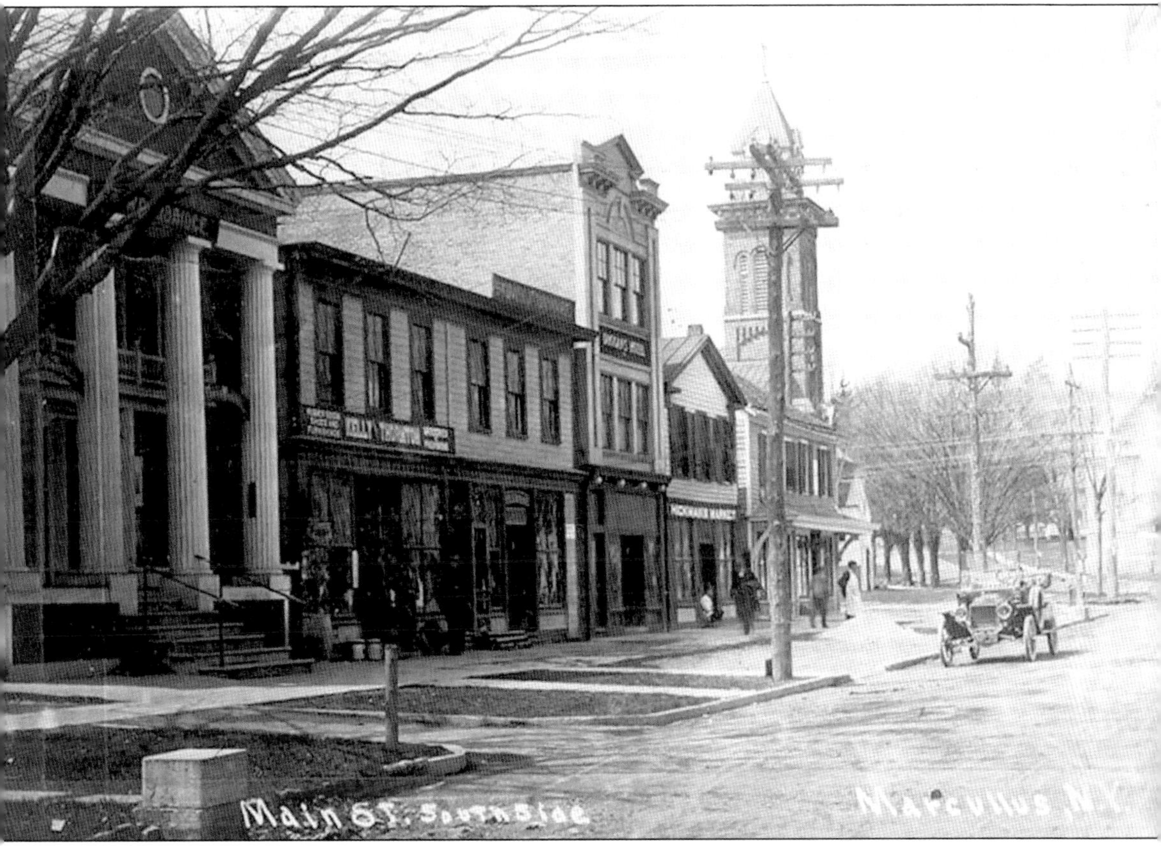

This is a view of Main Street, looking west, in 1916. The Woodbridge building is on the left.

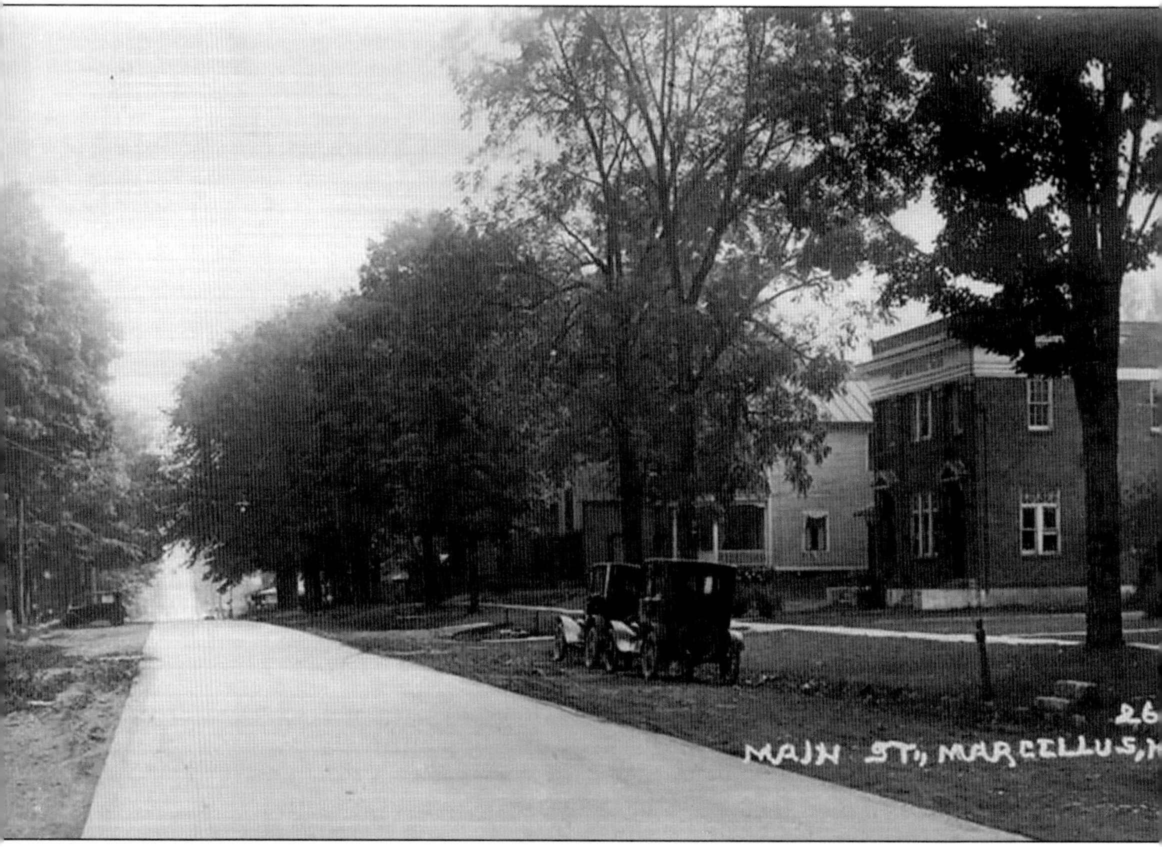

This photograph is of East Main Street in 1926. Notice the brick bank building on the right.

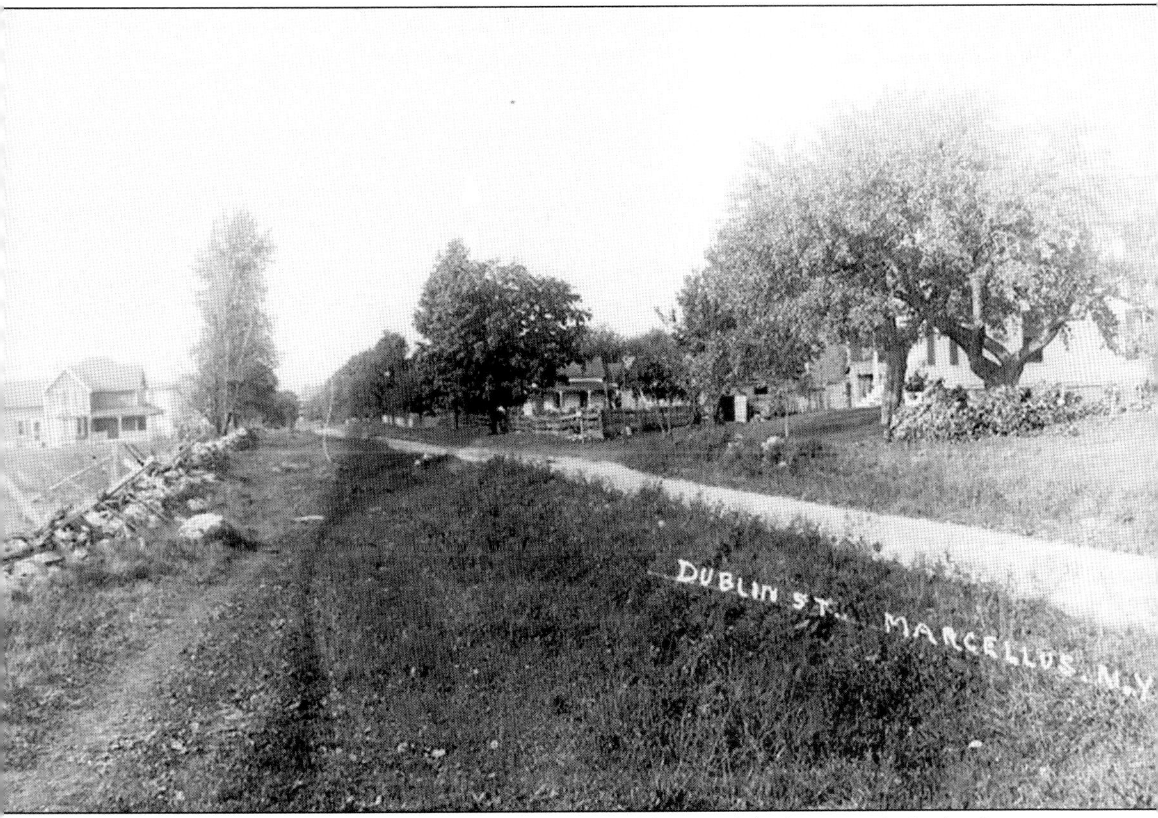

This photograph, taken between 1910 and 1915, is of Dublin Road, looking north. In the distance one can see the house on the left that was restored in the 1970s by the Weeks family.

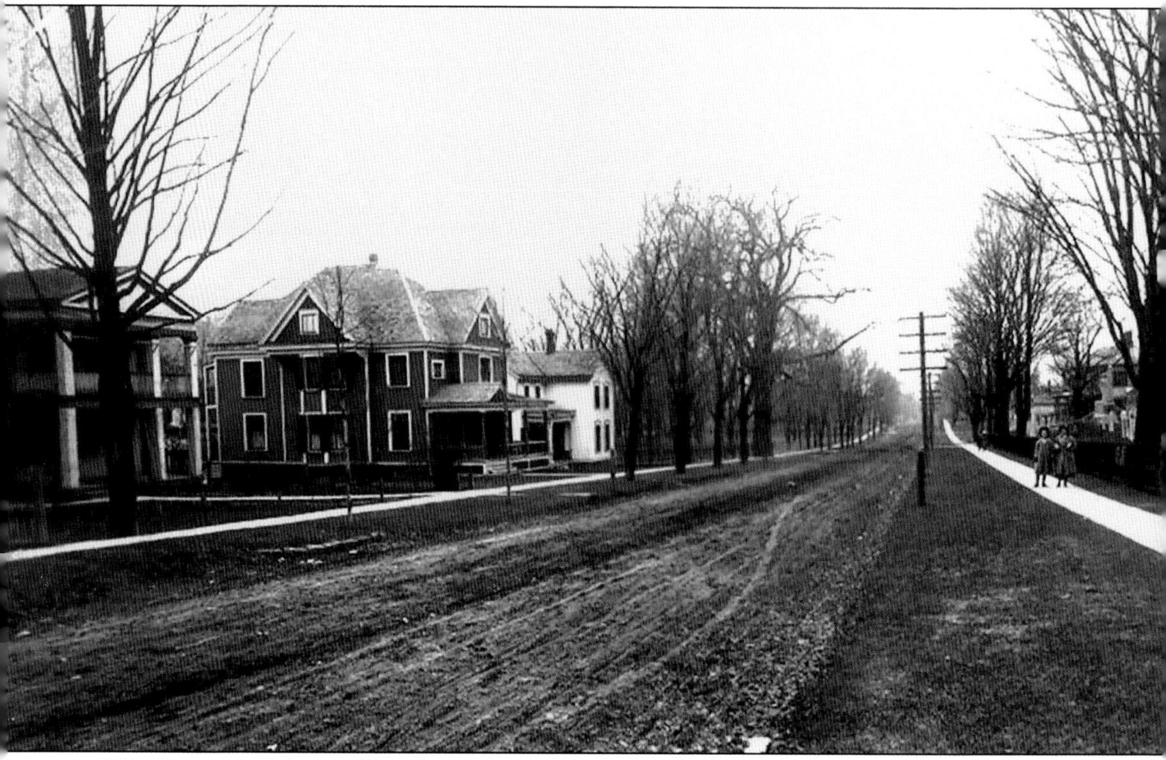

This is a view of the residential section of North Street across from the Village Cemetery in 1939.

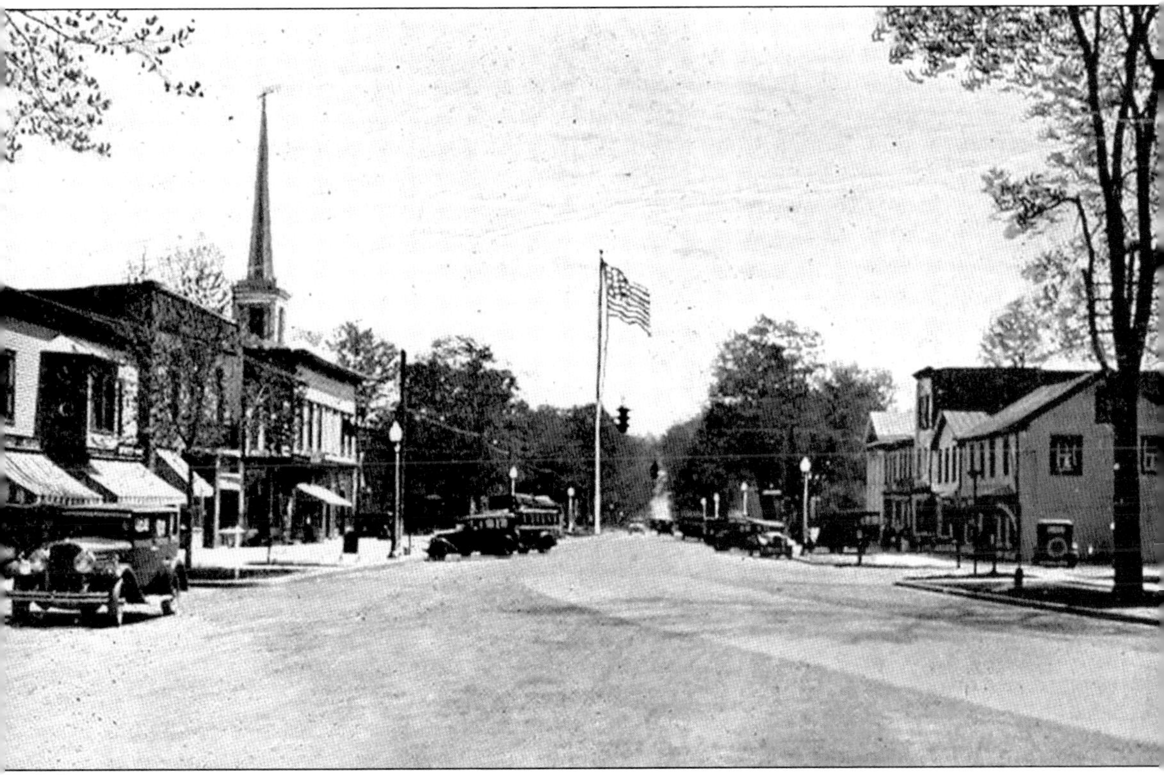

This 1937 photograph of the village center shows the first flag pole in the Alvord House Square.

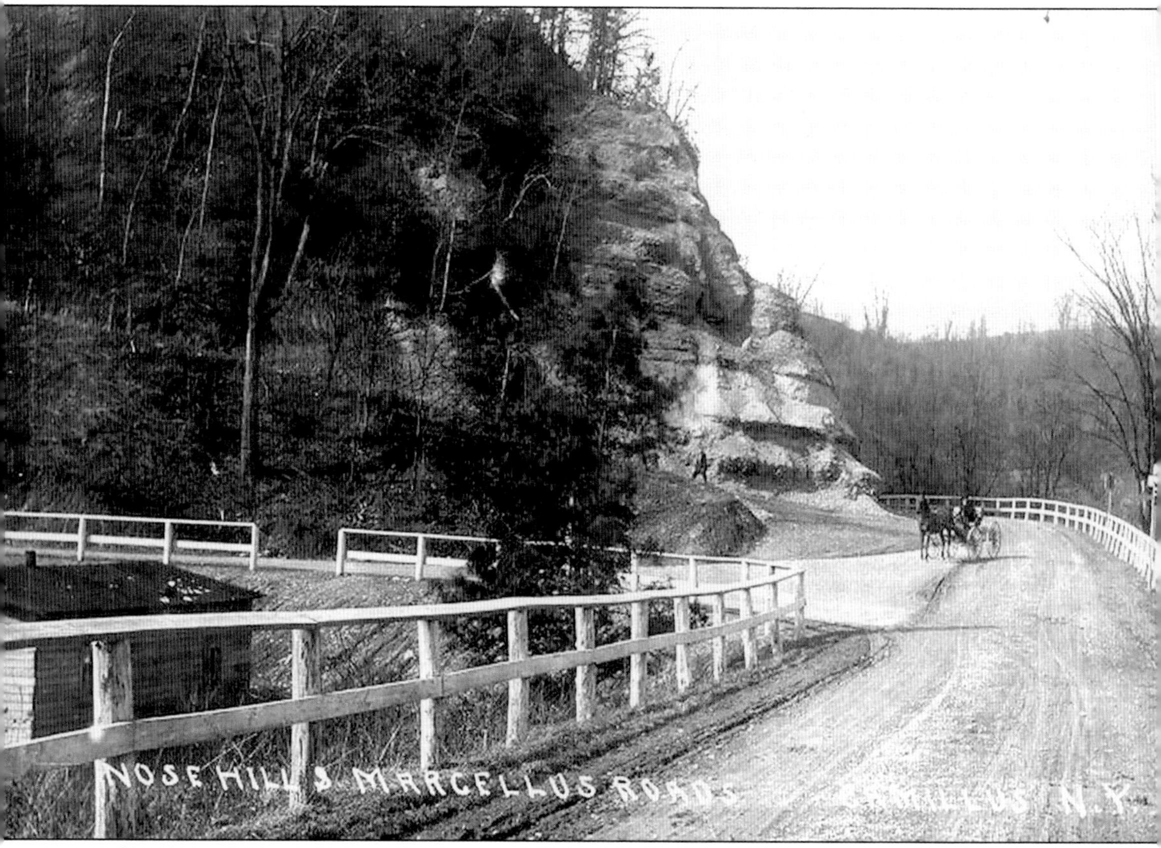

This photograph was taken of Nose Hill, along what is known today as Gorge Road.

Three

The People

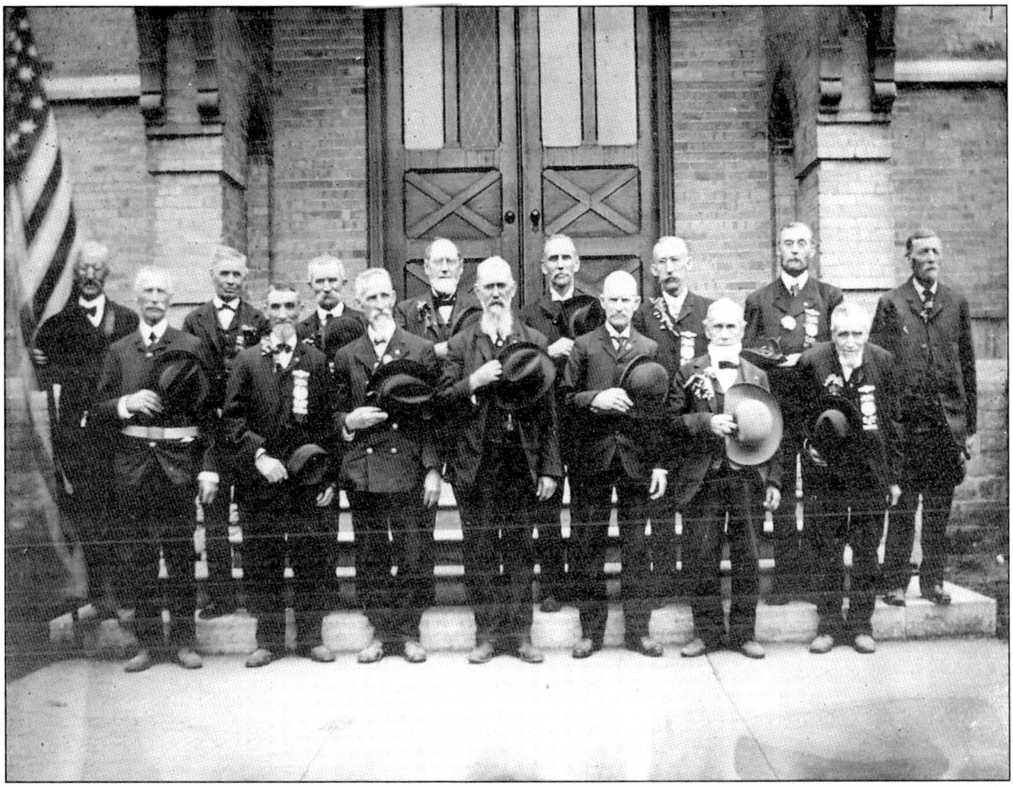

This photograph was taken on May 30, 1906, of the Civil War veterans. The photograph appeared in the *Marcellus Observer* on June 1, 1906. The veterans were with the Joseph Jones post of the Grand Army of the Republic. Their names from left to right are (first row) E. V. Baker, Isaac Richards, E. L. Arnold, Samuel Mead, Aaron Waldron, A. W. Beach, and Martin Hogan; (second row) Patrick Heenan, Irving W. Davey, John Kille, I. N. Sherman, E. D. Gillet, E. H. Baker, Belus F. North, and Washington Hedgeland (of Amber). This photograph was taken by Watson J. Matteson, the postmaster in 1906.

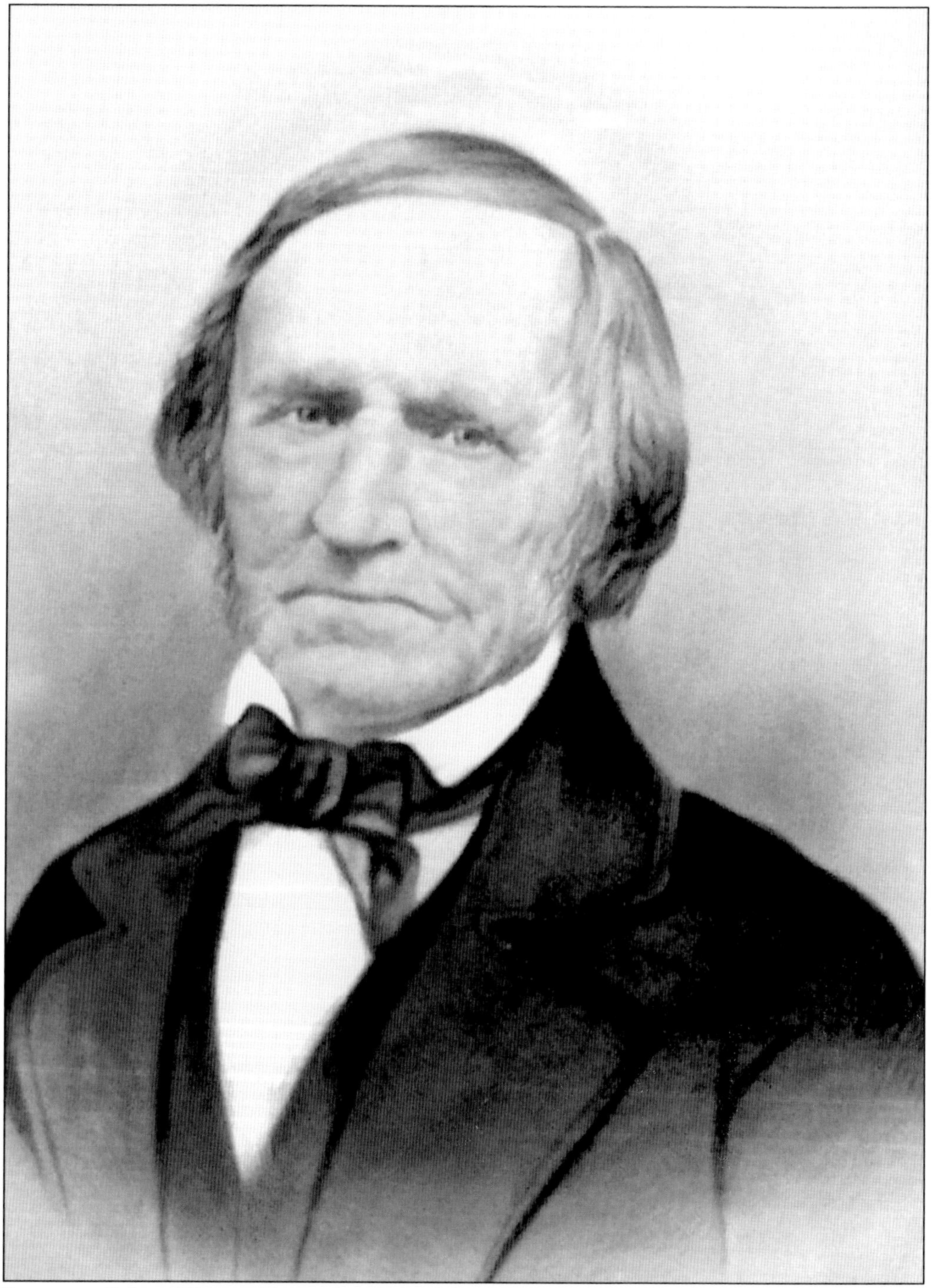

Benjamin Baker (1778–1864) purchased land from Phillip VanCourtlandt in September 1804. He was one of five brothers who moved here from Pelham, Massachusetts. Baker had three wives and 12 children. He died at the age of 86 in 1864.

On March 10, 1810, Nathan Kelsey Hall was born two miles west of the village of Marcellus on West Hill at the farm of Nathan Kelsey, where his parents Ira and Catharine Hall lived. Known to be honest, methodical, and loyal, Nathan was appointed postmaster general by his friend and colleague Pres. Millard Fillmore, who on August 31, 1852, nominated him as U.S. district judge of the Northern District of New York. Nathan presided over Buffalo for the next 22 years. He died in Buffalo on Monday, March 2, 1874, and is buried next to Fillmore at the Forest Lawn Cemetery in Buffalo.

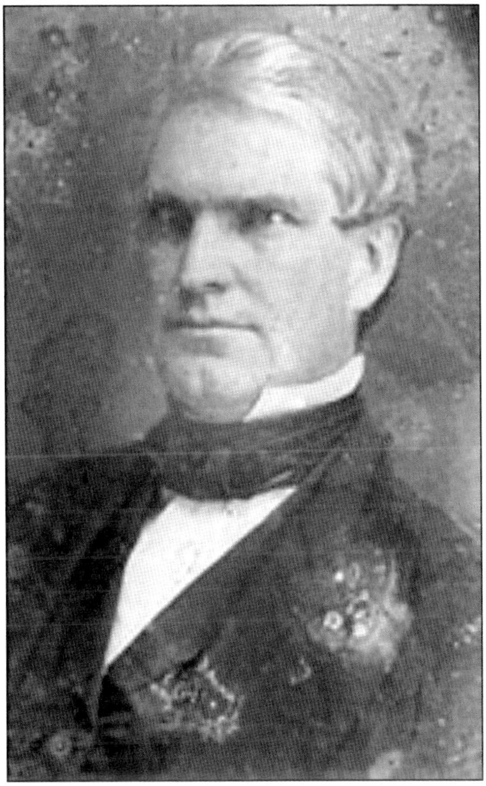

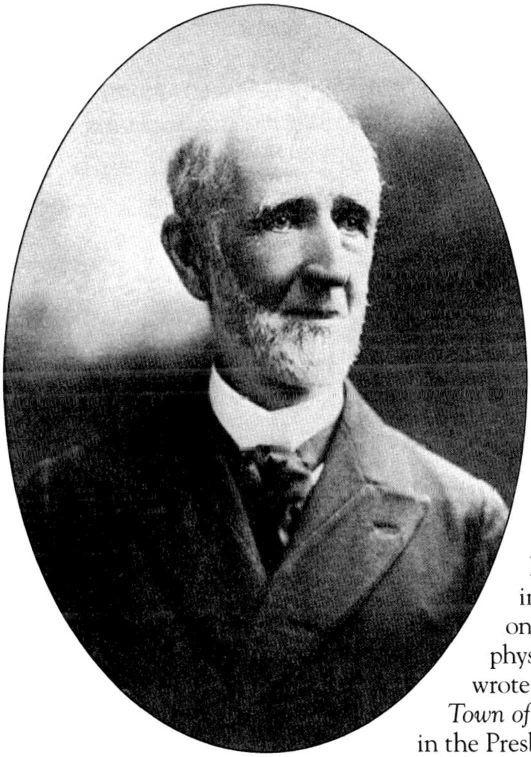

Dr. Israel Parsons (1821–1904) was a graduate of the College of Physicians and Surgeons of the University of New York. He was the son of Levi Parsons and the grandson of Deacon Samuel Rice. Levi was the first pastor serving the congregation of the First Presbyterian Church for 33 years. Levi was also instrumental in establishing the burial grounds on North Street. Israel was a well respected physician, minister, and local town historian. He wrote a publication entitled *Centennial History of the Town of Marcellus,* which he delivered on July 4, 1876, in the Presbyterian church.

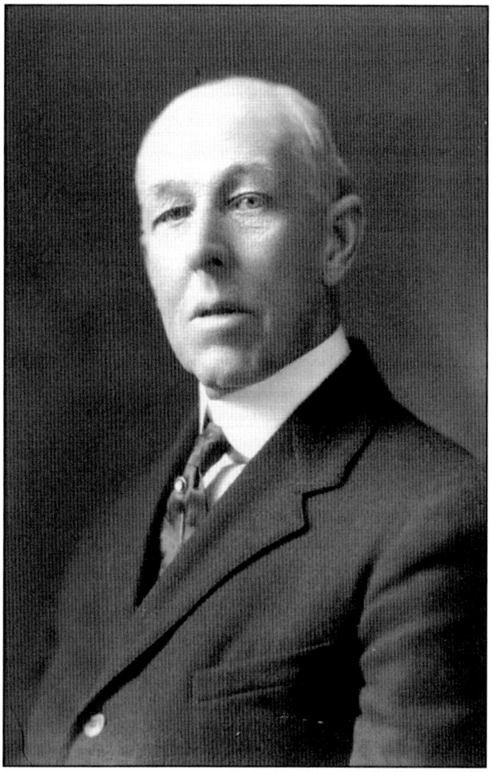

Dr. John Parsons followed in the footsteps of his father, becoming a physician for Marcellus. He used the same horse drawn carriage that his father used (which is now on display at the historical society). He became president of the Marcellus New National Bank in 1910 and was appointed village health officer from 1916 through 1930.

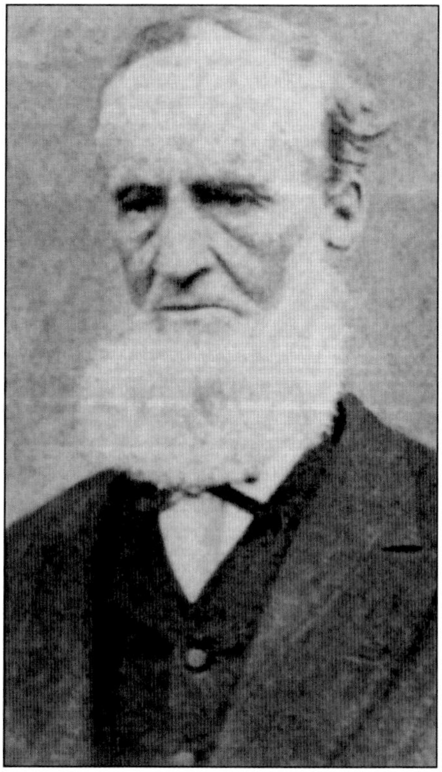

Dan Beach Bradley was born in Marcellus on July 18, 1804, to Rev. Dan Bradley and Eunice Beach Bradley. He graduated from the College of Physicians and Surgeons in New York City. He married Emelie Royce and in 1835, they arrived in Siam, Thailand, where he worked as a medical missionary. He established the printing press and introduced vaccinations to help control the small pox outbreak, which won him the confidence of the king. He was a very well respected physician in Siam. Bradley is said to be the prototype for a character in Margaret Landon's novel, *Anna and the King of Siam*, the novel upon which Rogers and Hammerstein based their musical *The King and I.*

Joseph C. Platt was a wealthy farmer, whose lands were on the south end of the village and are part of the current Marcellus Park. He served as a village trustee from 1863 to 1865. Platt was the father of Erminnie Adelle Platt Smith.

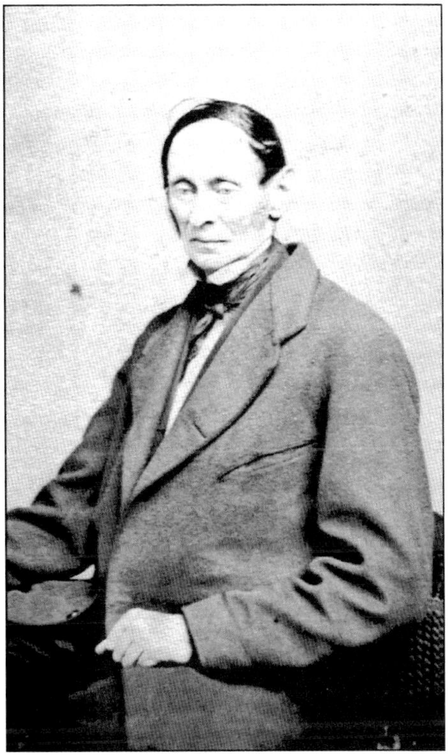

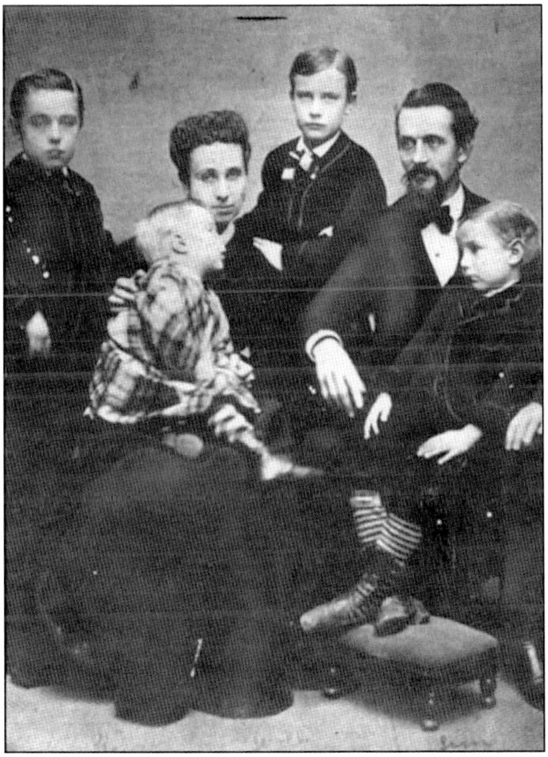

Erminnie Adelle Platt Smith was born in Marcellus in 1836 and graduated from Troy Seminary, New York, in 1853. She married Simeon H. Smith and had four sons (William, Carl, Simeon, and James). Erminnie and her family lived in Germany for four years in the 1870s so she could continue her studies in mineralogy and crystallography. She became an expert on the Six Nations of the Iroquois, specializing in their native languages, which led, in 1880, to her being retained by the Bureau of American Ethnology of the Smithsonian Institute in Washington, D.C. Erminnie was the first woman inducted into the American Academy of Science and was a member of the American Association for the Advancement of Science and the New York Historical Society. She was only 50 years old when she died on June 9, 1886, and is buried at New York Bay Cemetery. Vassar College received the mineral and fossil specimens that she had collected throughout her life.

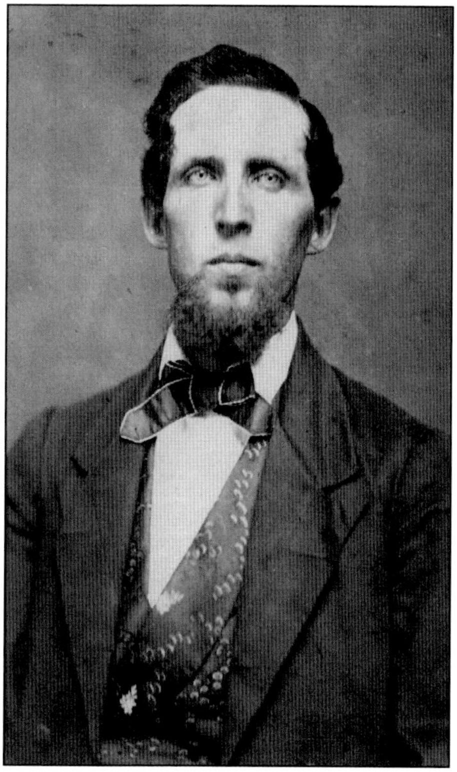

Henry H. Fellows was born in 1837 in Marcellus and enlisted in Company H, Regiment 12, New York Volunteers in the Civil War. He was wounded in the Battle of Malvern Hill and was taken as a prisoner of war. He died of his wounds in Libby Prison on July 13, 1862, at the age of 24.

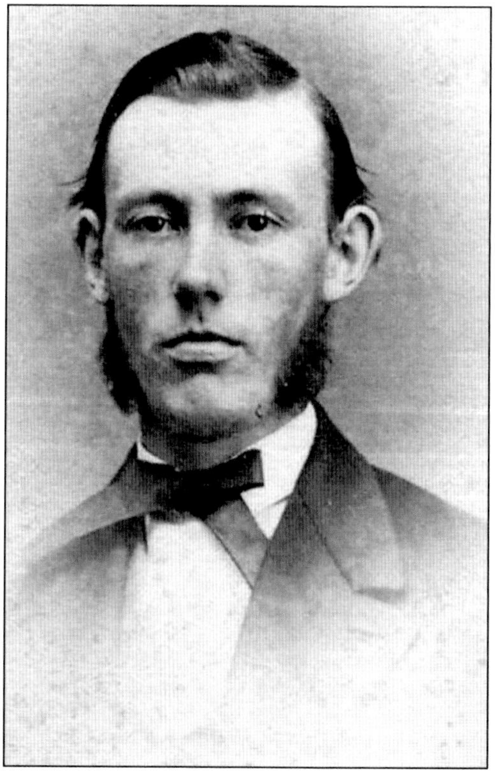

John H. Platt was born in Marcellus in 1829 and served in the Civil War. He was a captain aboard the USS *Huntington*. He died at the age of 43 in 1872.

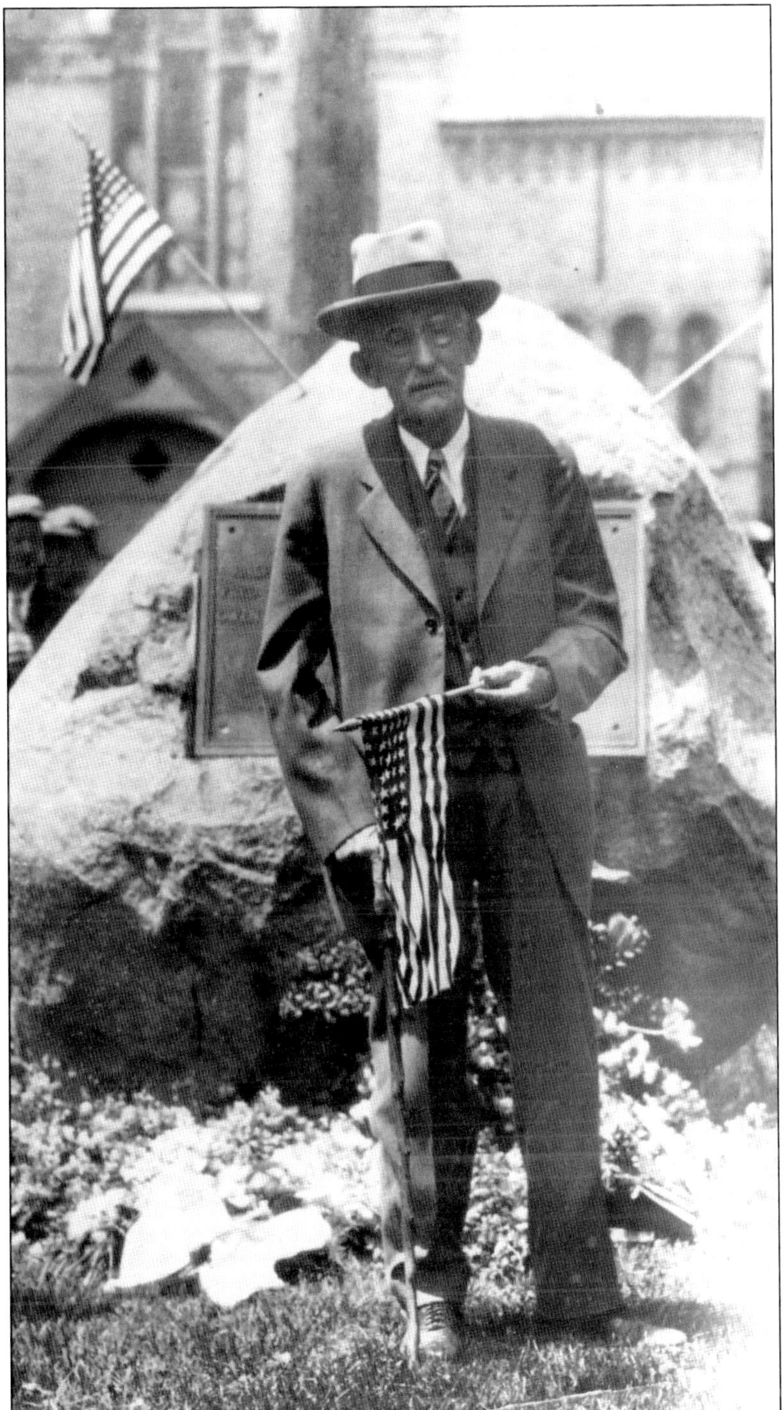

Elijah Baker was the last surviving Civil War veteran from Marcellus. He fought for the 122 Regiment, New York Volunteers, and was present at the surrender of General Lee. He lived in Marietta with his wife, Dena Baker, and although they had no children of their own, they were known by the neighborhood children as "Uncle Lige" and "Aunt Dean."

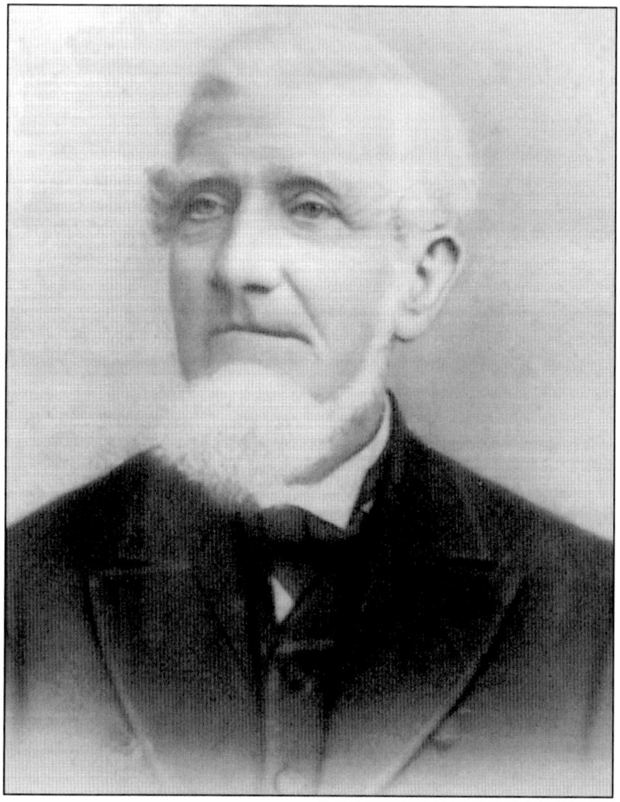

Samuel Hooper was born in England and came to Marcellus in 1848. He took over the furniture and undertaking business from N. C. Hoyt in about 1880. Hooper owned the Marcellus Furniture Manufacturing Company in partnership with William Gallup. The Marcellus Furniture Manufacturing Company burned to the ground in the late 1800s. Hooper also served as village trustee.

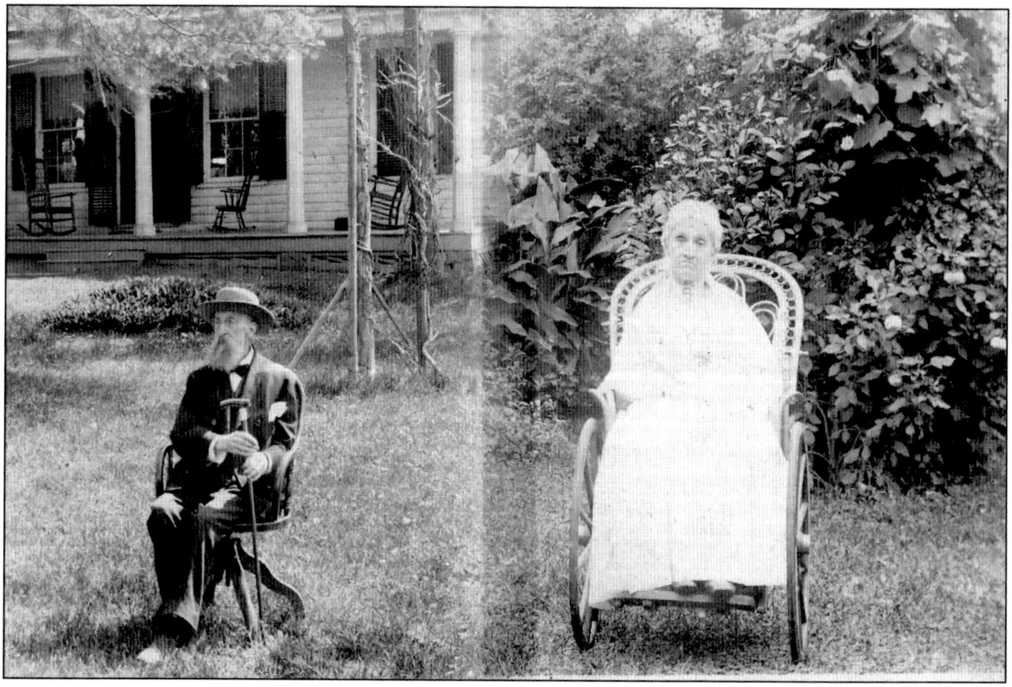

Isaac Bradley and his wife Mary are sitting out on their front lawn on South Street. Isaac was voted in as assessor in 1853.

Sidney Slocombe was born in England on December 18, 1856. He was the son of Samuel and Elizabeth Slocombe. He came to Marcellus in the spring of 1873, and spent three-and-one-half years as an apprentice and journeyman at his trade of tinsmith. He then started in business in Marcellus for himself, and his business gradually increased every year. He had a large store, and store rooms, containing a fine line of stoves, agricultural implements, and hardware. He married Urena Nettleton, daughter of Samuel Stafford Nettleton, of Arnprior, Ontario, Canada, and had four children. Sidney was village president from 1898 to 1901, 1909–1910, and 1921–1922.

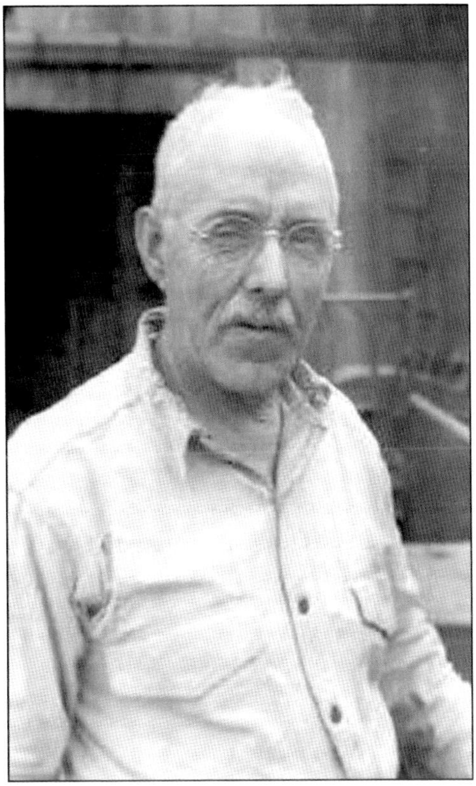

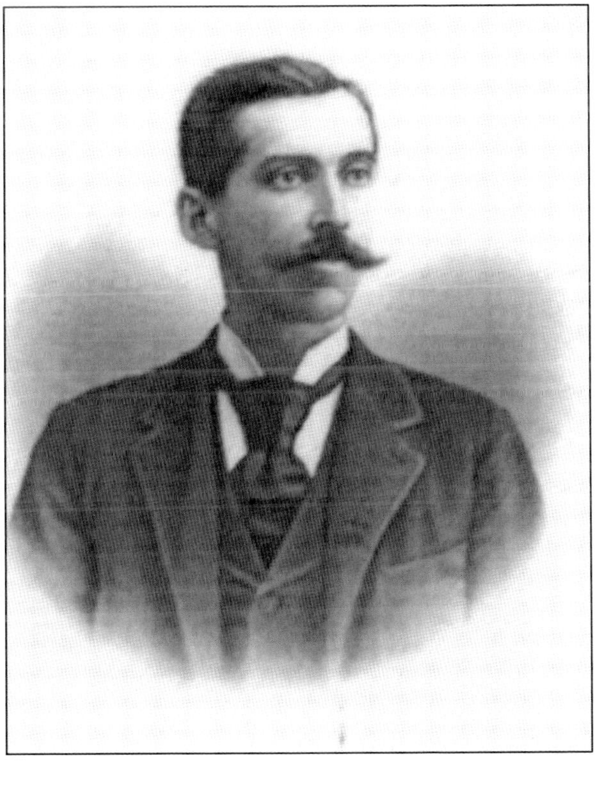

Frank B. Mills was born in Marcellus in 1866. As a youth he became interested in producing and classifying seeds of various plants and vegetables. He started his seed business and, due to the great volume of that business, the U.S. government saw the need for a post office and, in 1890, named Mills as the first postmaster of Rose Hill.

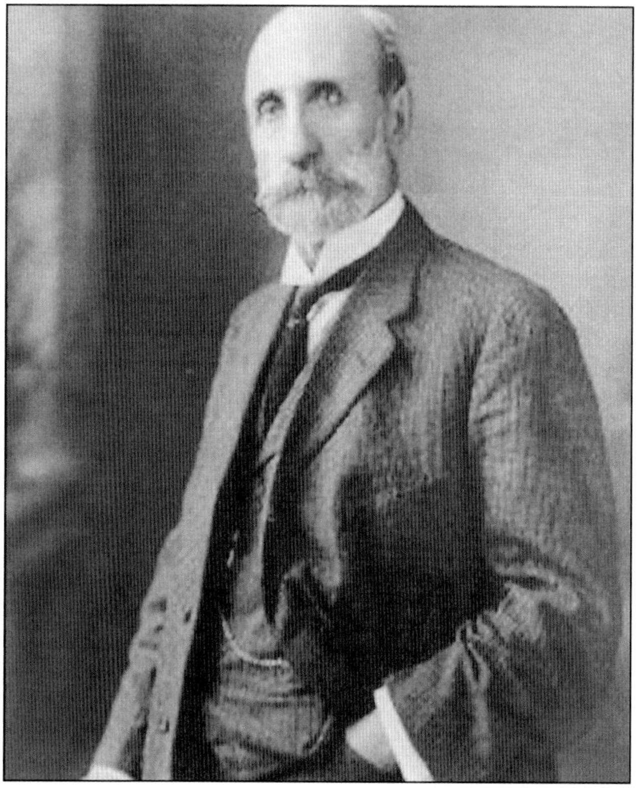

Edward Moir was born in 1846 in Galashiels, Scotland. In 1856, he immigrated to Ontario, Canada, where he attended school, received extensive experience in the woolen industry, and purchased and enlarged the Auburn Mills in Ontario. Recognized as being an authority in the woolen industry, Moir was brought to Marcellus by S. W. Barker, who made him superintendent, replacing Robert Waugh. Moir was elected village president and served from 1892 to 1893 and from 1905 to 1908.

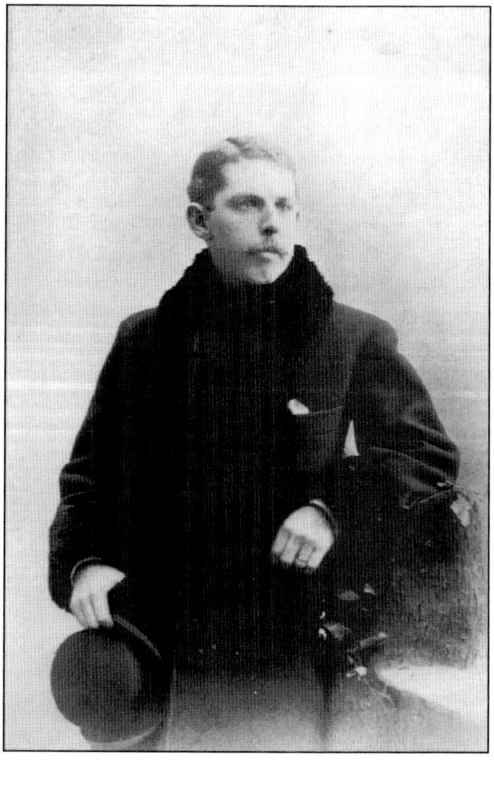

Edmund Reed was the son of Hiram and Martha June Glass Reed. He was born in October 1856 and died in May 1923. He founded the town's first newspaper, the *Marcellus Observer*, in April 1879. He also owned Reeds Novelty Factory in the late 1800s, which was located on West Hill. In 1888, he was elected supervisor and also acted as village president. His daughter Ruth Cummings lived with her family in her father's home after his death.

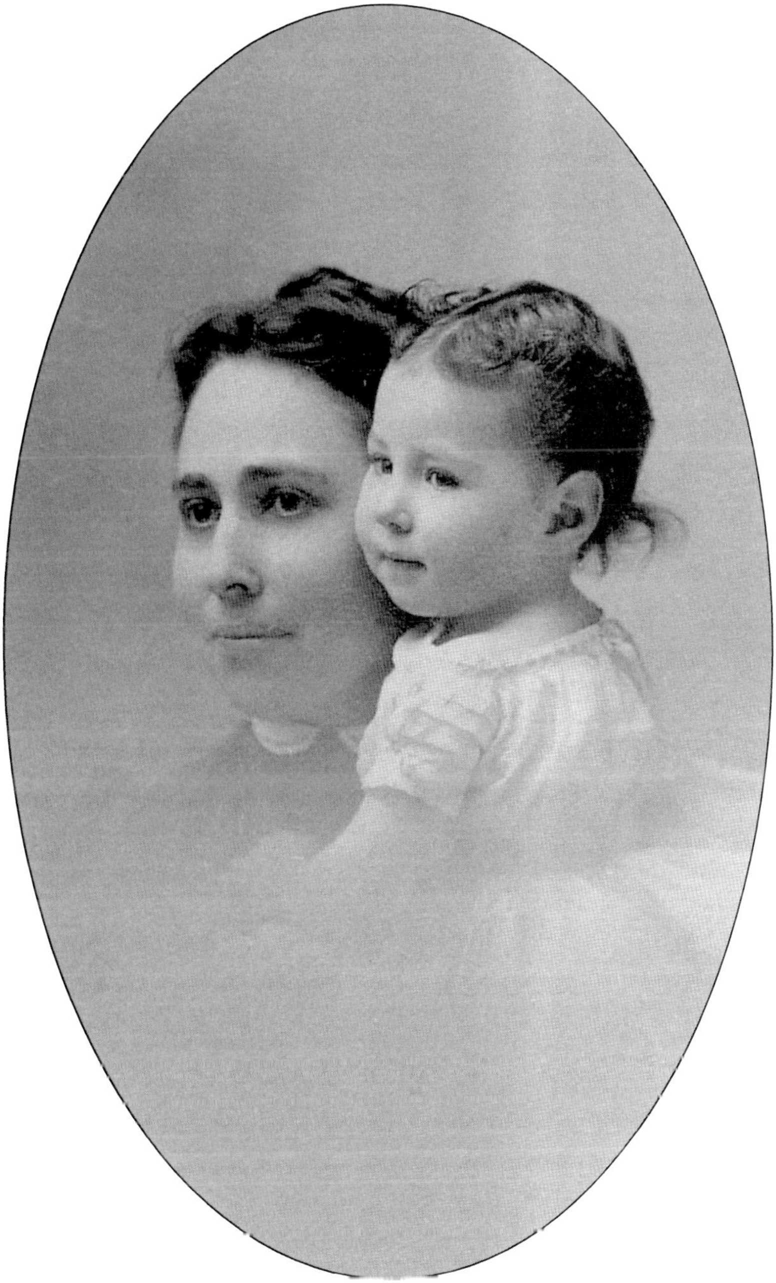

Hattie Daboll Reed was born in 1856. She became the wife of Edmund Reed, and had four children. She is shown here holding her youngest child, Ruth. The three living children were Hiram (1888), Martha (1892), and Ruth (1900). In 1925, Hattie developed the Reed Farm Tract as a new residential section of the village. This included the sale of over 130 building lots. She also raised High Bred Sicilian Buttercup hens. She won best display two years running in 1917 and 1918 in Madison Square Gardens.

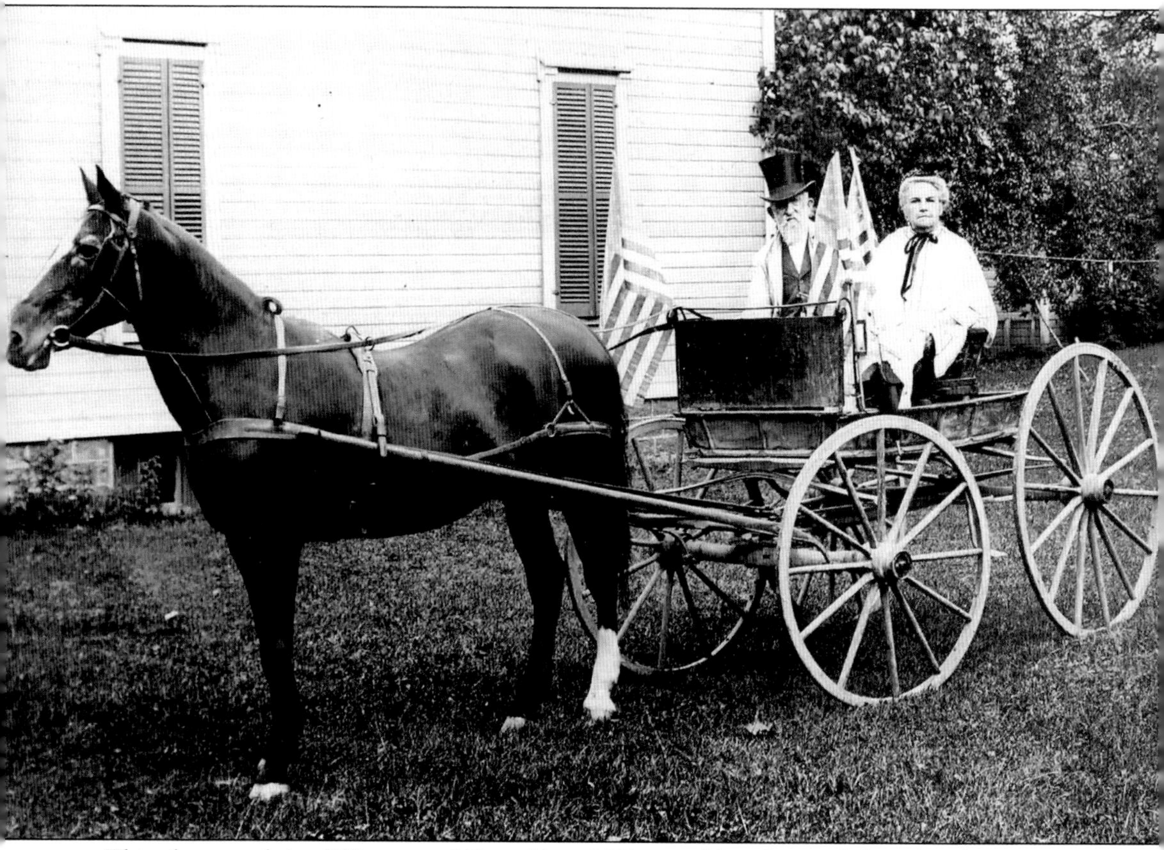

This photograph is of Warren and Eliza Alvord. Warren Alvord owned the Alvord House along with his brothers Calvin G. Alvord and Charles Alvord. The Alvords were born in Saratoga, and moved to Marcellus prior to the outbreak of the Civil War. Warren sat on the village board, and his brother Calvin was also a member of the village government.

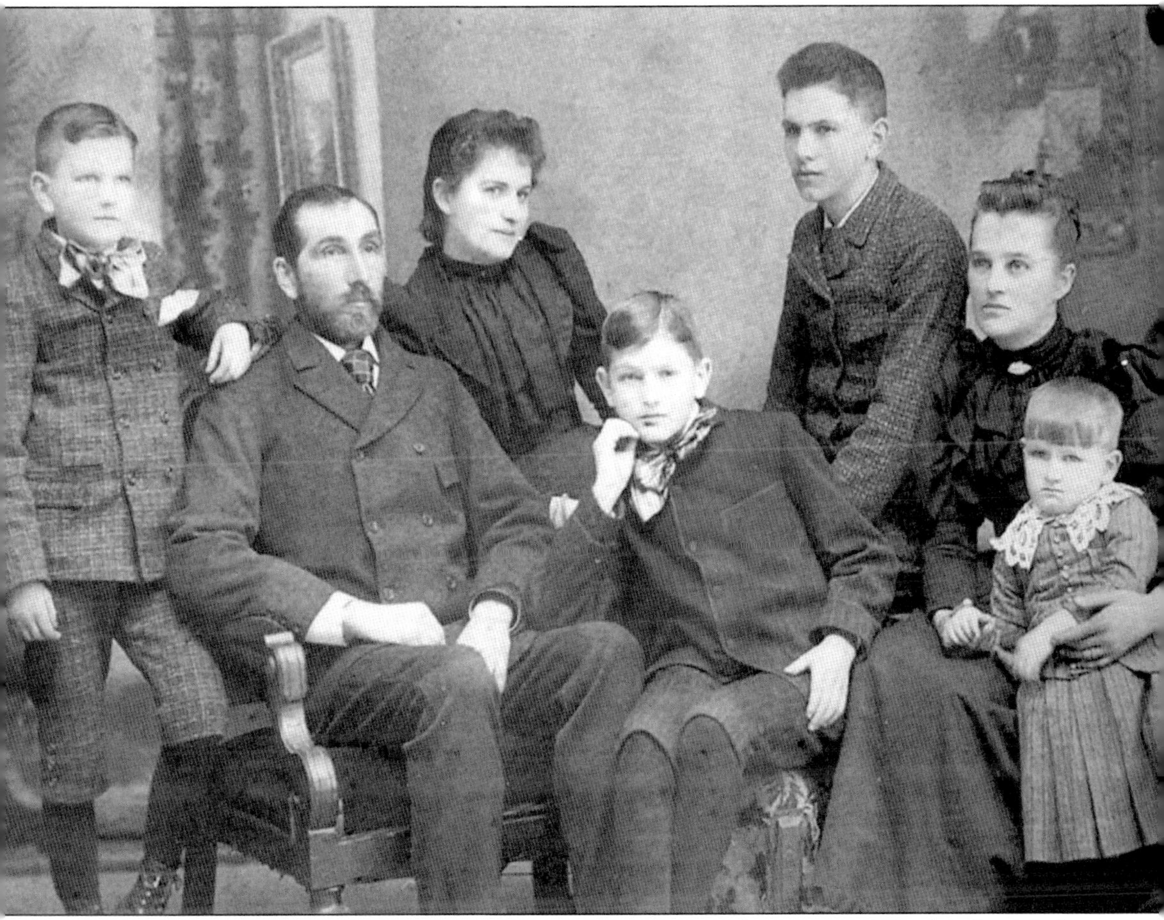

Rollin M. Stone is shown here with his family. Stone was a master horseman. He bred and trained coach horses. He was also the famous first baseman for the first baseball team in Marcellus. Family members from left to right are Dwight, Rollin, Grace, Robert, James, Mary, and Horace. Horace, the youngest son, became a prominent attorney and supervisor of the town of Marcellus and served 13 terms in the New York Assembly. Nominated for Marcellus's Most Useful Citizen in 1938, he died in 1944. Rollin's father, James, had owned the land where much of the Marcellus Central School campus is today. It was called Stone Farm, in Shelter Valley. James raised pure bread Holsteins and horses and also sold milk to the village and to Marcellus Falls. Stone Farm also hatched and sold 13,500 squab broilers (young chicks) in 1932 and annually produced and dressed between 2,000 and 3,000 broilers for the restaurant businesses in the area.

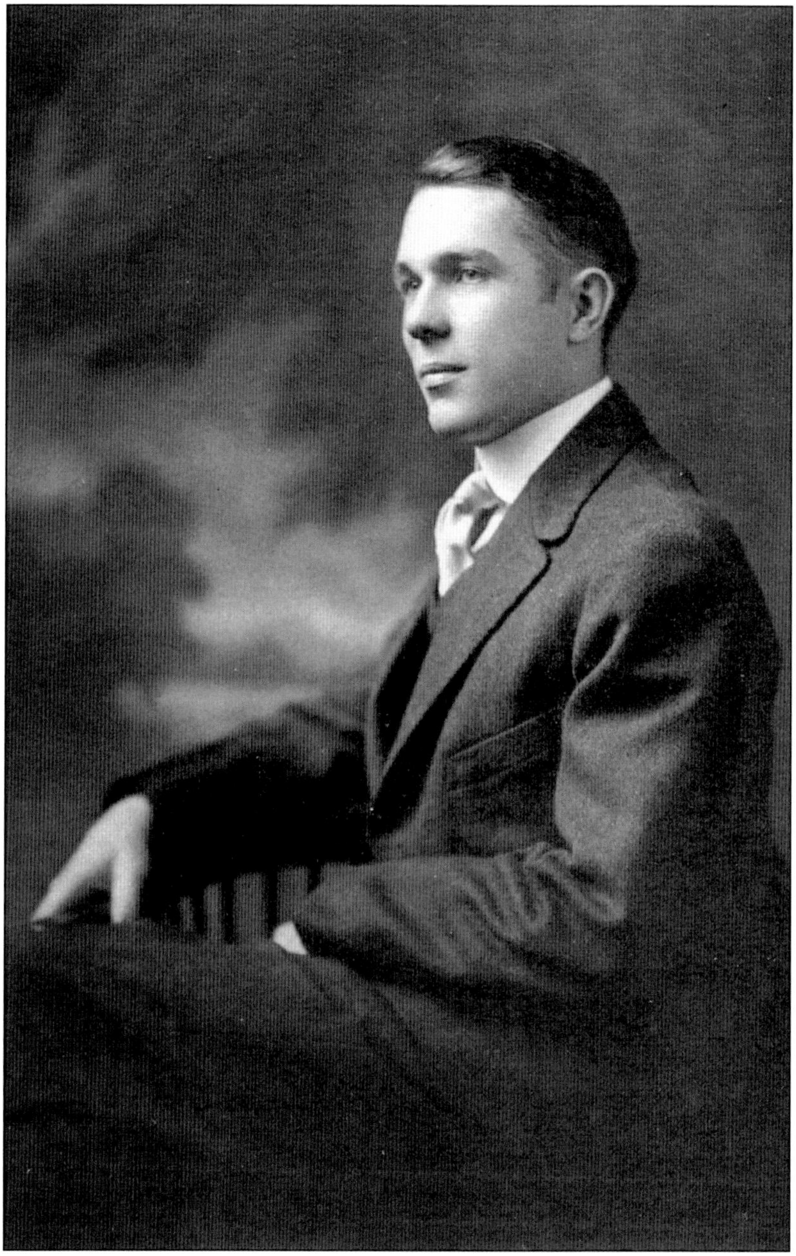

Robert Earl Baker, whose great-great-grandparents came from Massachusetts in 1809 and settled on a farm on Cherry Valley Turnpike and Slate Hill Road, was born in 1893 in a house at 12 North Street. Baker, whose father operated a wagon shop on the premises, grew up in Marcellus and graduated from Marcellus High School. After attending the University of Michigan, he worked as a chemical engineer with Allied Chemical Corporation. Baker's will revealed a perpetual trust fund, which he established in 1952, for educational and religious purposes. The beneficiaries are the Marcellus Free Library and the three Protestant churches in the village. He also funds scholarships to be awarded annually to graduates of Marcellus central schools. The recipients must be male, must be active members of one of the Protestant churches, and must plan on pursuing a career in medicine or engineering.

Stephen H. Hunt ran a grocery business in Navarino until he bought out Fred Schoonmaker and moved his store to 19 East Main Street. Hunt served as village trustee from 1930 until 1944.

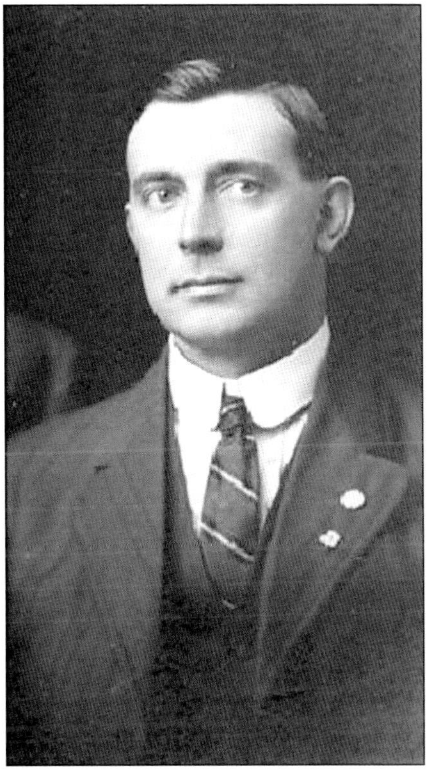

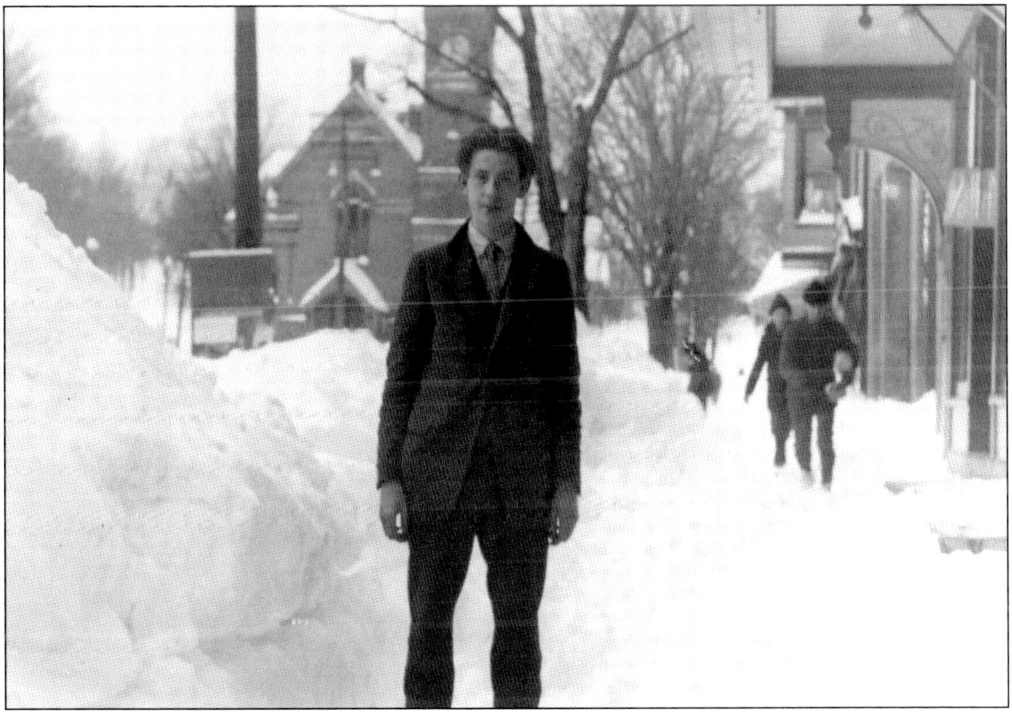

Frank Longworthy is pictured here in the winter of 1925. He worked at Marble and Spaulding Drug Store.

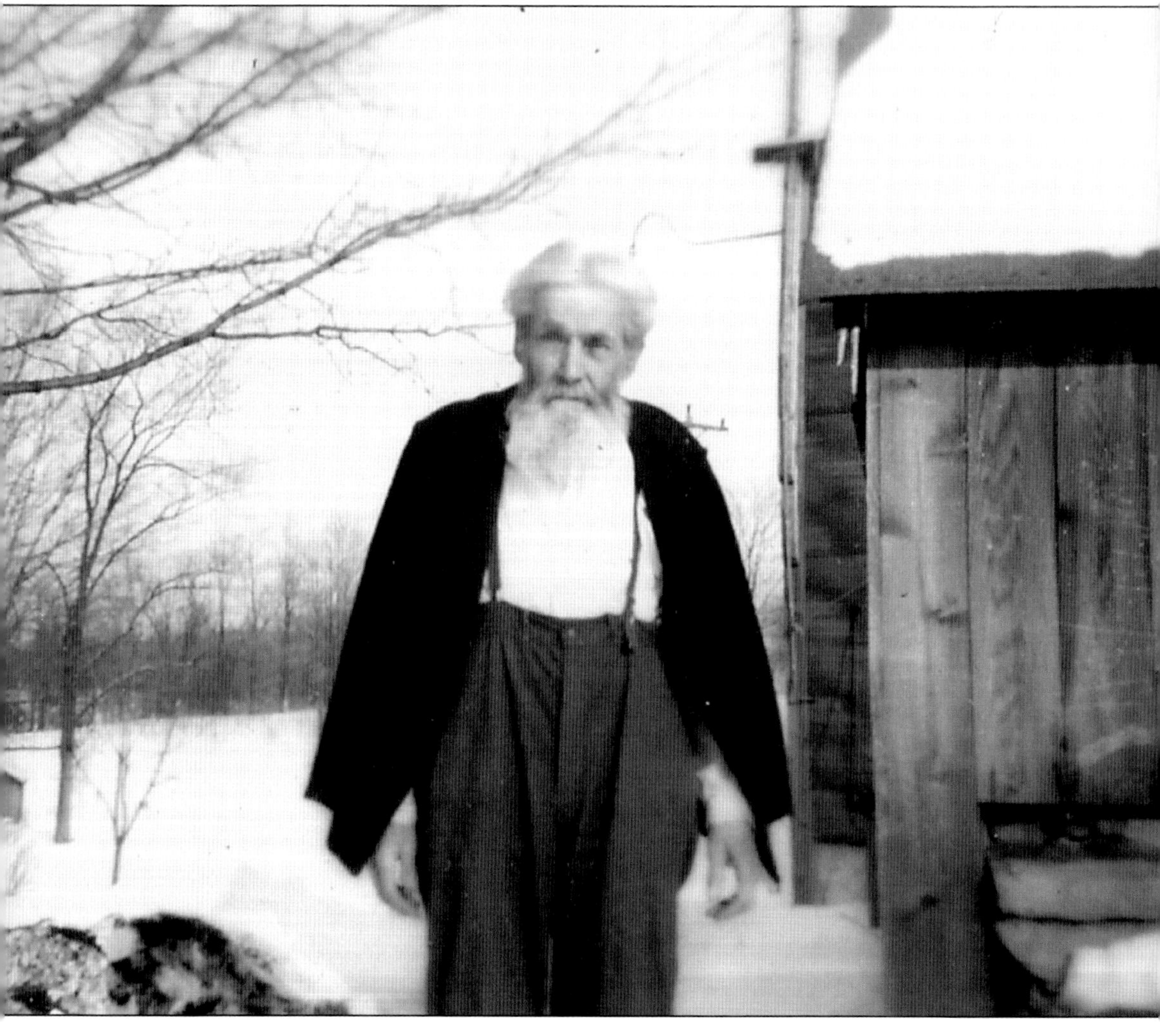

James W. Walker, a master carpenter, assembled the prefabricated trolley rest stops. When in his late 70s, he built his own home on Howlett Hill Road. Built by hand, the house was 14 feet by 20 feet and had a unique mode of construction. When the house was completed, he began work on erecting outbuildings.

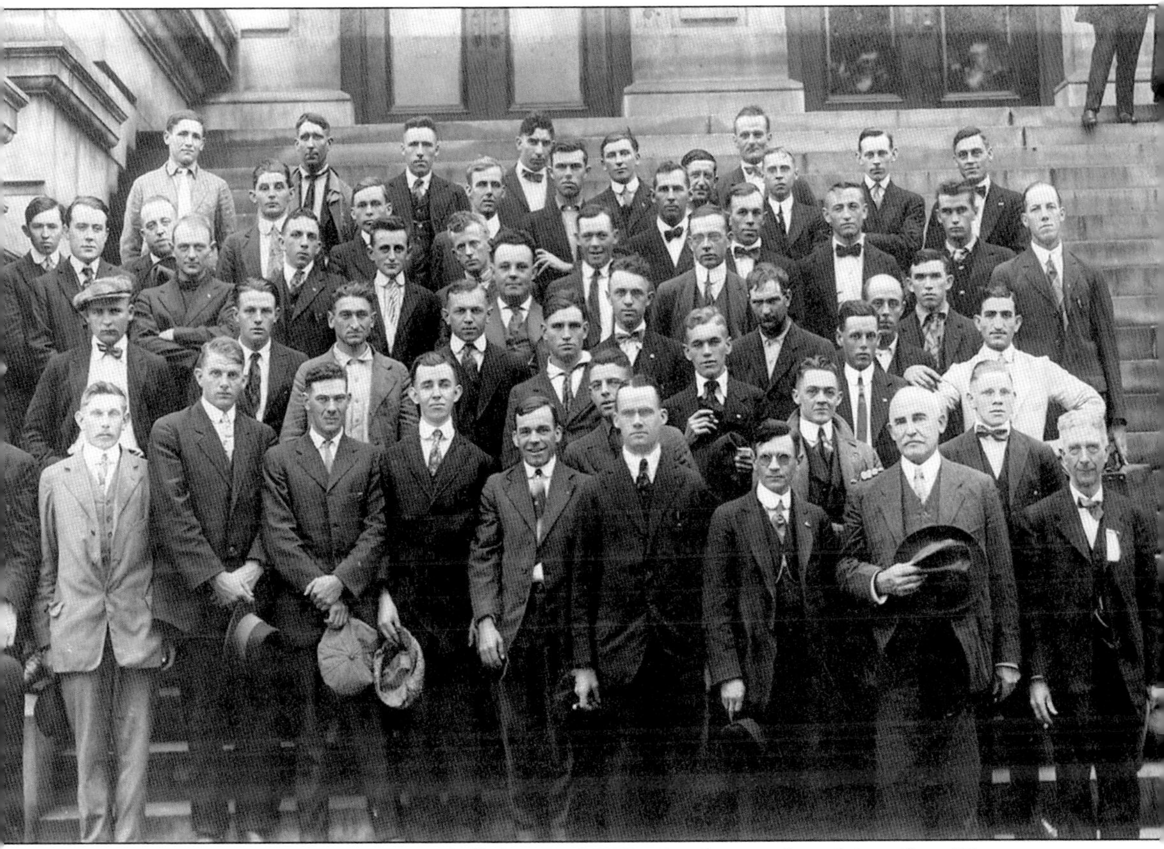

This is a photograph taken in 1917 of all the World War I inductees from Marcellus. The roster, printed in the appendix of *Nine Mile Country* by Kathryn C. Heffernan, listed 68 names of men on the Roll of Honor for World War I.

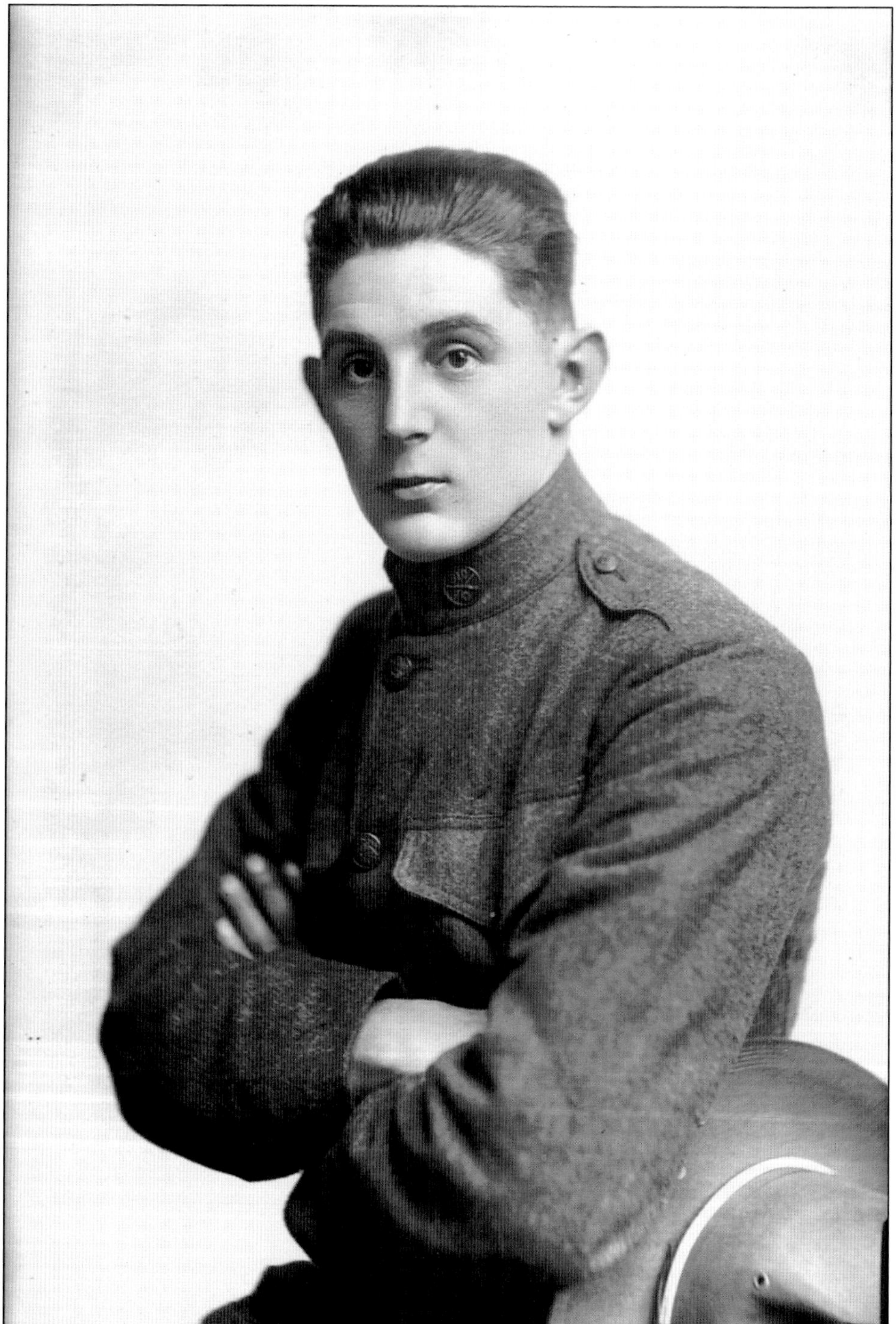

Ralph Cameron Share was a private in World War I with the 23rd Regiment, Company 6th, U.S. Marine Corps. He was killed in action on October 4, 1918, at Champagne Front, France. He was the first Marcellus native to be killed in World War I. The American Legion post in Marcellus bears his name today.

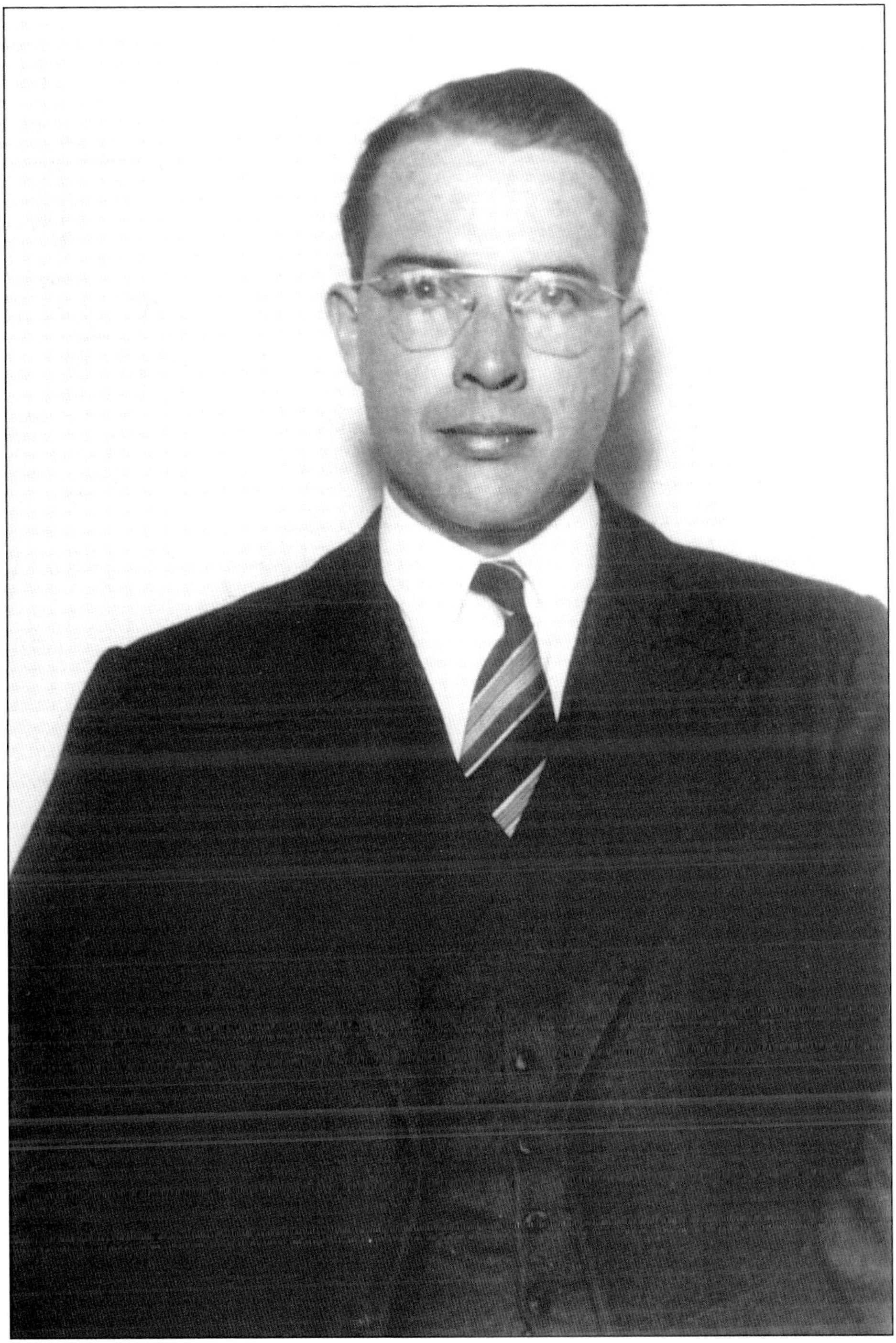

Lester Norris was a prominent figure in Marcellus politics. He was first a trustee and then mayor, the longest-serving mayor (1955–1982) in the history of the village. He was a volunteer fireman and he owned Norris Funeral Home, a business originally started by Samuel Hooper in 1848. The succession of owners were: Hooper and Jones, Jones and Uttley, and then Uttley and Norris. The Norris Funeral Home opened in 1938 and today is known as the Norris-Plis Funeral Home.

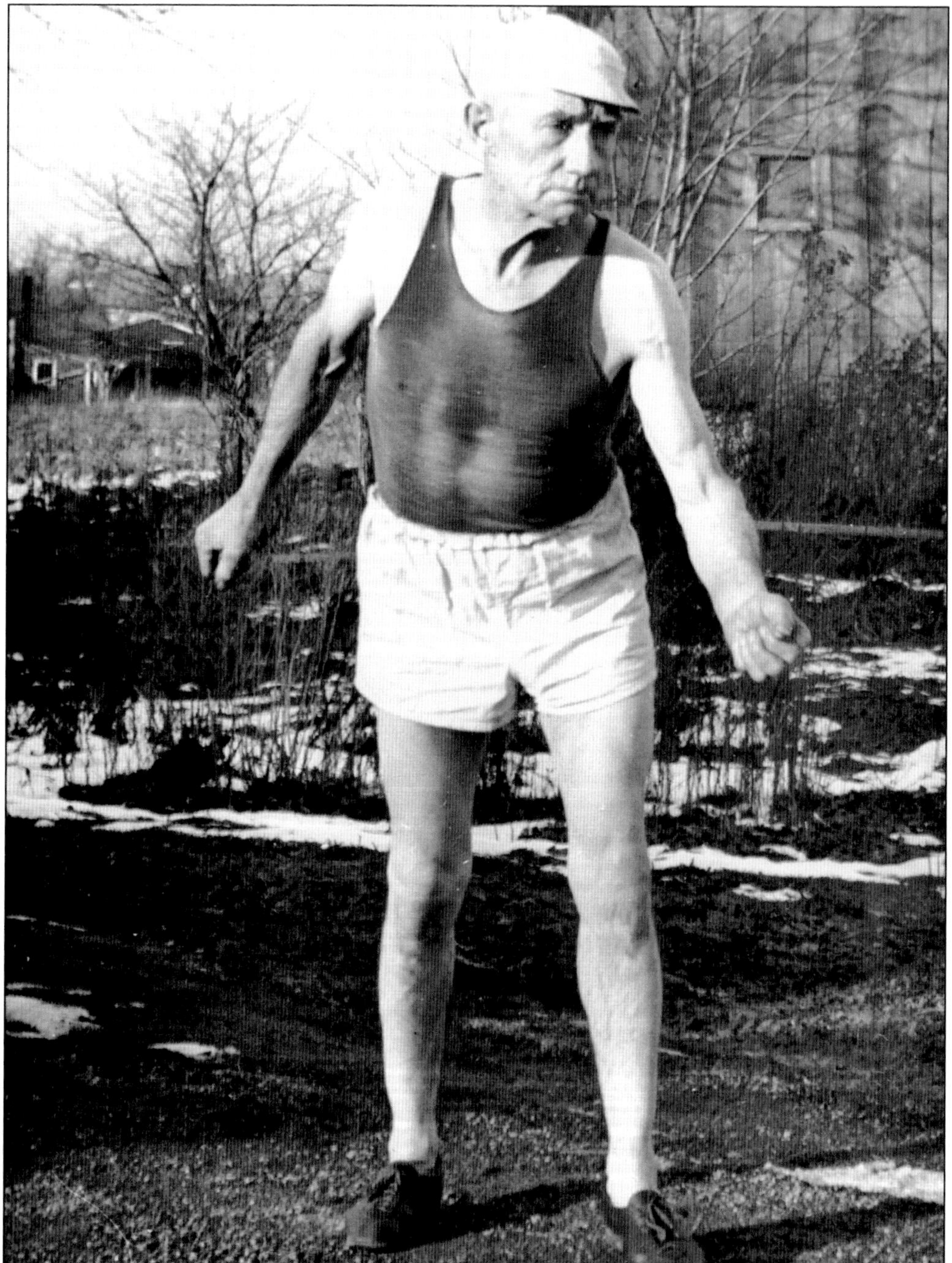

John L. Sullivan worked at the woolen mills in Marcellus, but was also an amazing track star. He once took a $10 bet that he could beat a doctor's horse from Camillus to Marcellus. Sullivan won the bet. Unfortunately, the horse collapsed and died after the race. His physical makeup was a medical marvel for all the physicians who studied him. He was often sought out for his expertise in track by Syracuse University athletes. He was known for his superior strength, speed, and stamina, and he won victories over the best athletes in the United States and in Canada.

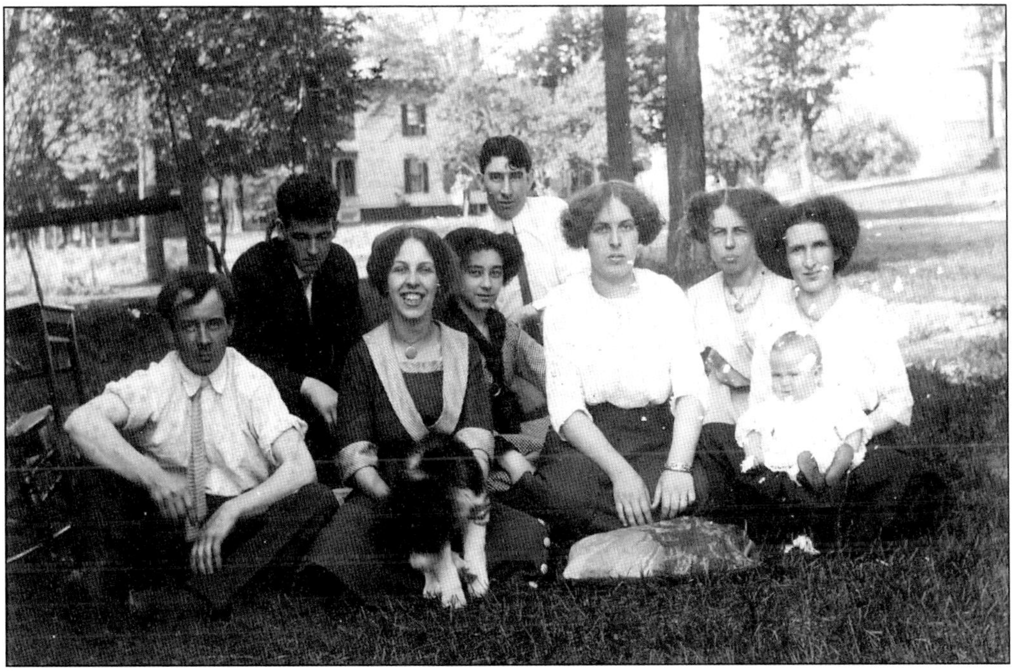

This photograph shows, from left to right, Norman Buffan, Thomas Campion, Viola Campion, Minnie Haney, Thomas Haney, Flossie Bagley, Eva Owens, Elizabeth Owens, and infant John Campion.

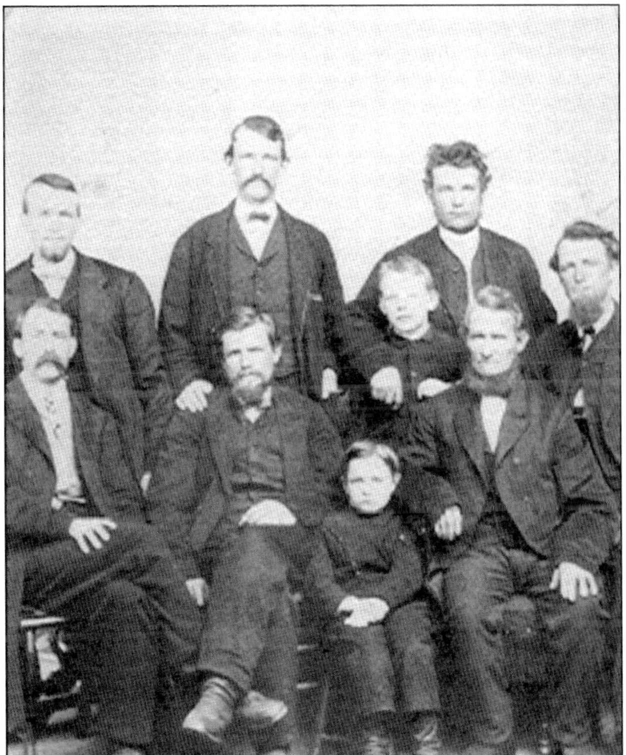

The Spinks men are, from left to right, (first row) Charles Spinks, I. Spinks, Jeffie Spinks (small boy), and Grandpa John Spinks; (second row) George Spinks, Page Spinks, E. Spinks (small boy), Isaiah Spinks, and John Spinks.

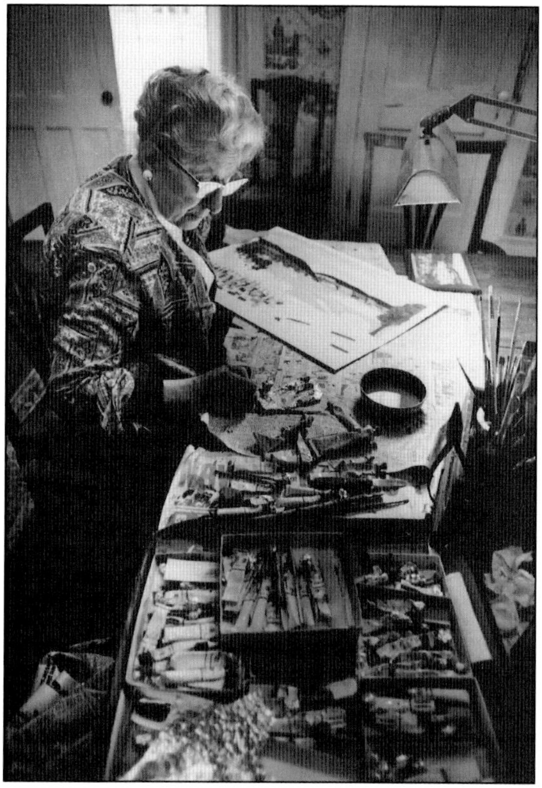

Ruth Reed married Lloyd Cummings and lived in her father's home on North Street. Together with her sister, Martha, she bought and sold antiques and also began a candy business. Her husband assisted her in the candy business as well, and in later years she became a primitive-style painter. She was lovingly known as "the Grandma Moses of Marcellus."

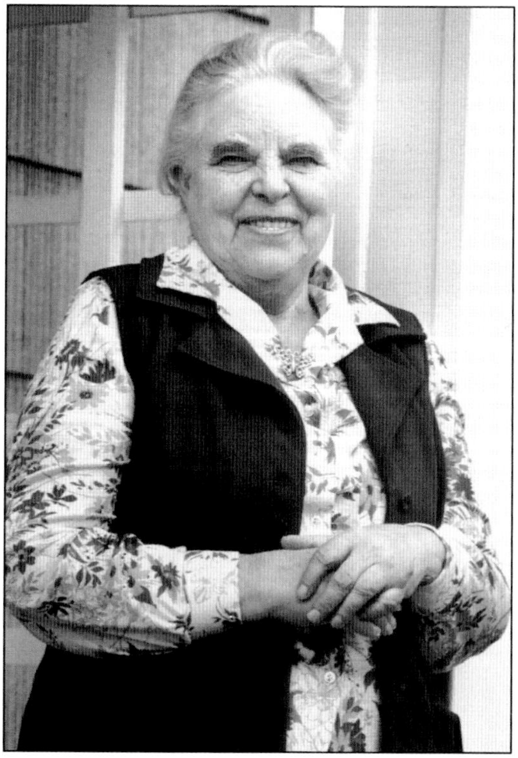

Lucy Sweet was much loved throughout the Marcellus community. She taught school from 1936 to 1973. She was also the town's historian and was secretary to the Marcellus Community Council. In 1960, she was voted secretary and treasurer for the newly formed Marcellus Historical Society. Through her tireless efforts, the historical society has grown to become the wonderful resource it is today.

Four
Home Sweet Home

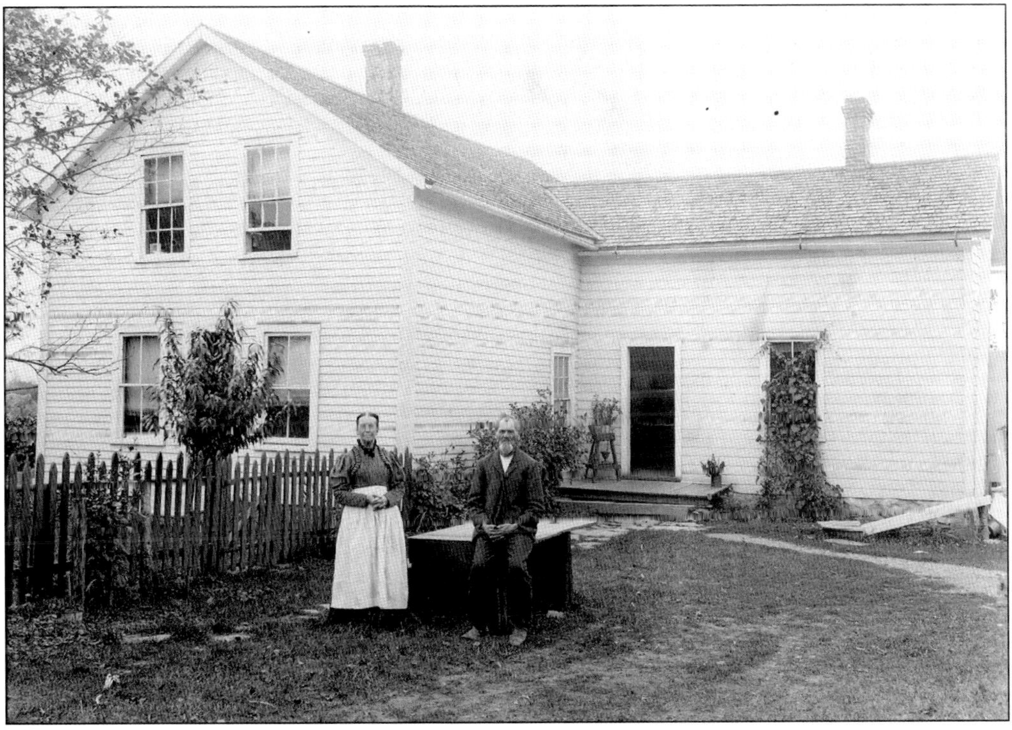

This is the home of Shubael Kenyon in 1868. It was located at lot No. 56, just south of Marcellus. Mary Kenyon, shown here with her husband, was a dressmaker.

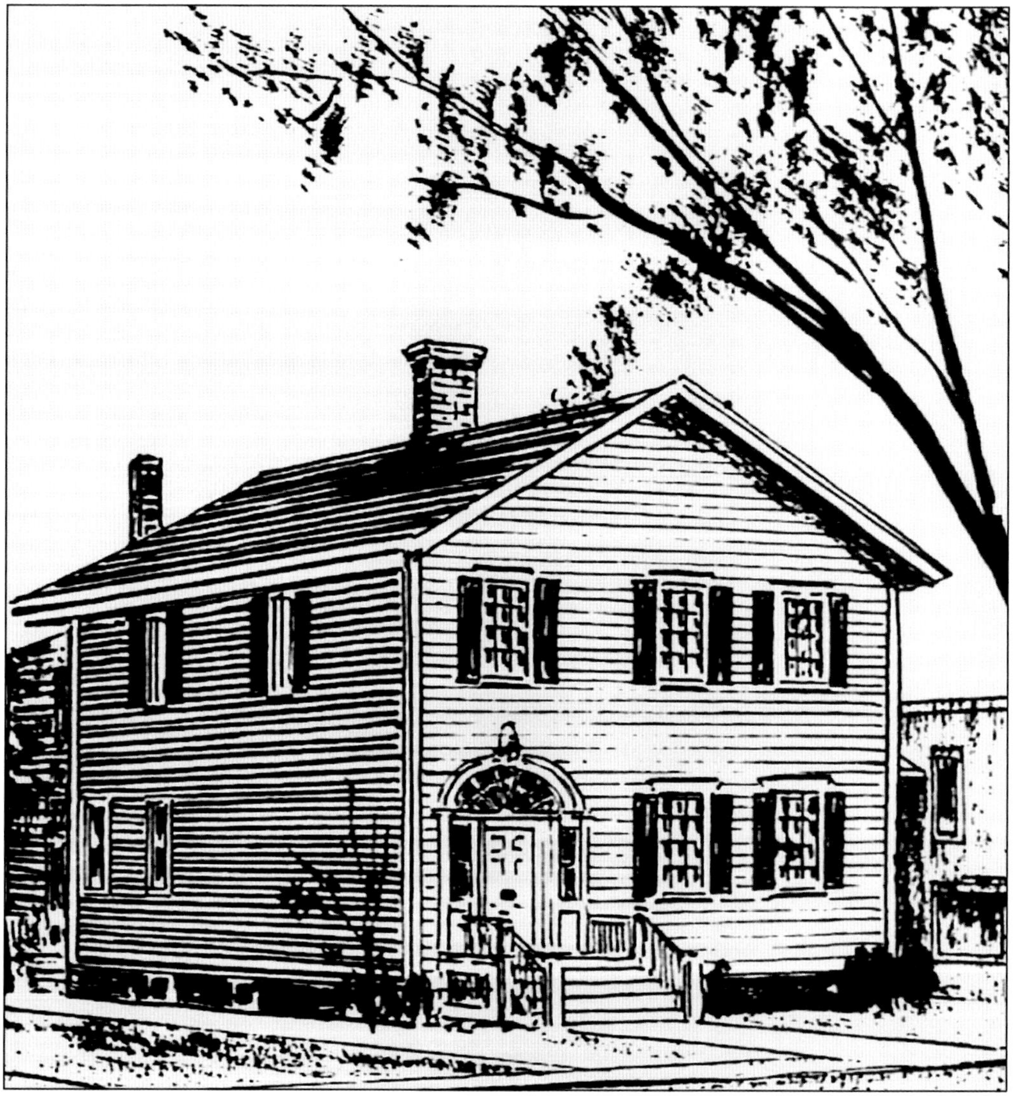

The library found a permanent home in 1937 when the Smith home (originally built by the Gasper family in the early 1800s) came up for sale and was remodeled to fit the needs of the library. The Clift sisters, May and Mattie, started an endowment fund of $6,000 in memoriam to their father, Hiram Clift.

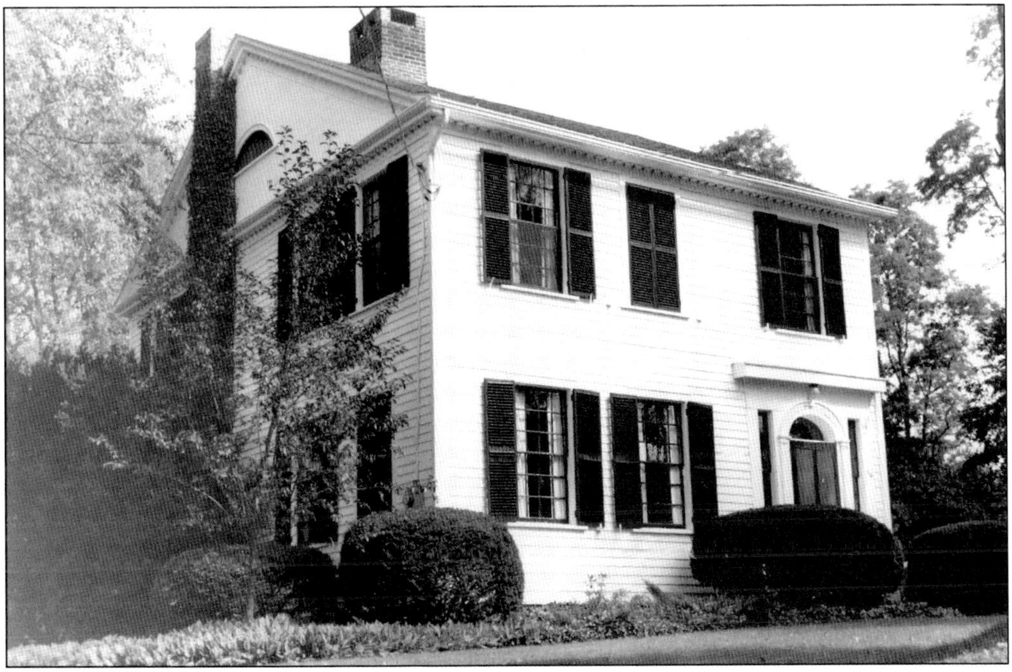

This is the Dan Bradley home at 59 South Street. The house was built between 1798 and 1800 and is the only house in the village on the National Register of Historic Places. The house has poured glass window panes, seven fireplaces, and a cellar kitchen with a flagged hearth and a crane and bake oven. After selling this two-story home in 1828, Bradley moved into a smaller home at 13 South Street. He died in 1838. His son Isaac lived in this house until his death in 1904.

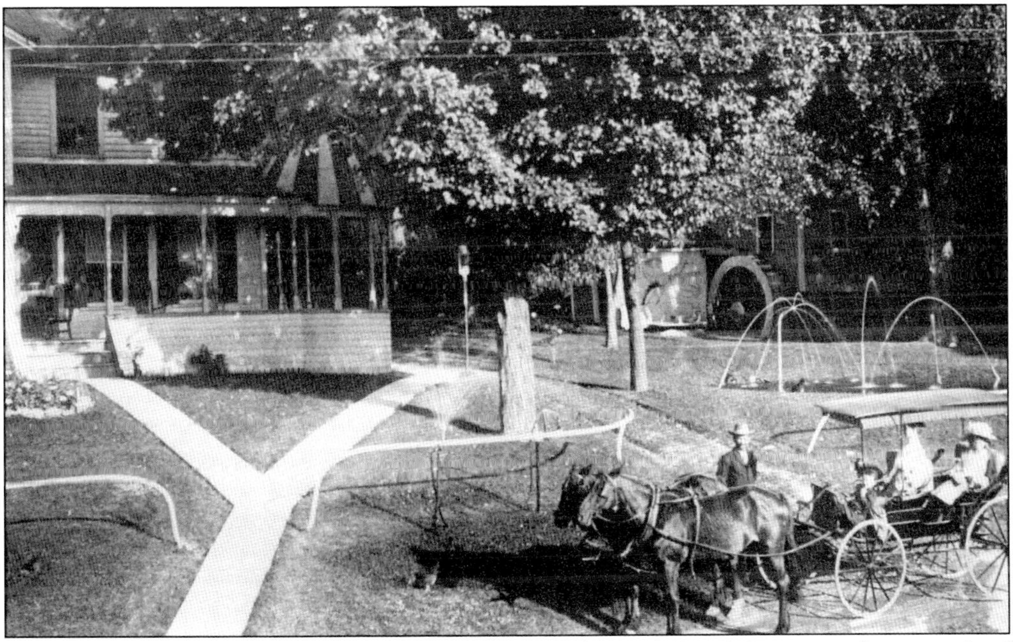

This is the home of A. G. Cornwell, in 1889, on South Street Road. It was on the east side of the road, north of Seal Road. The large water wheel seen in the background on the right was operated by the water from the stream draining from Rockwell Reservoir.

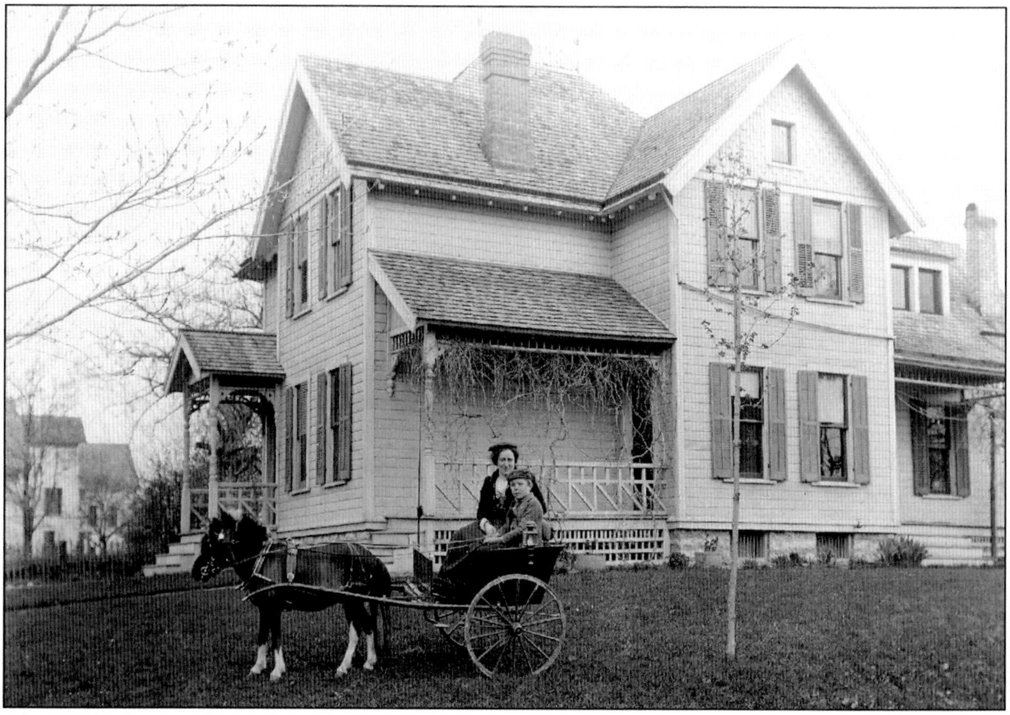

This is the home of Dwight Baker on North Street. Baker ran a wagon shop behind his home. His son Robert E. Baker is in the buggy out front with his nurse Kip Kennedy.

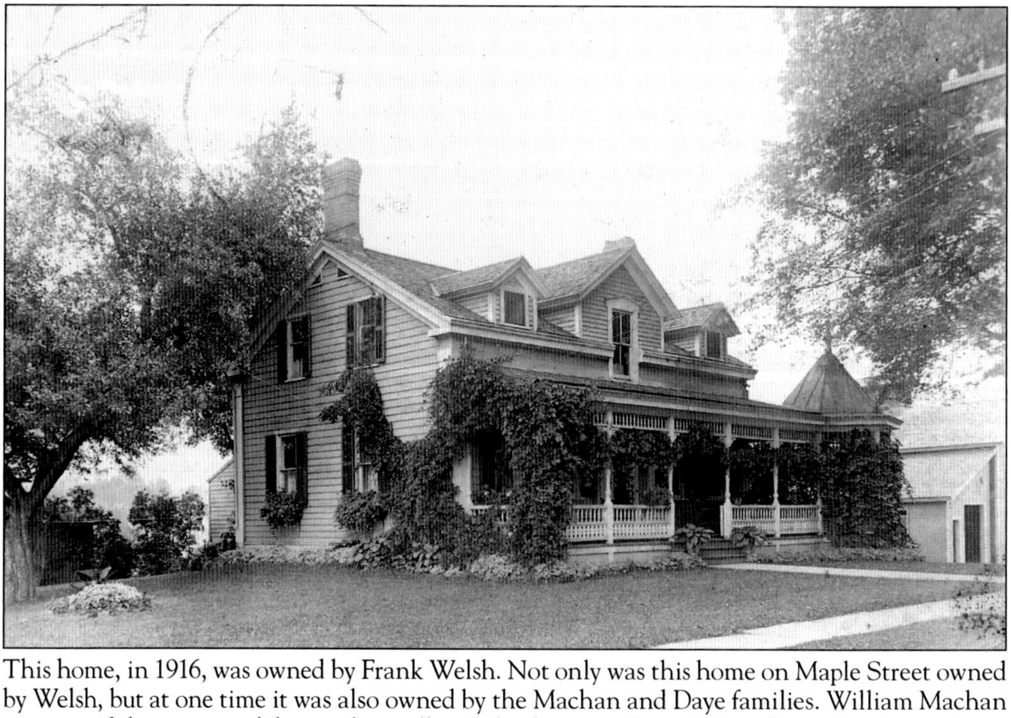

This home, in 1916, was owned by Frank Welsh. Not only was this home on Maple Street owned by Welsh, but at one time it was also owned by the Machan and Daye families. William Machan was one of the owners of the woolen mill and the first president of the village.

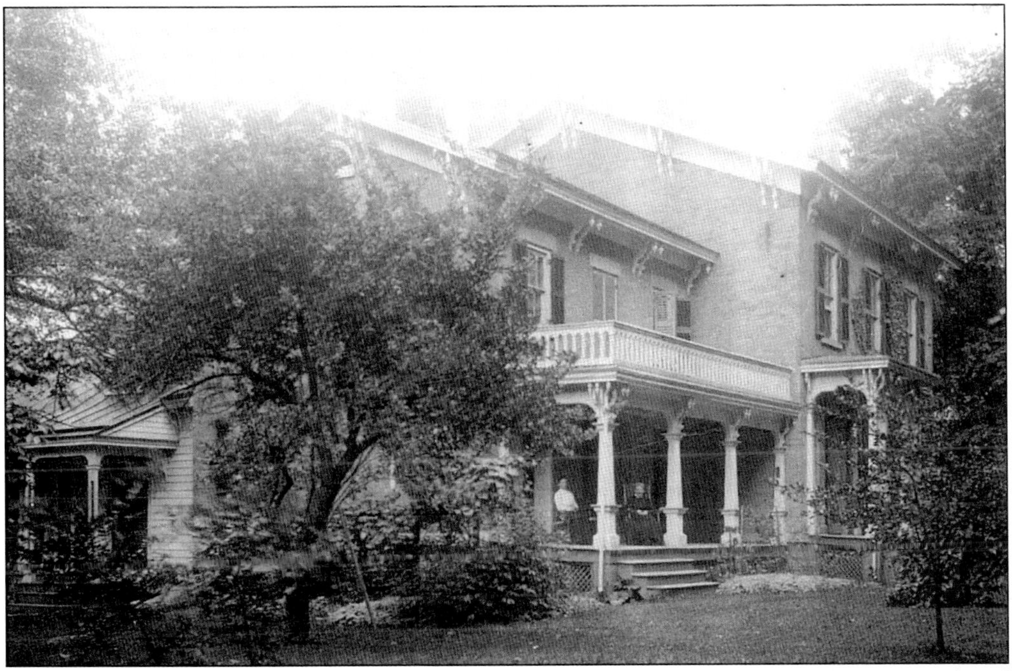

The Talbot-Case home was originally built in 1835. The home was the residence for Edward Talbot, one of the owners of the old stone mill at the lower end of East Main Street. Talbot's daughter Mary Elizabeth married Newton G. Case, who purchased the home in 1854. It is now the site for the Masonic temple.

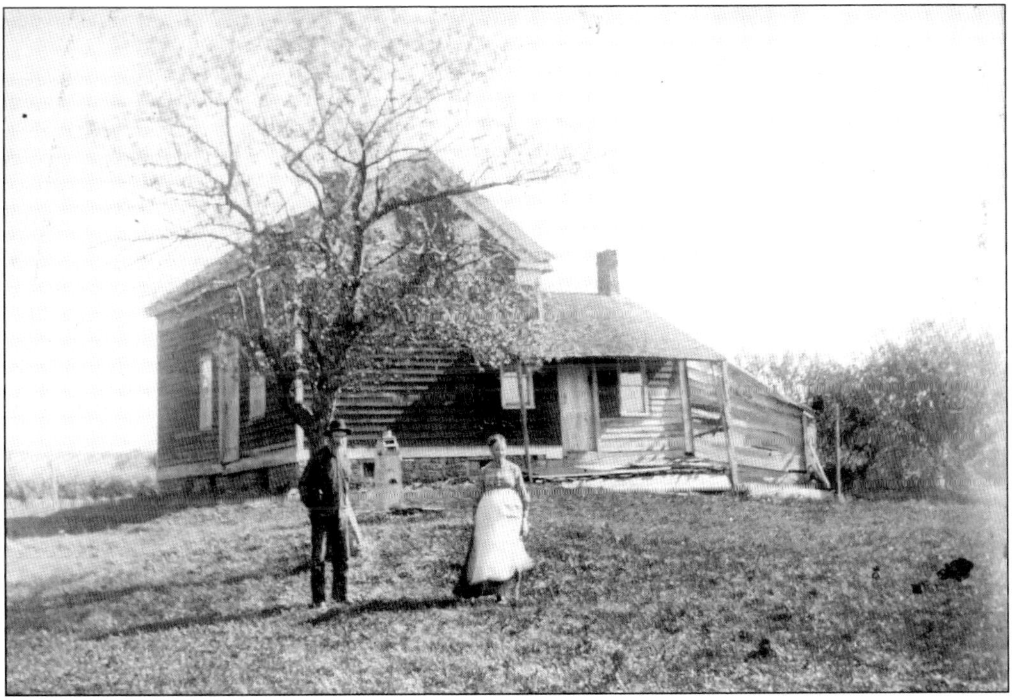

This photograph was taken in 1890 of George and Nancy Webber outside of their home on Route 20.

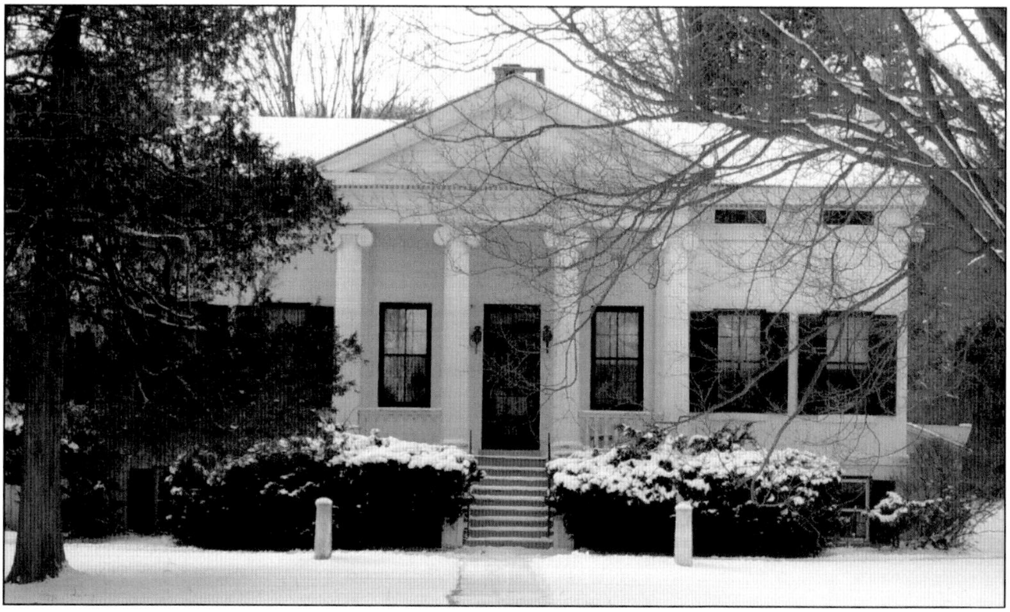

The Arthur Wilson home, built by Curtis Moses at 36 South Street, dates back to 1838. The brick for the house was manufactured locally and originally the house had a basement kitchen and dining room with floors made from the brick. The house has wide plank floors of mahogany, a Belgian marble fireplace in the dining room, and a curving flight of stairs made from cherry.

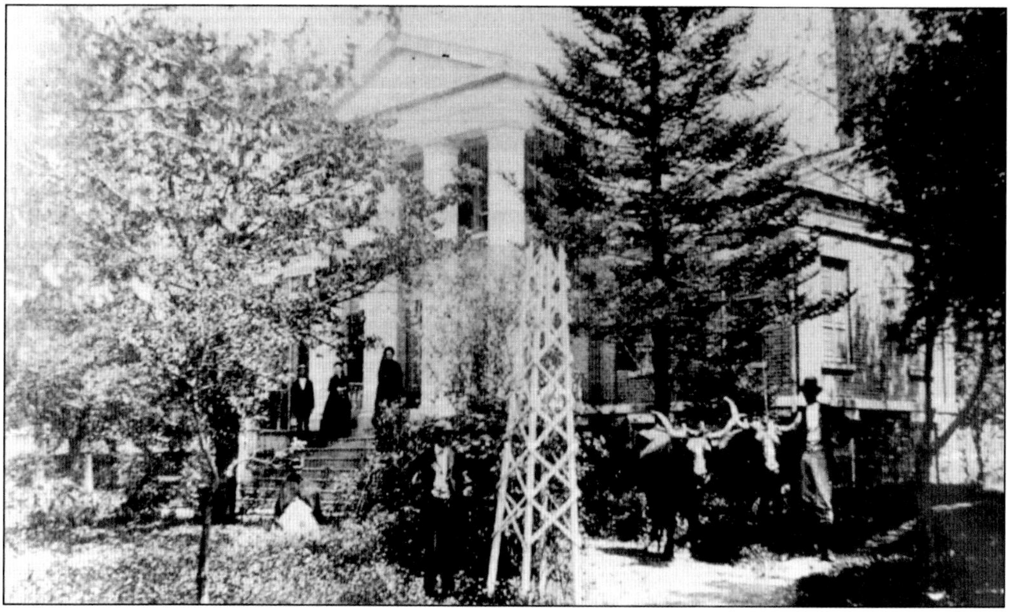

The North House was built by Dr. Lake I. Tefft. Tefft, originally from England, purchased part of a farm on what is now North Street and built a Greek revival–style home in 1827. The house contained six fireplaces. The pink brick used for the exterior originally came from England as ballast in a ship. The ship sailed up the St. Lawrence River and then down the Black River. The brick was then brought over land to Marcellus. Wesley Clark bought the house in 1947, and it has since changed hands a number of times. The current owners have rebuilt the four pillars on the front of the house to resemble the original structure.

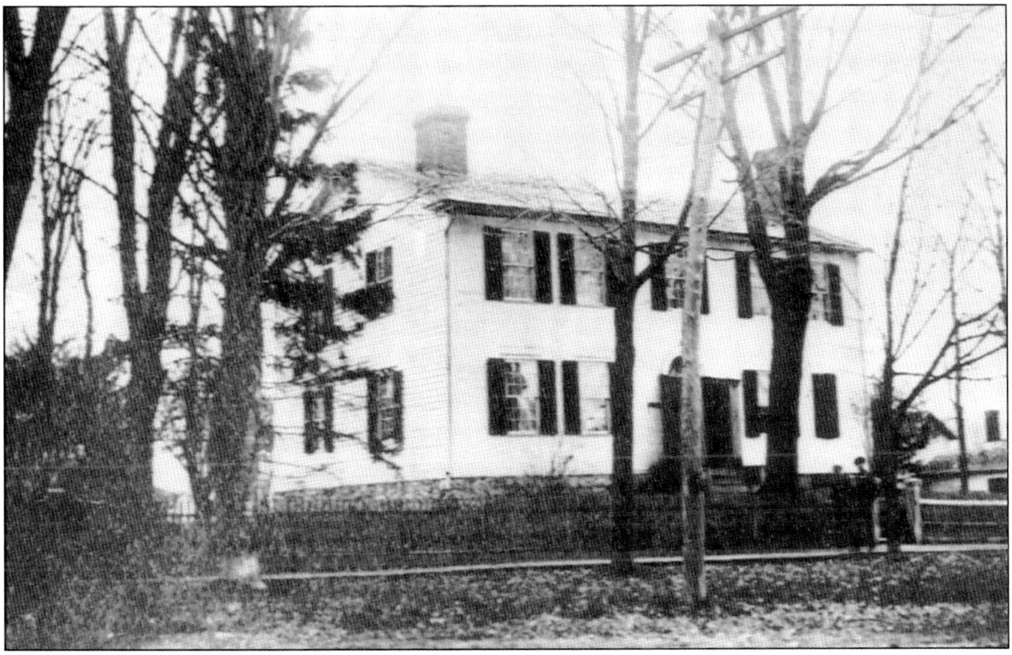

This beautiful home was that of the Parsons family on the corner of Orange and Main Streets. This home was later razed to build a gas station.

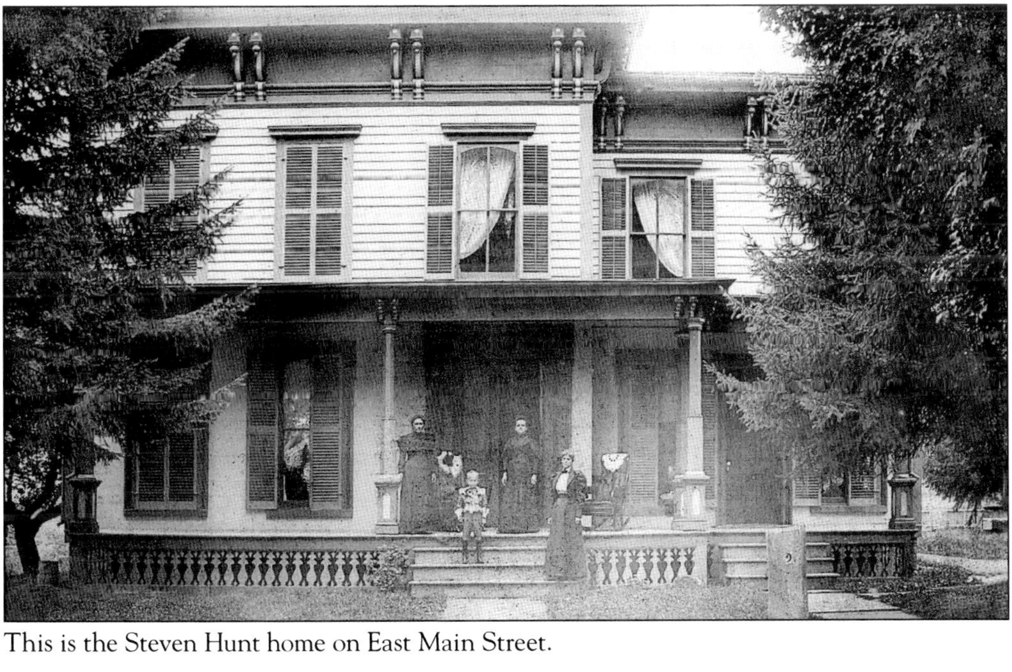

This is the Steven Hunt home on East Main Street.

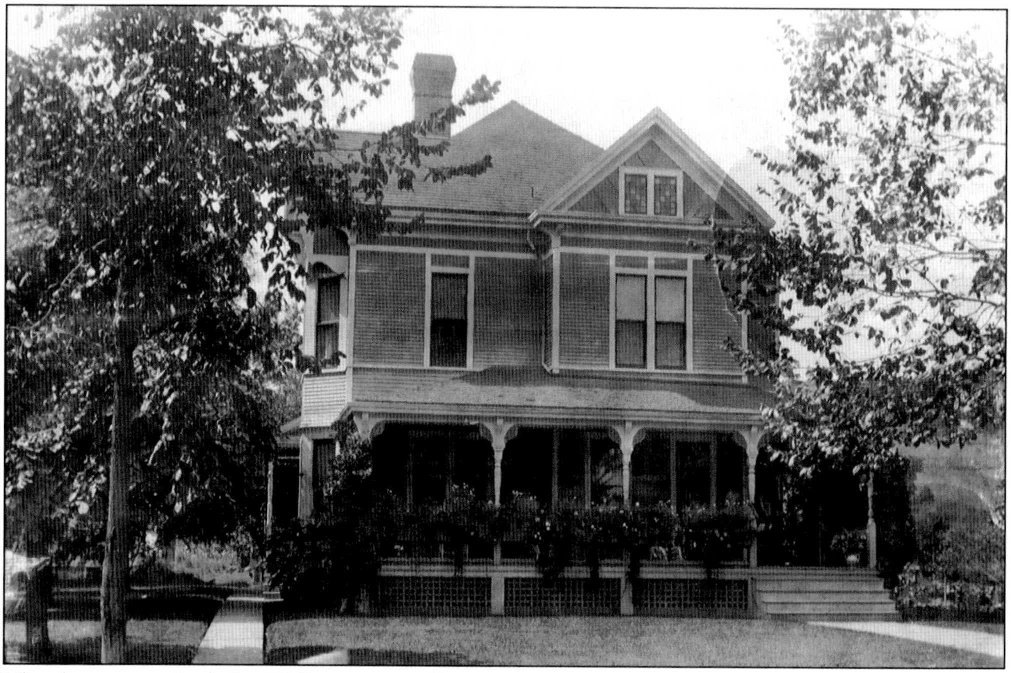

This home was built by William H. Gallup. Gallup was a lawyer, businessman, and political figure in Marcellus. The home is now the site of the Norris-Plis Funeral Home.

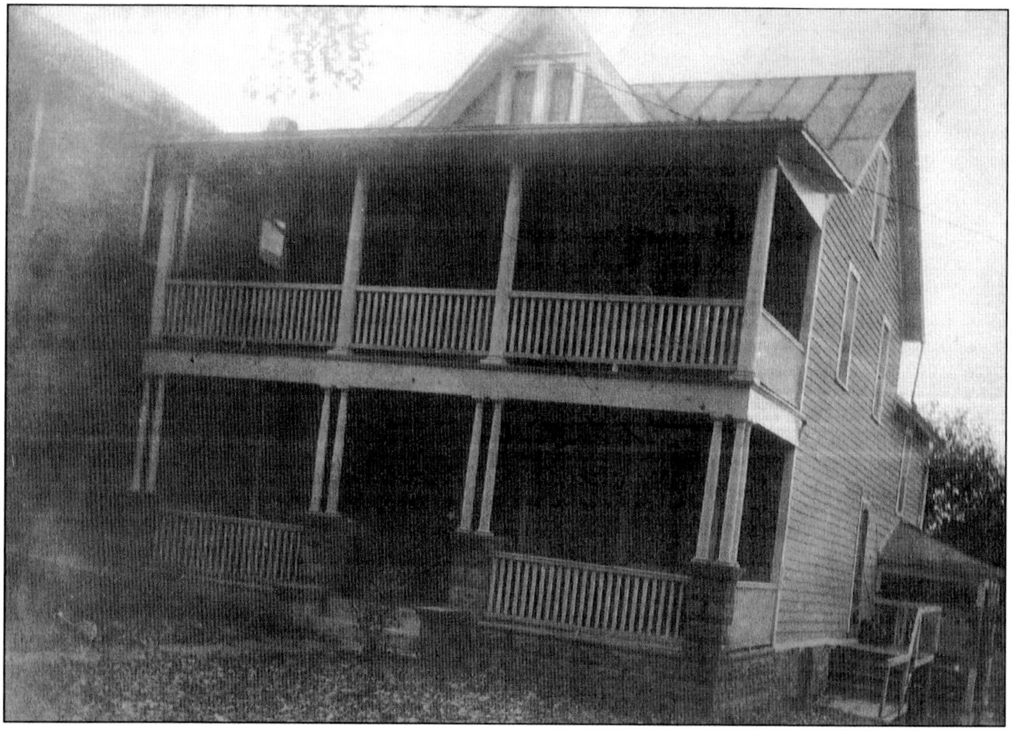

This photograph is of the Coyne-Tierney home on East Main Street. It was a beautiful home with double porches overlooking the main drag. It was demolished in 1972 to make way for the Marcellus Pharmacy.

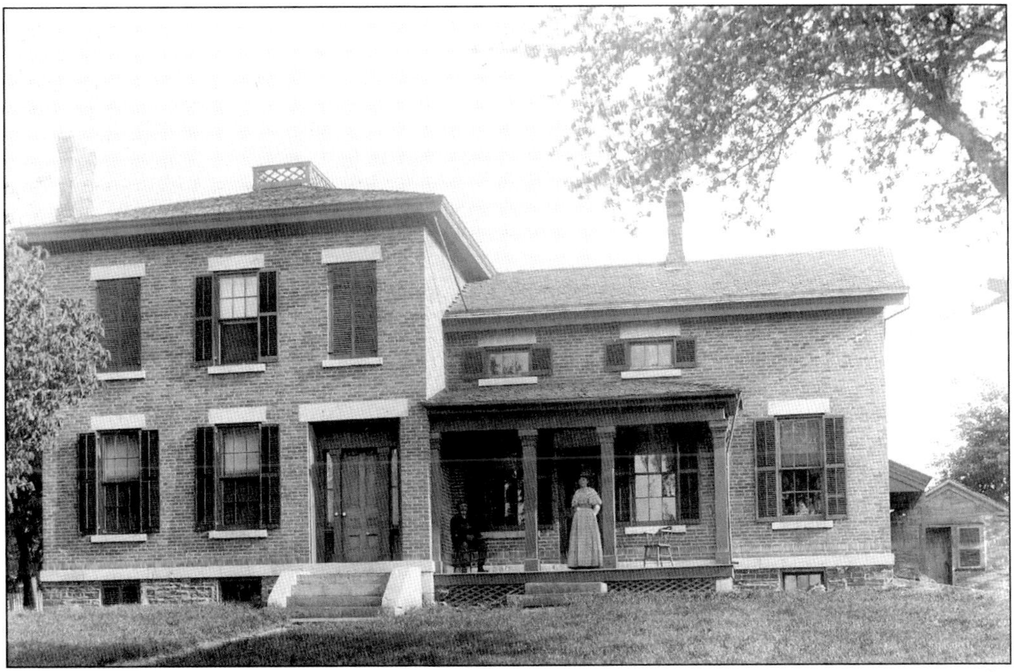

This handsome brick home was built by Robert McCulloch, a Revolutionary War veteran, for his daughter Mary and her husband Harry Fellows. Their son Henry died in the Civil War. Their other son George and his descendents lived in this house until the early 1900s. A very similar brick home on Frank Gay Road was also built by Robert McCulloch for his other daughter, Amanda, and her husband, Edward Austin.

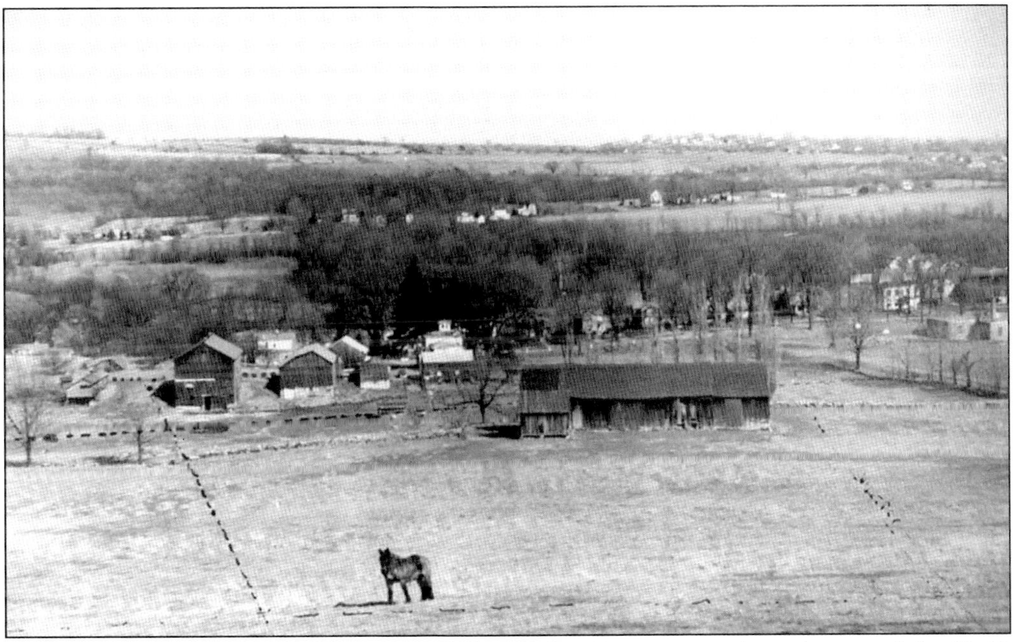

The James Stone Farm, also known as Shelter Valley Farm, currently is the site of the K. C. Heffernan Elementary School and the lower "pit" athletic field. Their home, with the cupola on top, was off North Street.

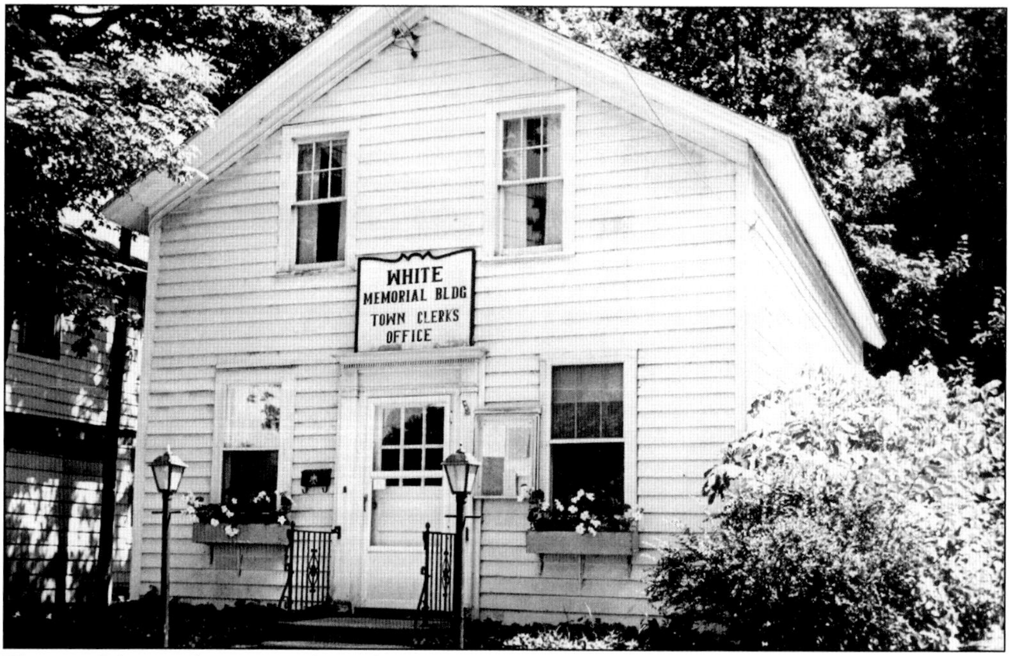

The small house, known as the White Memorial Building, dates back to about 1810. In 1818, Jeremiah G. B. White, a hatter by trade, came from Elbridge to work for a man named Copeland Moore. Shortly afterwards, he bought out Moore and made fur and wool hats for a great many customers until 1852.

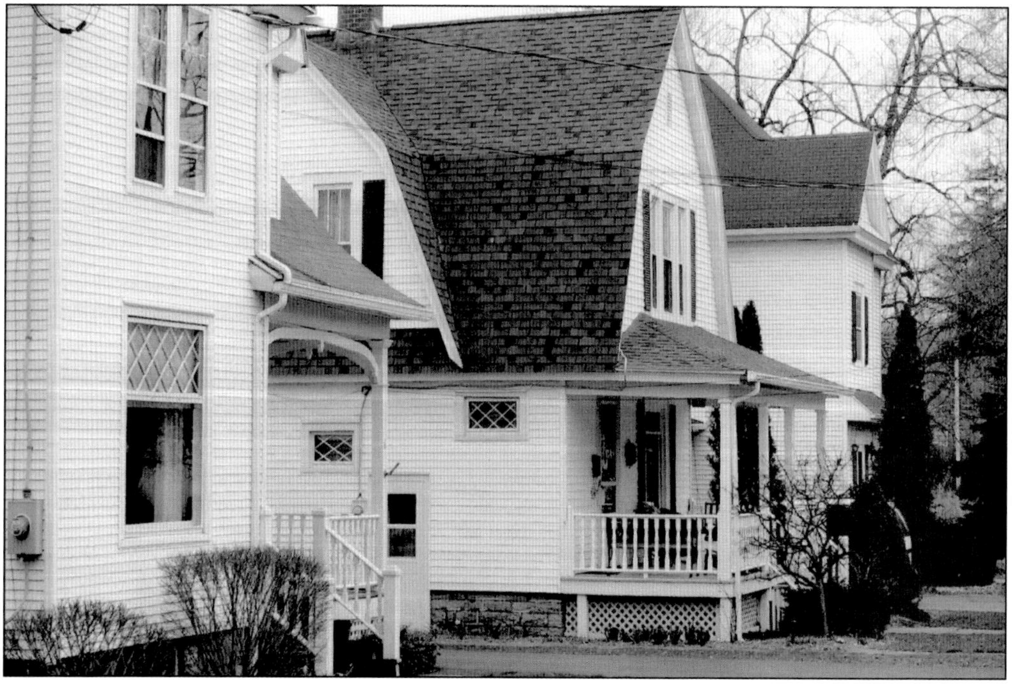

These homes along Reed Street were built by prominent citizens of Marcellus. The first home on the left, No. 6 Reed Street, belonged to the Kelley family. Next door, at No 4, lived the Moak Family, and next to them, at No. 2 Reed Street, was the Frank Knapp home.

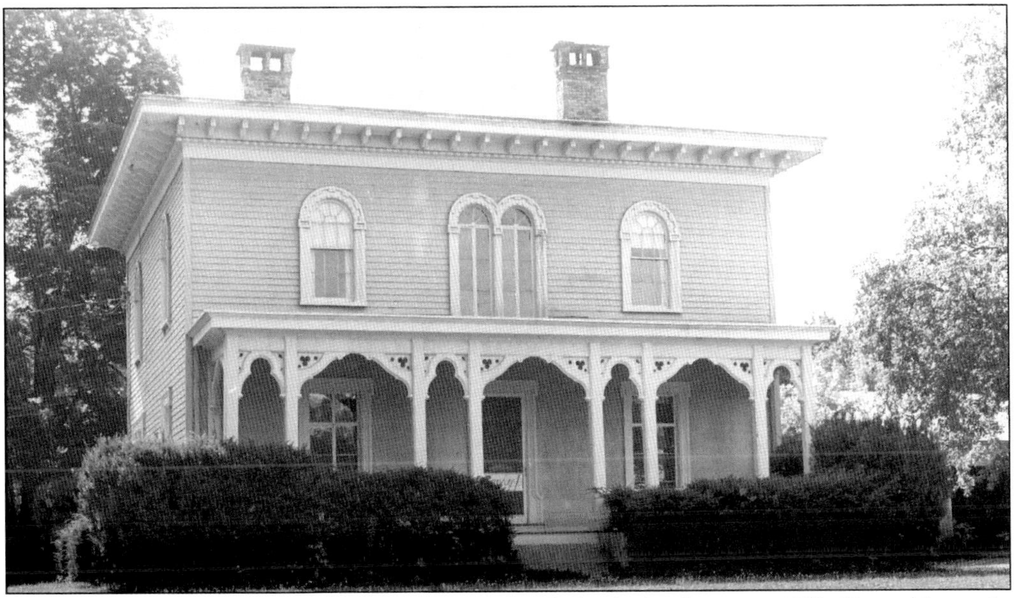

Hiram Reed, son of Jonathan Reed and Rhoda Cody, built this home in 1853. He and his wife, Martha Jane Glass Reed, built their home on a farm tract encompassing all the area between Reed Avenue and Reed Parkway and extending west beyond Highland Drive. Besides the house, there were several outbuildings including a tobacco barn, carriage barn, granary, and hay barn. What is now Meadow Street was the lane up to the Reed cow pasture. In 1940, Lloyd Cummings and Ruth R. Cummings donated the land for Second Street, to further the village's need for expansion.

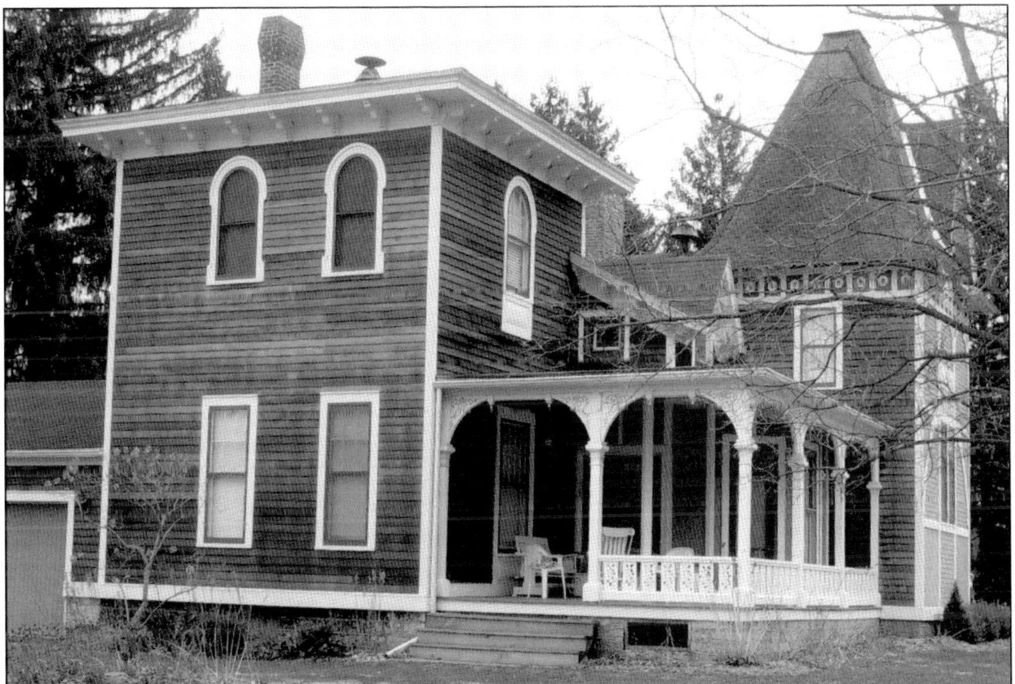

The Moir family home was built on Orange Street. It was a magnificent home with a stunning library. The home was situated just above the Upper Crown Mill, which the Moir family owned.

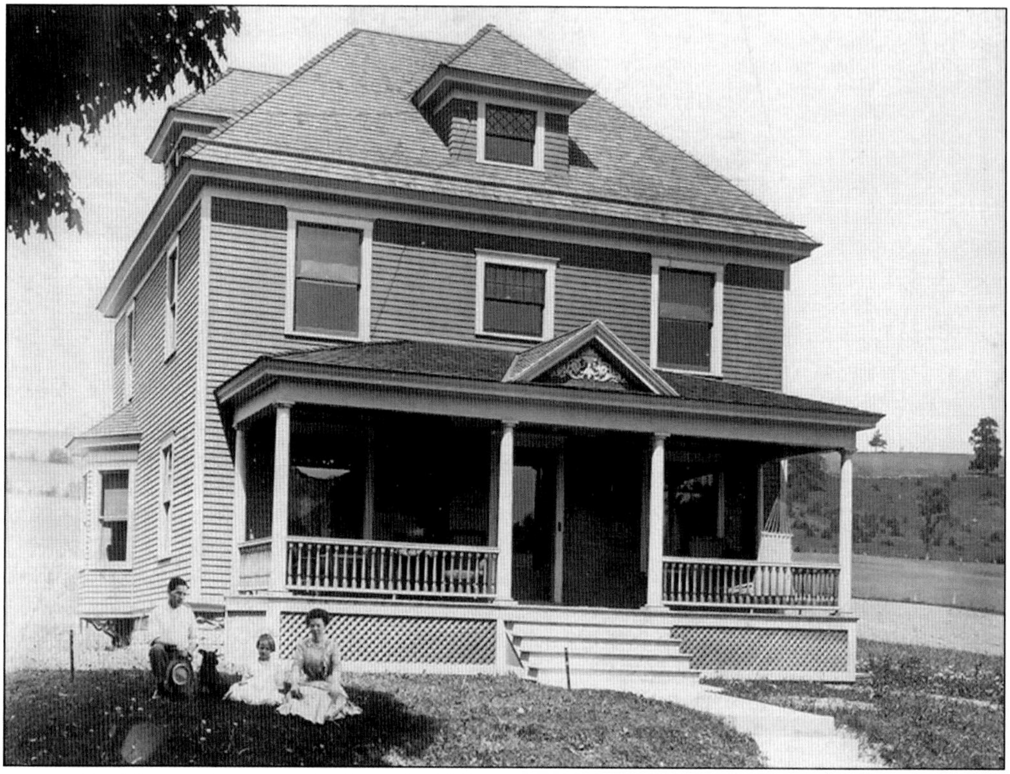

Austin Marble had this home built in the Ward Wellington Ward style around 1910. Ward was a notable architect practicing in Syracuse at that time. This home is located on the corner of First and Reed Streets. Seen in this picture are Austin Marble (left), with his wife Ethel (right), their daughter Dorothy Woodford, and their dog.

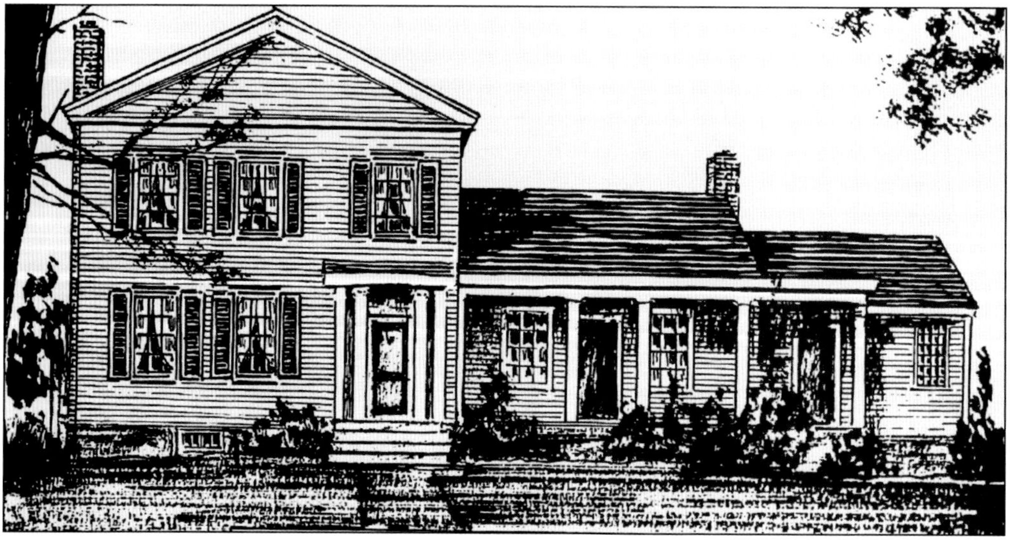

This etching is of the Tuscarora Home on Munro Road. It was built in 1819 by Calvin Bingham. Calvin Bingham grew the first primate apple and a tree in the yard bears a bronze plaque saying, "On this farm, Calvin D. Bingham about 1840, produced the marvelous Primate apple, named by Charles P. Cowles. God's earth is full of love to man."

Five

Houses of Worship and Eternal Resting Places

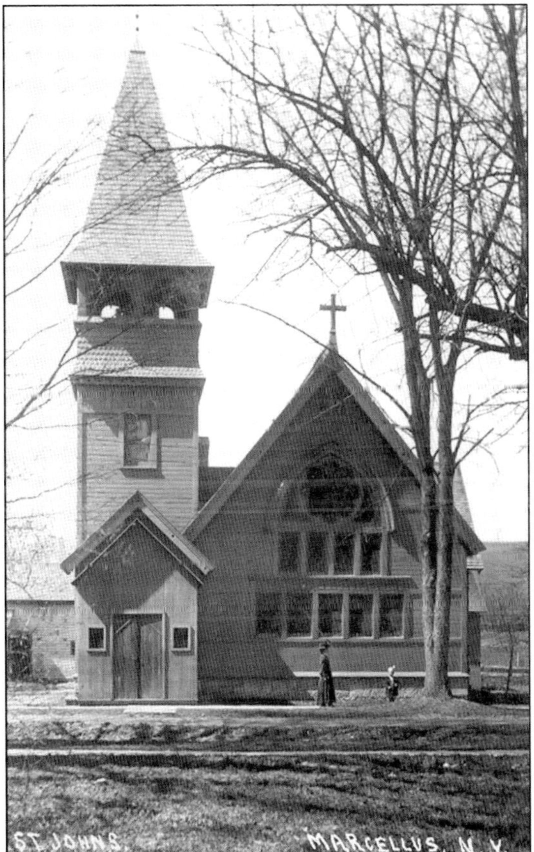

St. John's Episcopal Church was incorporated on February, 8 1824. A lot was donated to the church by Jeremiah White, on the corner of North and Main Streets. The church itself was built in 1833. In December 1866, the little church was destroyed by fire. Without any insurance, the congregation had to rally to raise money to rebuild. Once again, on July 3, 1879, St. John's church was destroyed by fire. The lot was sold for $500 and a lot on Orange Street was purchased (which is now the back side of Nojaims Market). This picture was taken in 1881.

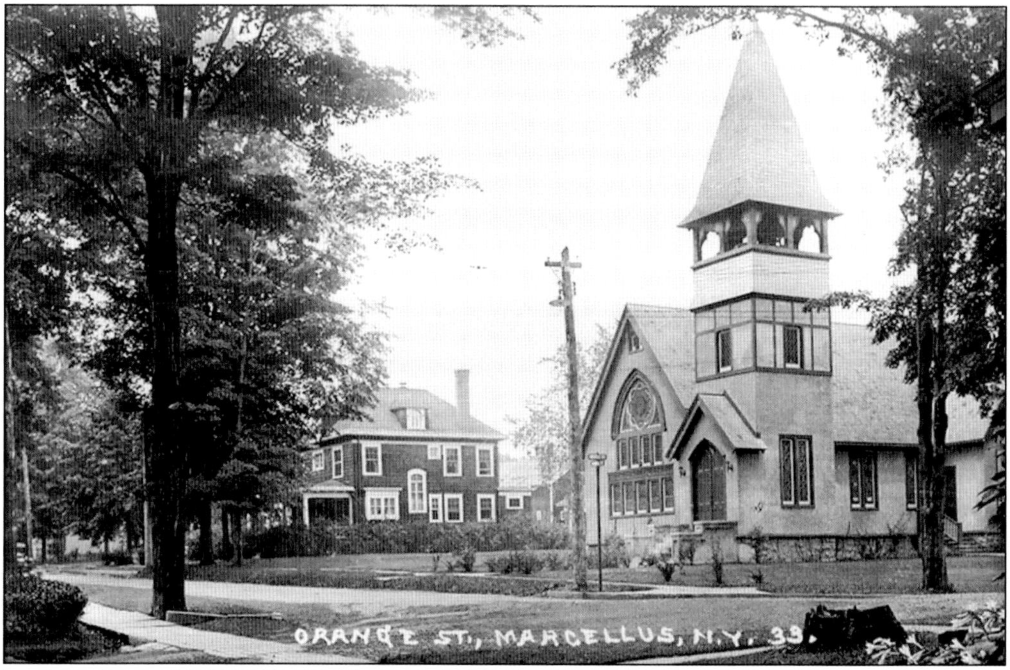

In 1904, Edward Moir offered a donation of $1,000 to St. John's parish on the condition that the congregation demolish the two houses on the property that faced his home and build a new church. On November 25, 1913, the congregation opened its new parish house on the corner of Orange and Maple Streets. This picture was taken in 1924.

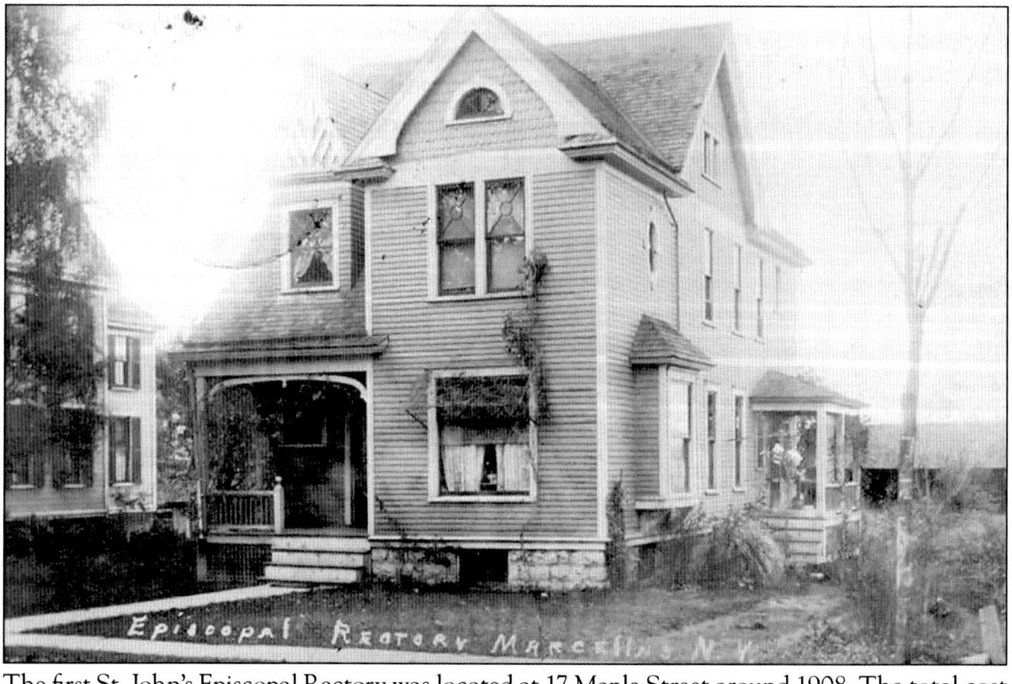

The first St. John's Episcopal Rectory was located at 17 Maple Street around 1908. The total cost of the house was $19,096.

The Methodist chapel was built around 1824 on the land of what is now the old St. Francis Xavier cemetery. It was a plain stone building, 30 by 40 feet, with no steeple. Worshipers wore a well trodden path up the hill from the village to attend services.

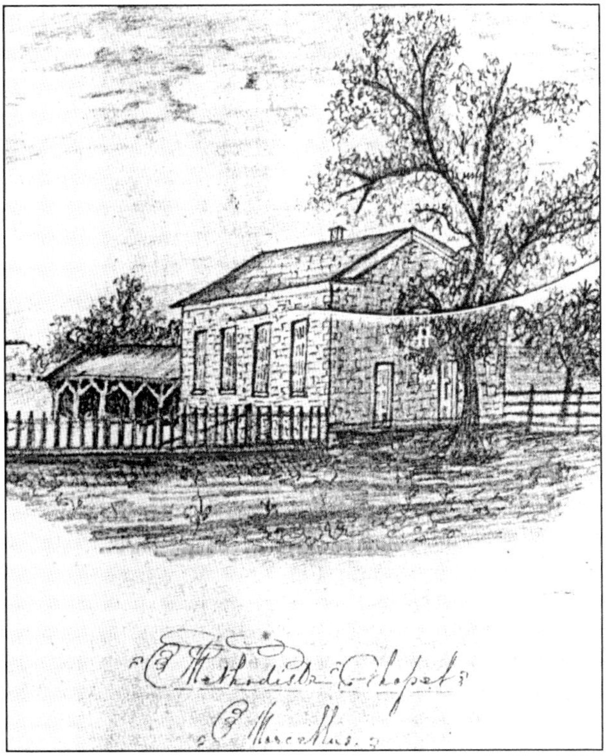

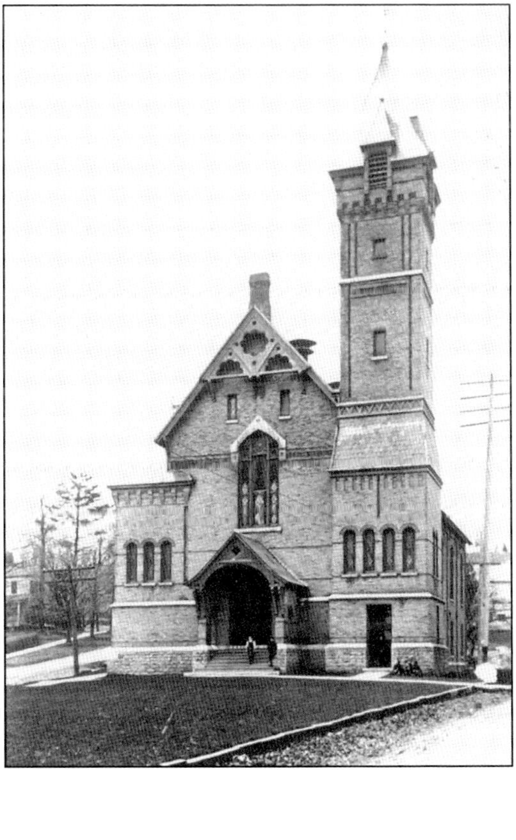

The Methodist Society first began around 1823 and the first meetings were held at the home of Stephen Cobb. The first Methodist brick church was built in 1858. It burned on January 25, 1877, and the present Methodist church was built in its place in 1878. This picture was taken in 1900.

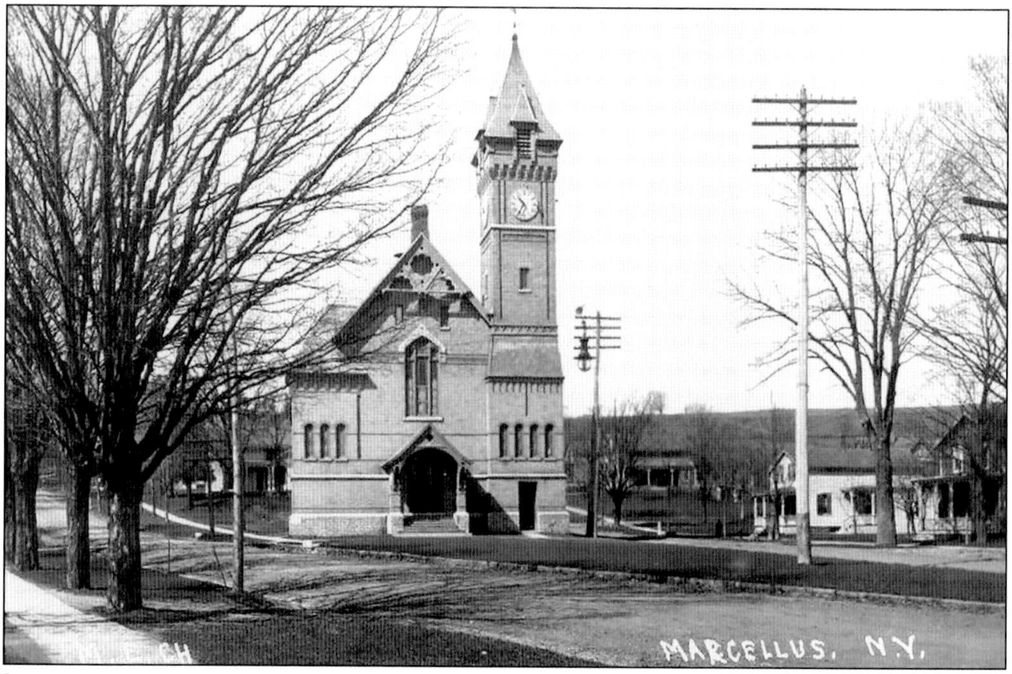

In 1909, George W. and Marion Case presented the Methodist Church with the gift of a clock to be installed in the church tower. What inspired Marion to donate the clock was when she was a child, she often hurried up West Main Street to school, not knowing whether or not she would be late.

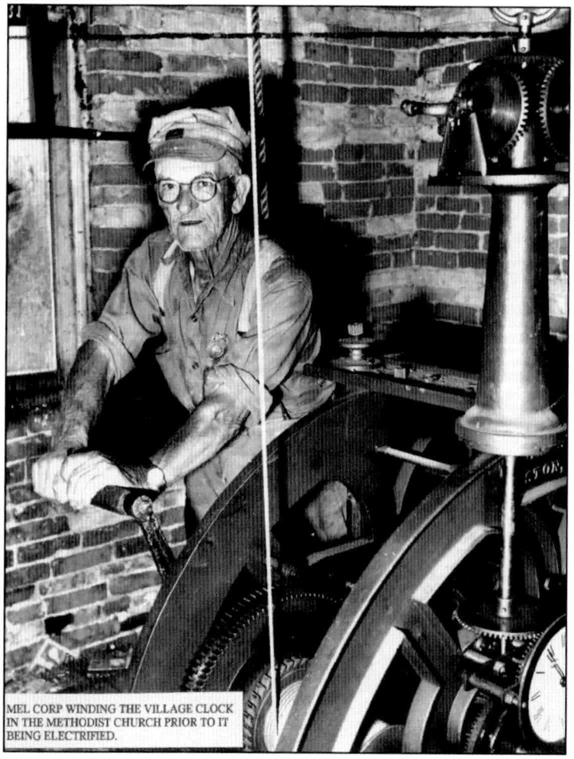

MEL CORP WINDING THE VILLAGE CLOCK IN THE METHODIST CHURCH PRIOR TO IT BEING ELECTRIFIED.

For years the clock would have to be wound by hand until 1962 when the Citizen's Club, the Rotary Club, and the village board shared the expense of electrifying the clock. Mel Corp, shown here in 1952, was the last person to wind the clock in the Methodist church.

Shortly after the settlement of Marcellus in 1794, the Presbyterian Church was established. The original house of worship, erected in 1803, was the first church building constructed in Onondaga County. Daniel Bradley donated the acre of land on the corner of North and Main Streets. The present sanctuary was built in 1851. Major renovations took place in 1950 when the body of the church was raised and a finished basement was constructed. The first pastor was Levi Parsons, who served for 33 years.

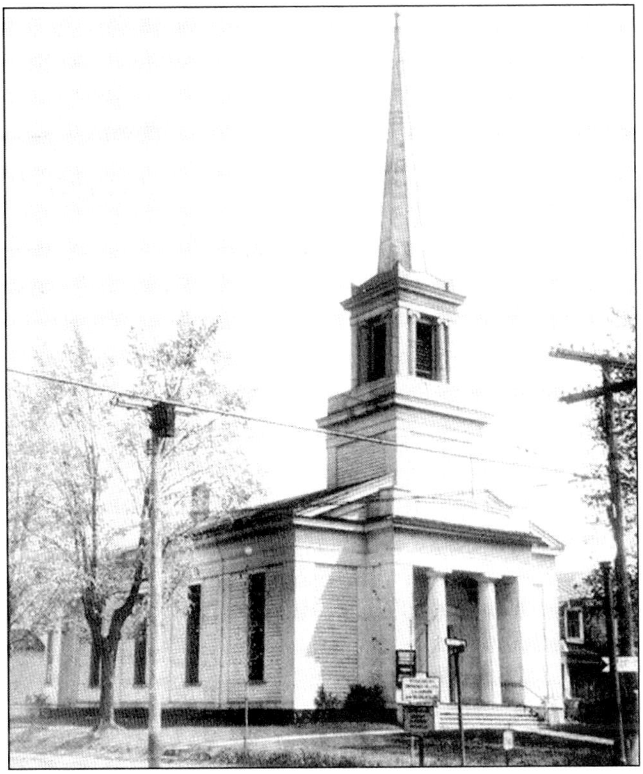

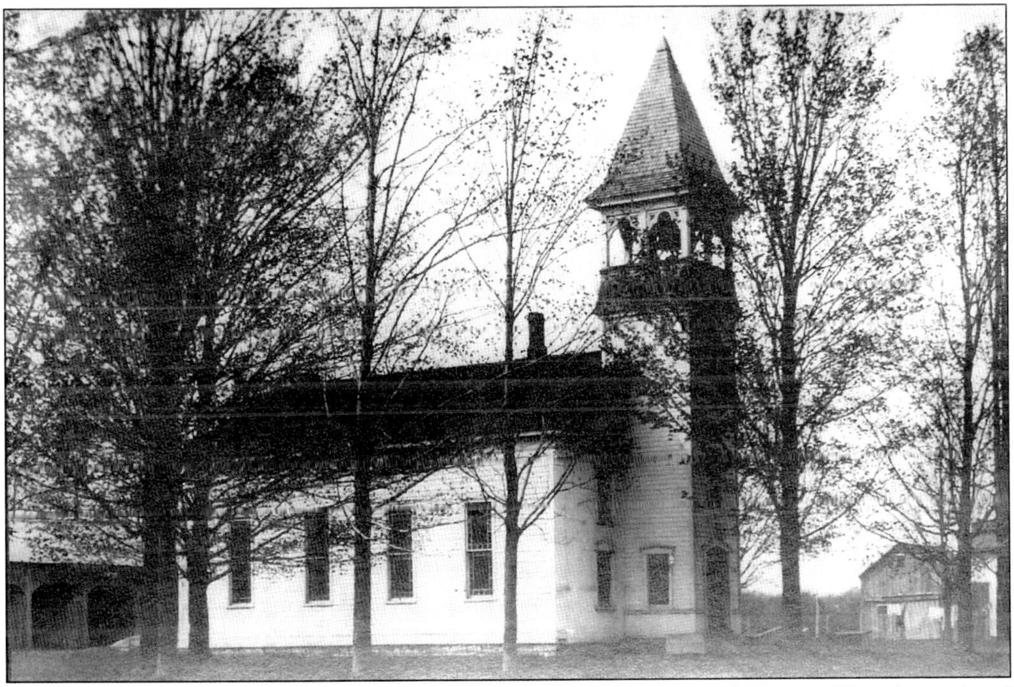

This is Rose Hill Baptist Church. The earliest records of the Rose Hill Baptist Church are dated in 1806. The first pastor was Elder Elias Harmon. The first meeting house was built around 1816 and added to in 1849. The bell tower was constructed in 1886.

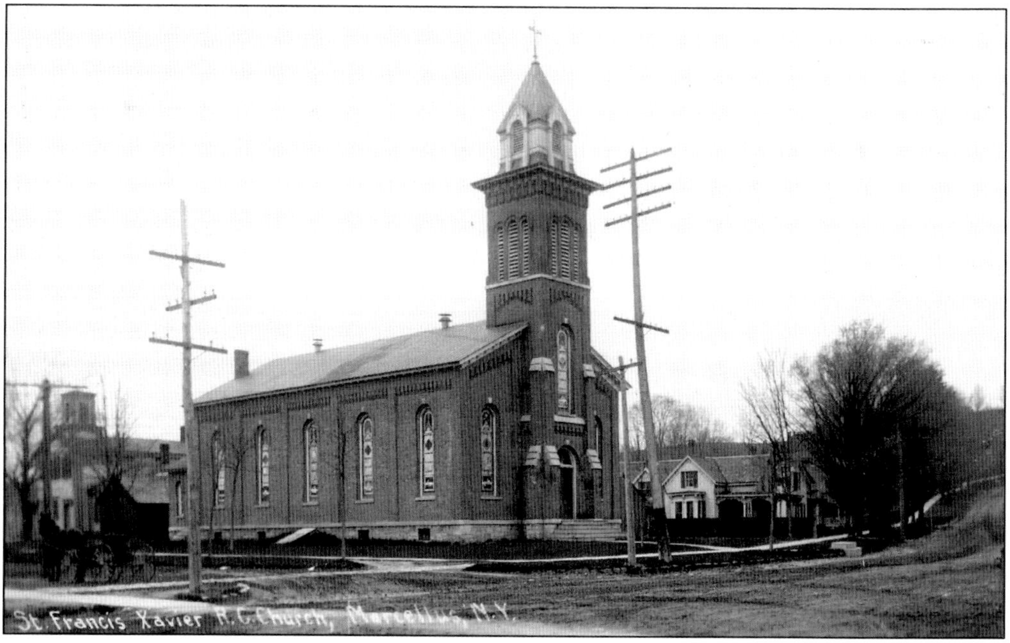

St. Francis Xavier Catholic Church was completed in 1868 at the cost of $15,000. The church sits on the corner of Main and South Streets, on the site of the old tavern owned by Deacon Samuel Rice. The original rectory for the church was located on East Main Street. Eventually it was sold to John Shay for $3,000. Today it is the site of the village laundromat.

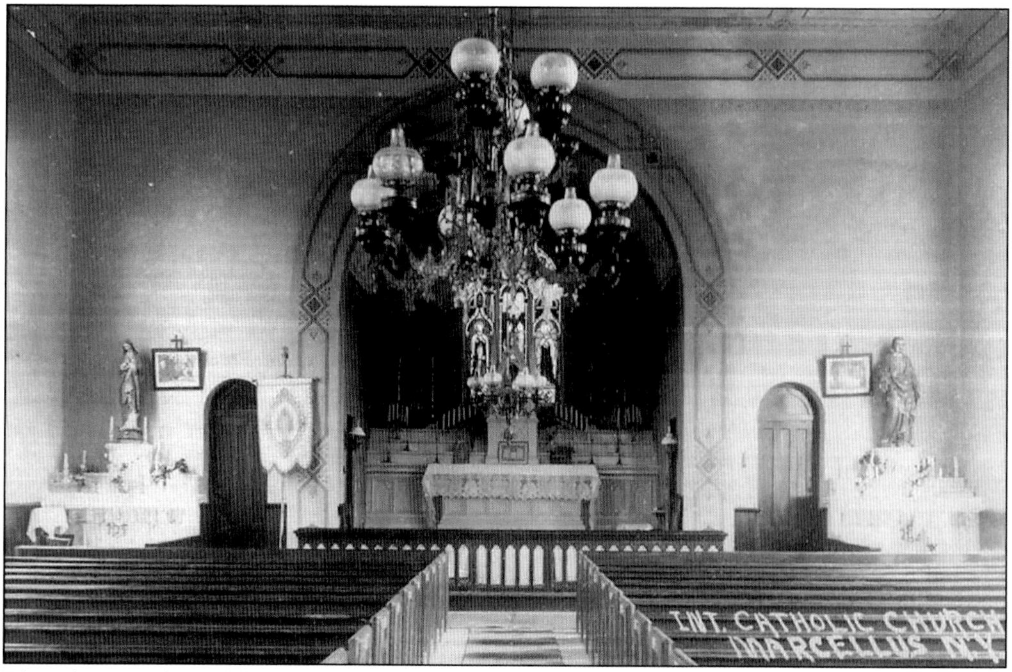

This photograph is of the interior of St. Francis Xavier Church in 1907.

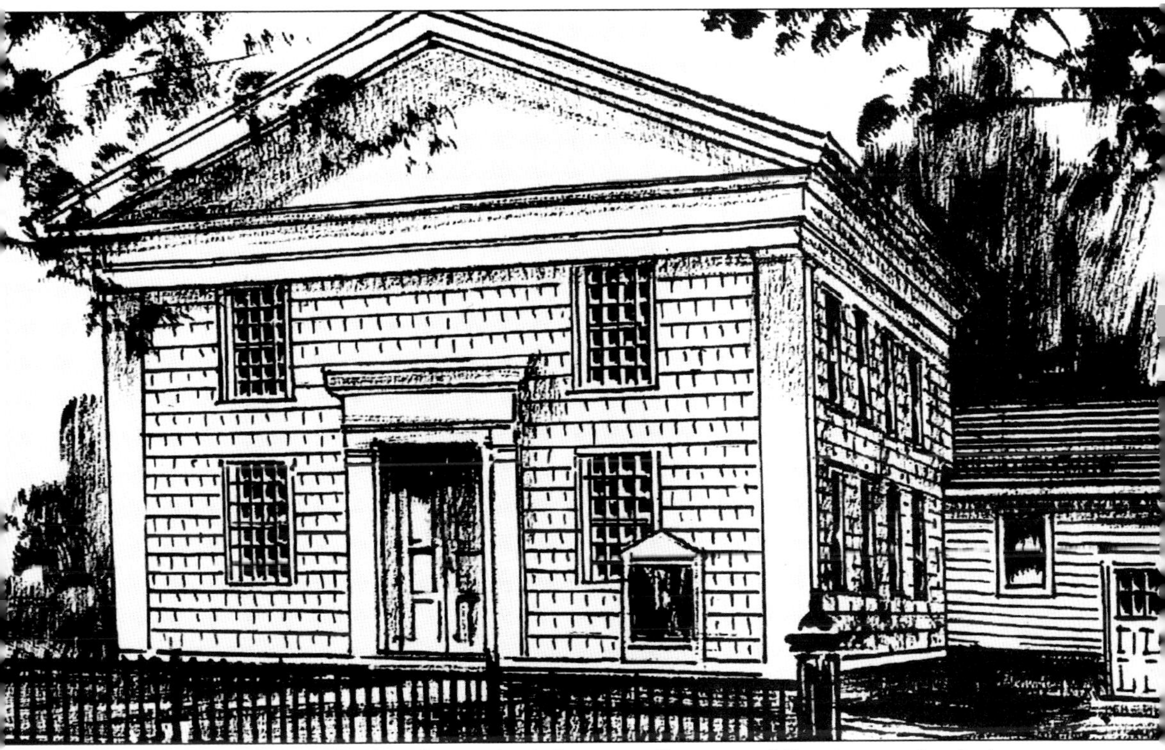

In 1821, the Howlett Hill Church was built by a small group of Baptists on land given to them by Leonard Caten. The first Baptist Church of Onondaga had been organized in 1804 with a congregation of six men and seven women. The Baptists left, and a number of years after the close of the Civil War in 1865, the church became a mission church of the United Presbyterian denomination.

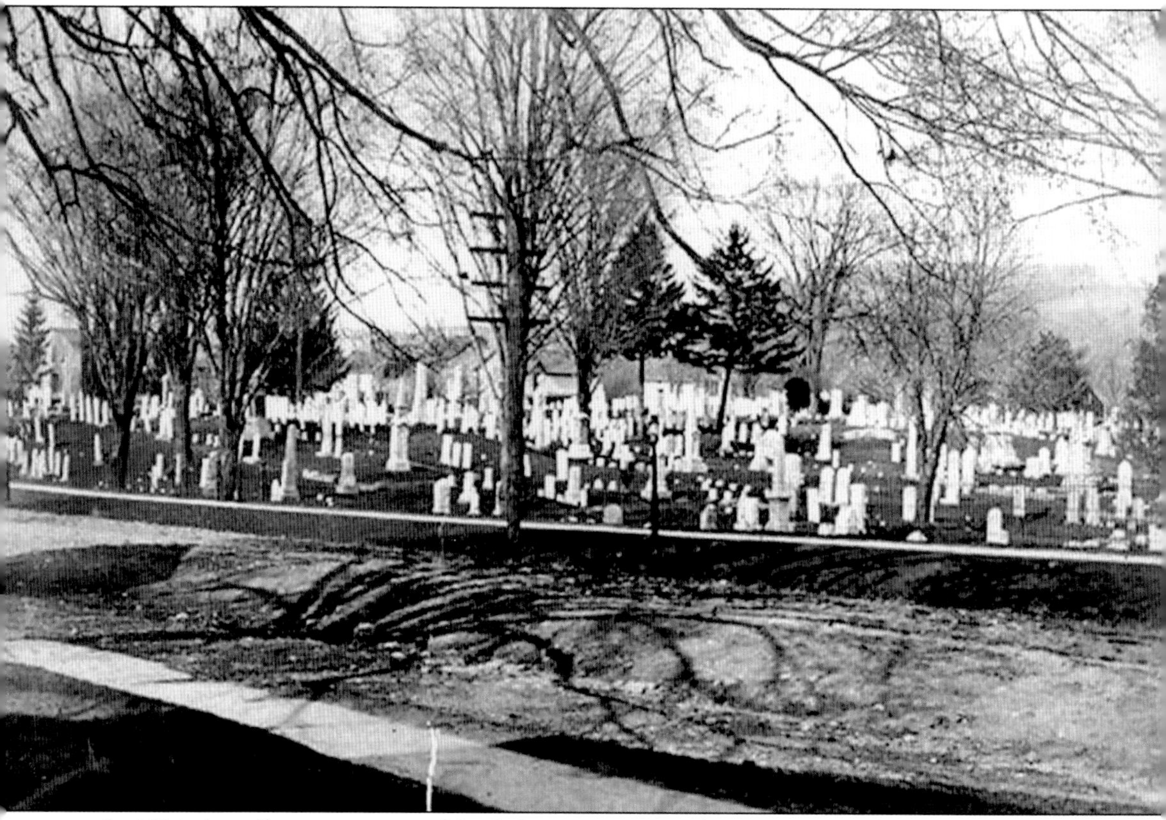

In 1804, the village cemetery on North Street was opened. In 1857, an addition to the southwest corner was purchased from Harry Kennedy. After many years of fund-raising, an iron fence was erected around the perimeter of the cemetery. Improvement work continued on through 1976, and as a result, well over 200 headstones were raised, repaired, and straightened. Dr. Centrone, along with his daughter Betty, developed a scale map using the 1899 map of Belus North as a primary source. Among the graves are 47 veterans of the Revolutionary War, 19 veterans of the War of 1812, 1 veteran of the Mexican war, 17 veterans from the Civil War, and 1 veteran from World War I.

Six

Old Schools, Students, and Teams

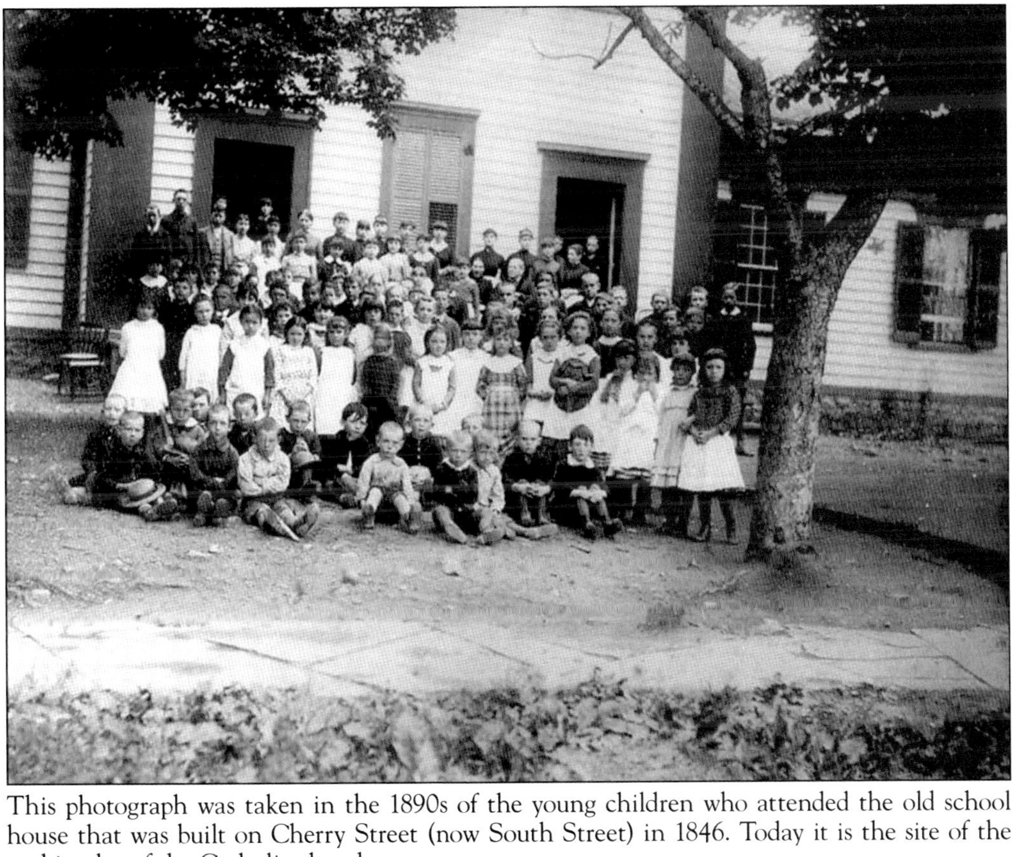

This photograph was taken in the 1890s of the young children who attended the old school house that was built on Cherry Street (now South Street) in 1846. Today it is the site of the parking lot of the Catholic church.

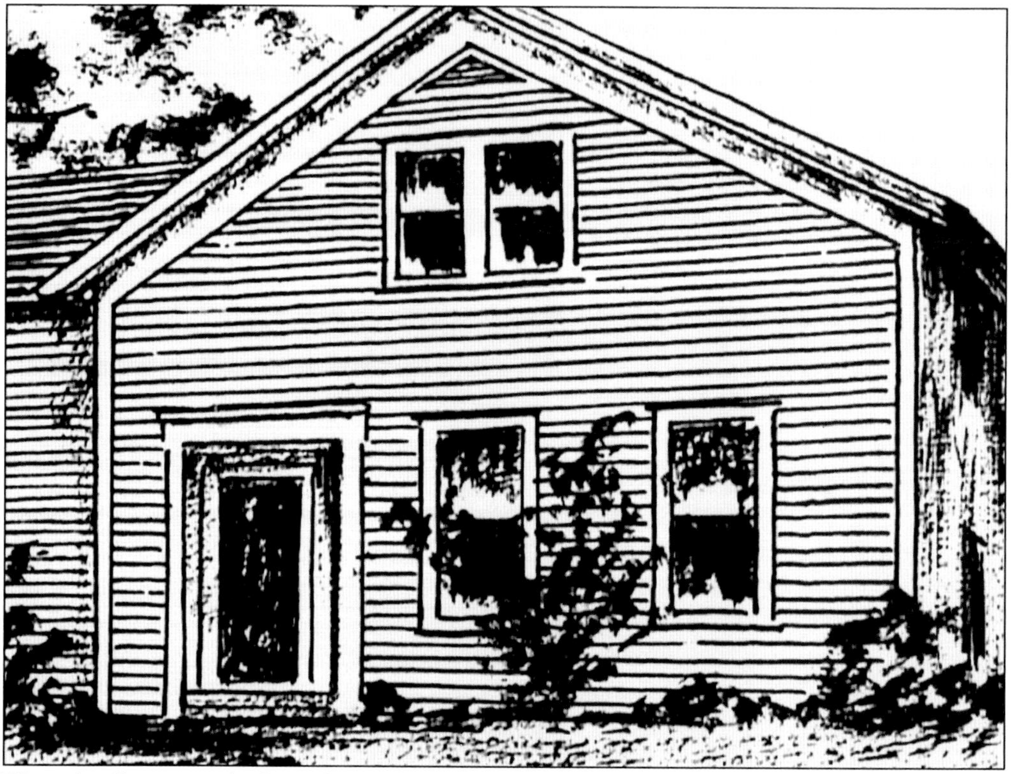

This schoolhouse was built on the south side of Seneca Turnpike, and was District No. 8. It served the children until 1891, when the district joined with the village to form the Union School.

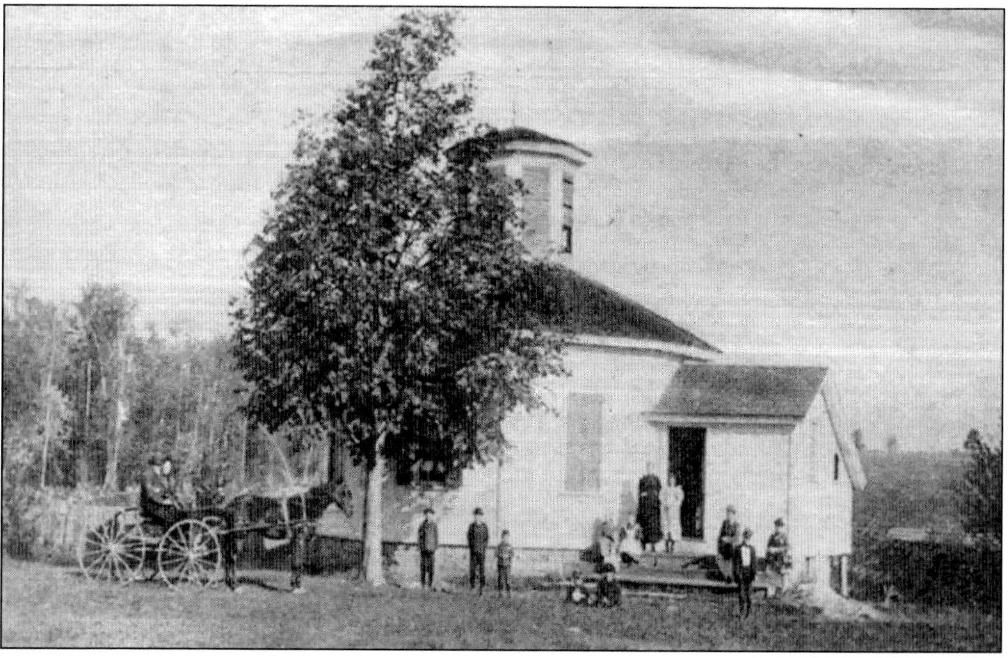

District No. 9 was an octagon schoolhouse located east of Marcellus, between Cards Corners and the village on Seneca Turnpike. It was built in 1867 to replace an earlier log schoolhouse.

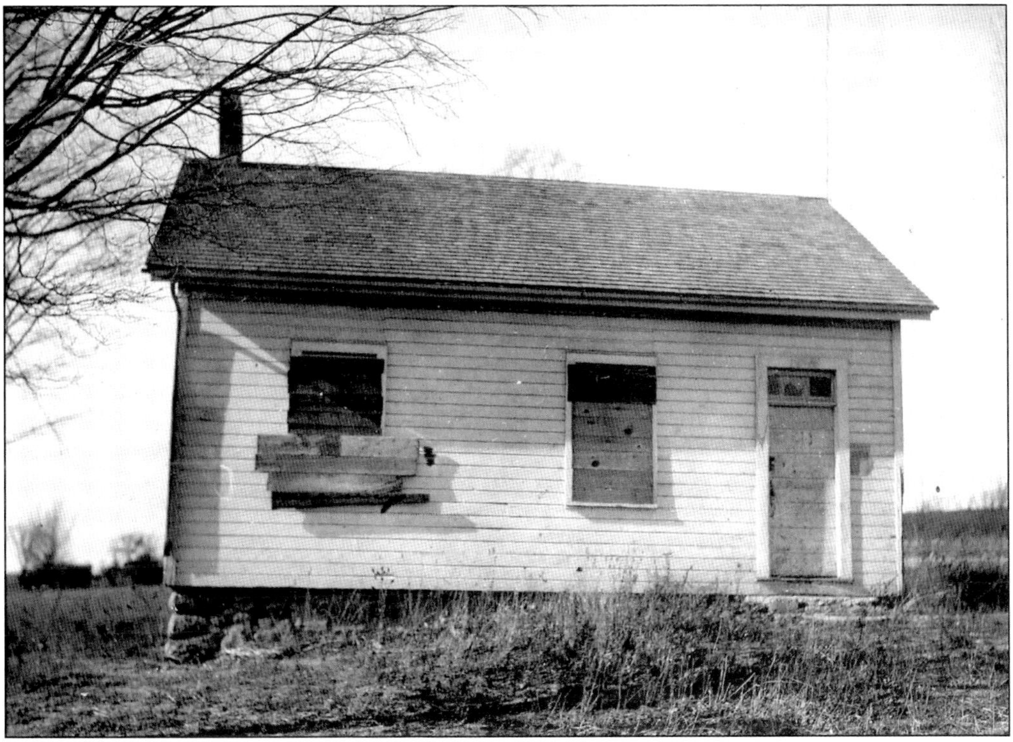

This is Marcellus School District No. 4. The schoolhouse was located on the corner of Lawrence Road and Bishop Hill Road.

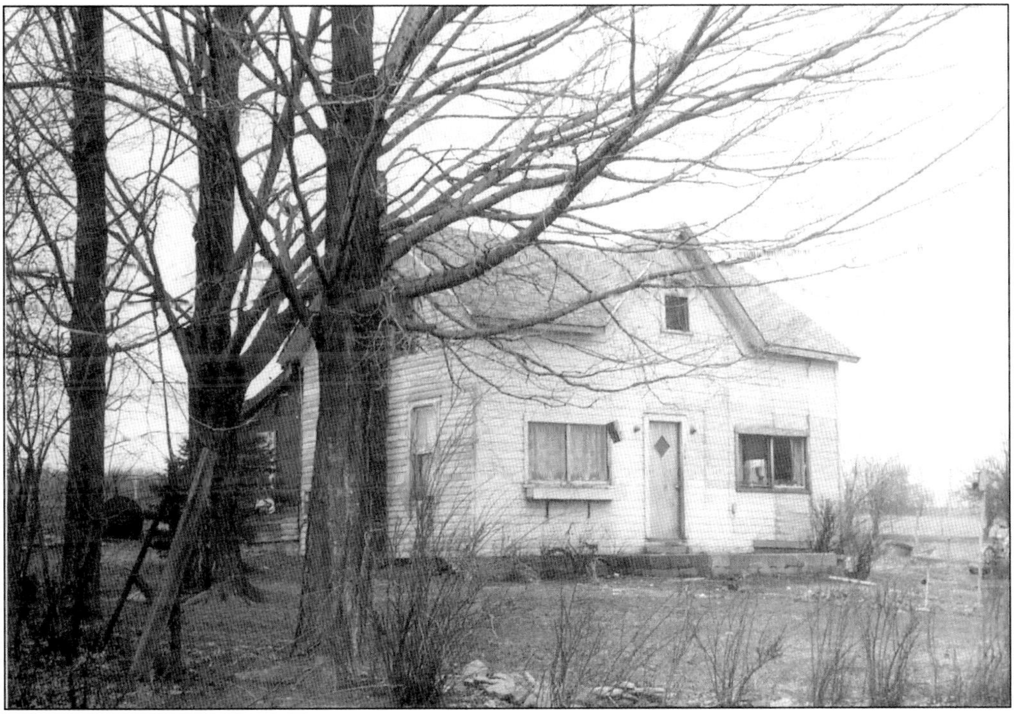

This is a photograph of the Marble Road schoolhouse, District No. 6.

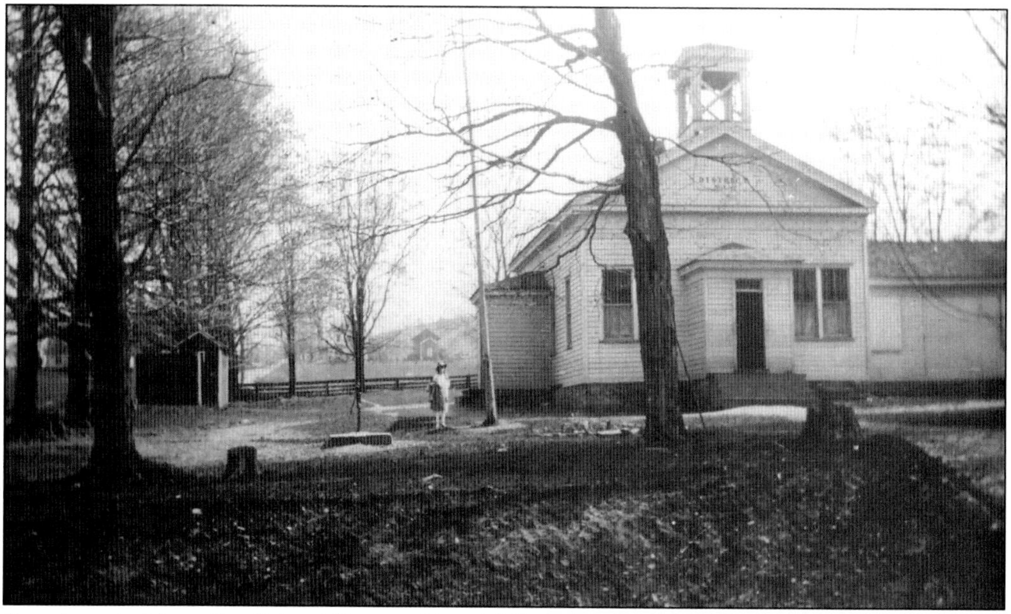

Seen here is Marcellus School District No. 4. The schoolhouse was located on the corner of Howlett Hill Road and Beef Street. The building is now a private residence.

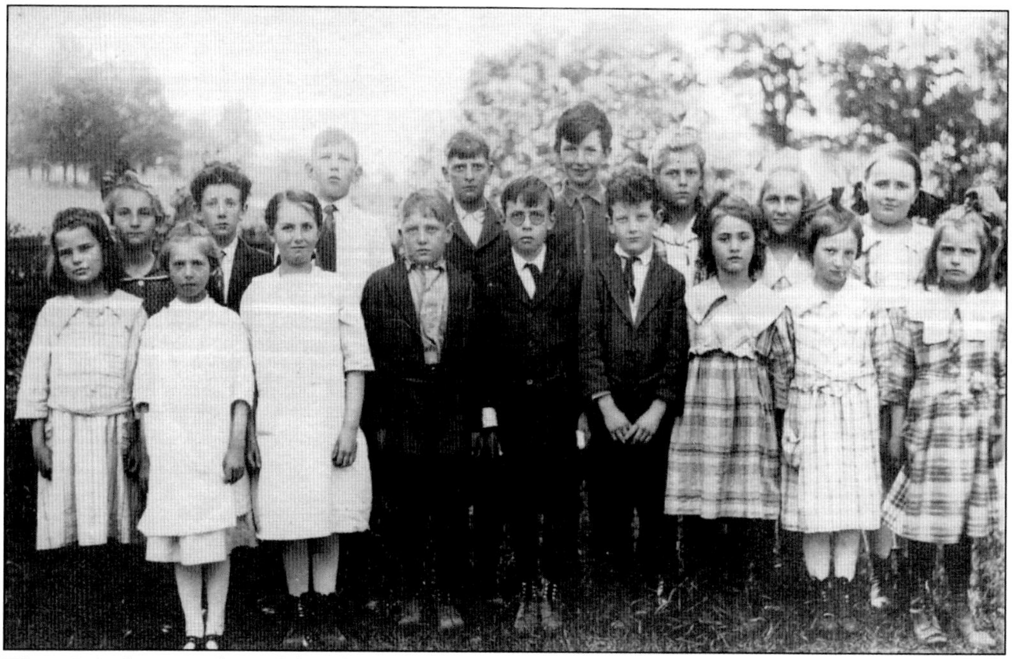

This 1919 photograph is of the children who attended Howlett Hill School, District No. 4.

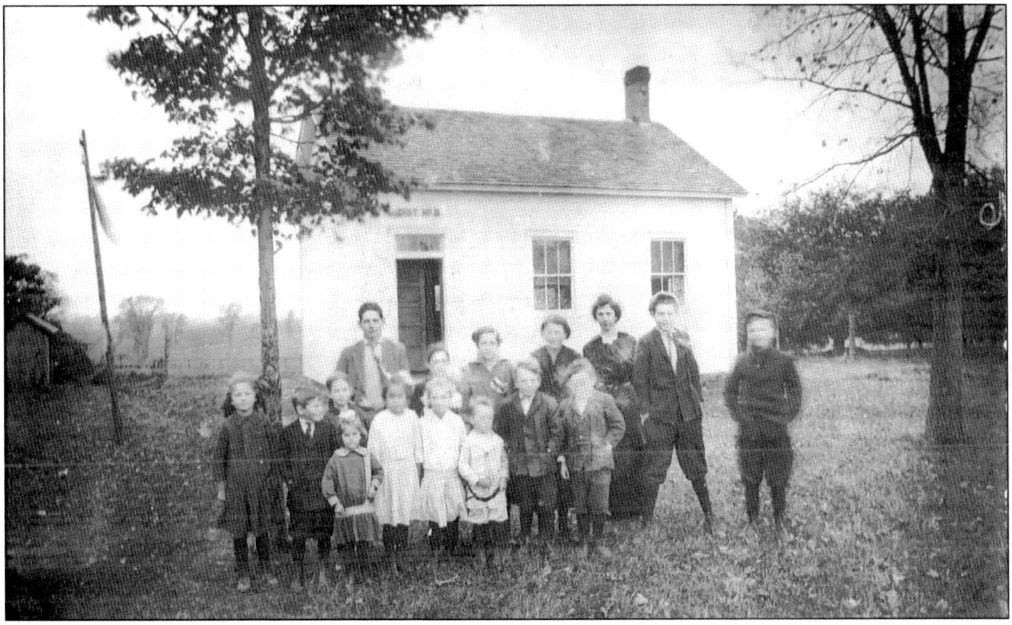

This photograph was taken at the Marcellus School District No. 8, which sat in the valley just west of Cedarvale Road on Seneca Turnpike. Pictured from left to right are (first row) Lena Horsford, Louise Horsford, Ruth Gray, Howard Roberts, George Roberts, and Elias Roberts; (second row) Ruth Seeley, Fred Seeley, Mary Louise Fitzgerald, unidentified, Charles Fitzgerald, Mary Roberts, Maggie Vincent, teacher Barbara Conroy, Ed Seeley, and unidentified.

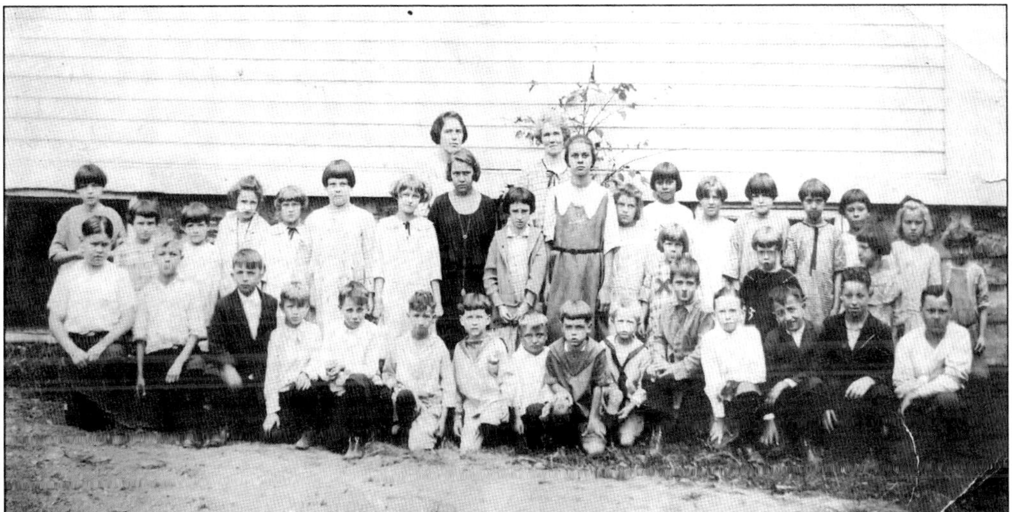

These children attended the Marcellus Falls School in 1923. The teachers were Elizabeth Glover and Bridget Kelly. The children are identified as William Lavey, Peter Prosonic, A. Kennick, Art Waters, Francis Waters, Leslie Seymour, Carlton King, ? Kennick, Leo Hayes, Henry Steele, J. Staparro, Joe Kelly, Mike Fridja, Oliver Pelchy, Charles Chrysler, Mary Fenlon, Margaret Aherin, Agnew Brennan, Alice Brennan, Agnes Giles, Margaret Lavey, Ruth Giles, Florence Seymour, Elizabeth Aherin, Catherine Prosonic, M. Kennick, Mary Prosonic, Helen Hopkins, Margaret Fenlon, Iva Pelchy, Julia Prosonic, A. Kennick, and Irene Pelchy.

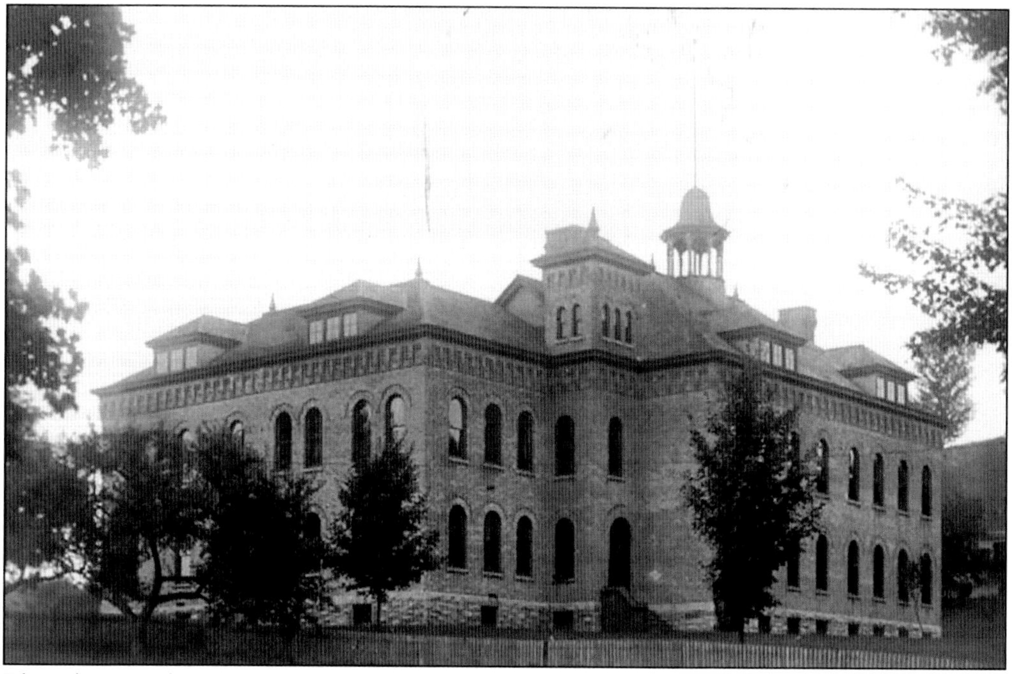

This photograph is of Marcellus Union Free School in the 1920s. The school was formally opened on December 3, 1892, with Matthew I. Hunt as the first principal. In September 1939, the old building was sold to L. D. Paul for $2,500. Paul dismantled the old school and sold off the remnants of it. He built his own home, and several others, on the site.

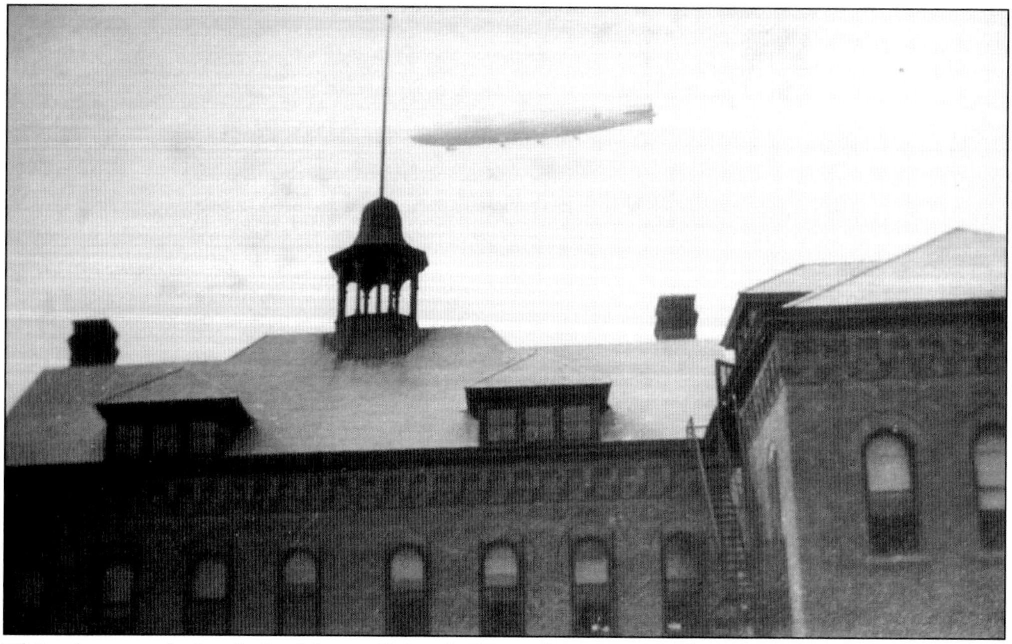

This photograph is of the Union School. Note the zeppelin flying overhead at the top of the photograph.

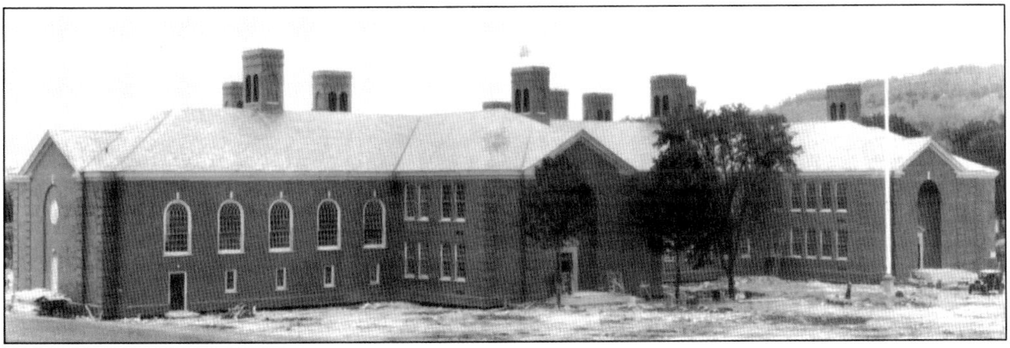

This is the high school on Reed Parkway that replaced the Union Free School on West Main Street. The school was built in 1936 and opened for classes in September 1937. This building was dedicated to its past principal Chester S. Driver and now houses the middle school, grades four through eight.

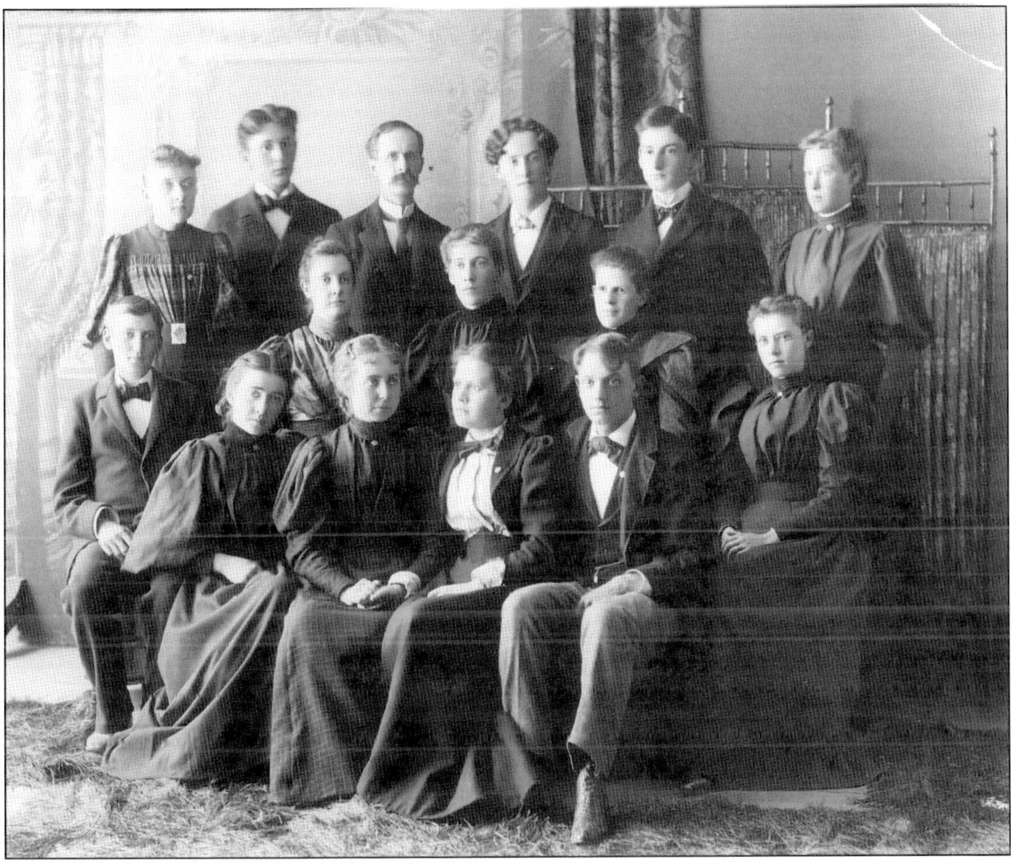

This is the Marcellus Union Class of 1895. Pictured are, from left to right, (first row) Anna Hennessey, Lena Jewel Krebs, Maud Conover, and Willis Cuddeback; (second row) Ralph Weeks, Miss Cobank, Miss Brigham (teacher), Miss Stuart (teacher), and Laura Williams; (third row) Annie Simmons, J. Charles Williams, Prof. W. F. Miner, Leland Colton, Harvey Nary, and Mable Thomas.

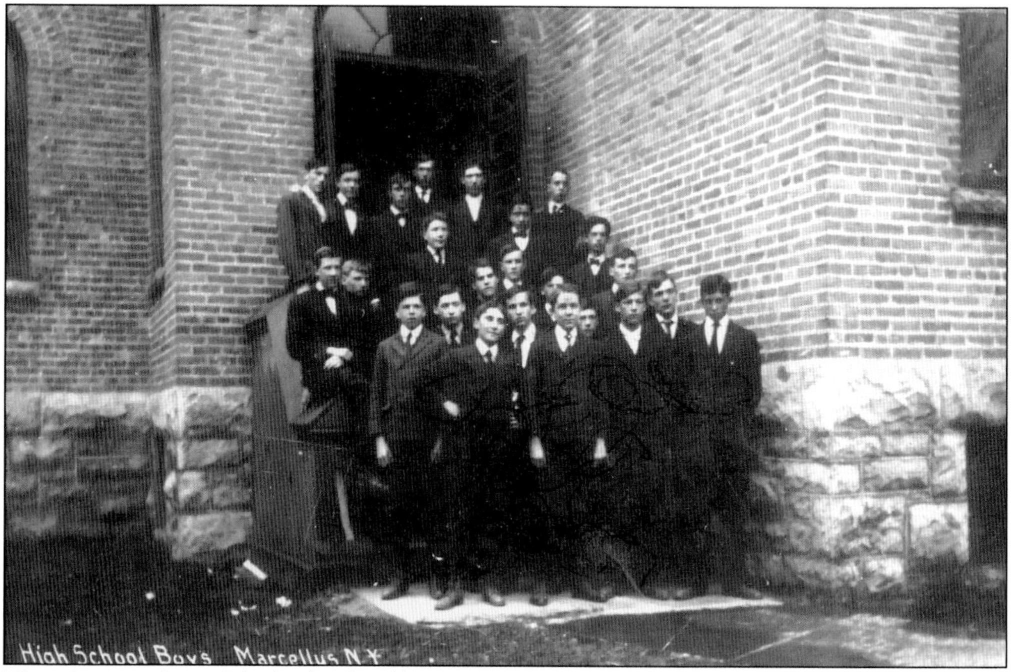

This photograph is of the high school boys. They are Edmund McHale, Charles Dillon, Tolman Spaulding, Seymour Evans, Earl Baker, Frank Allen, Earl Weidman, Edward Amidon, Emmett McNally, Roy Jewell, William Spaulding, William Curtin, Harry Kennedy, Earl Church, and Joseph Matteson.

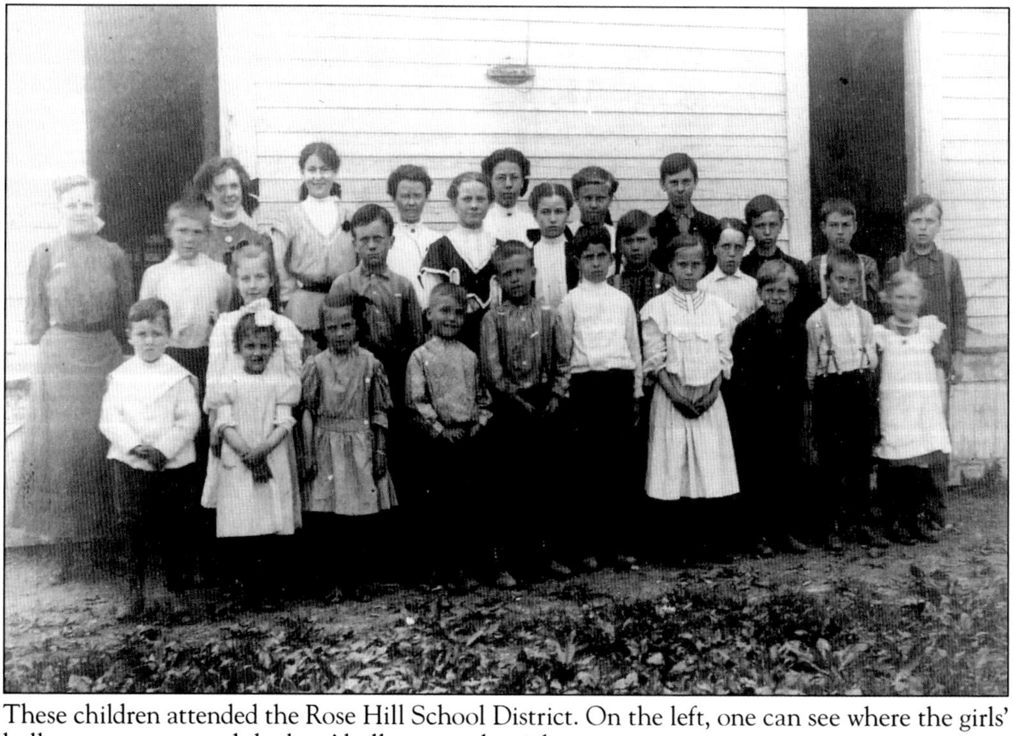

These children attended the Rose Hill School District. On the left, one can see where the girls' hall entrance was, and the boys' hall was on the right.

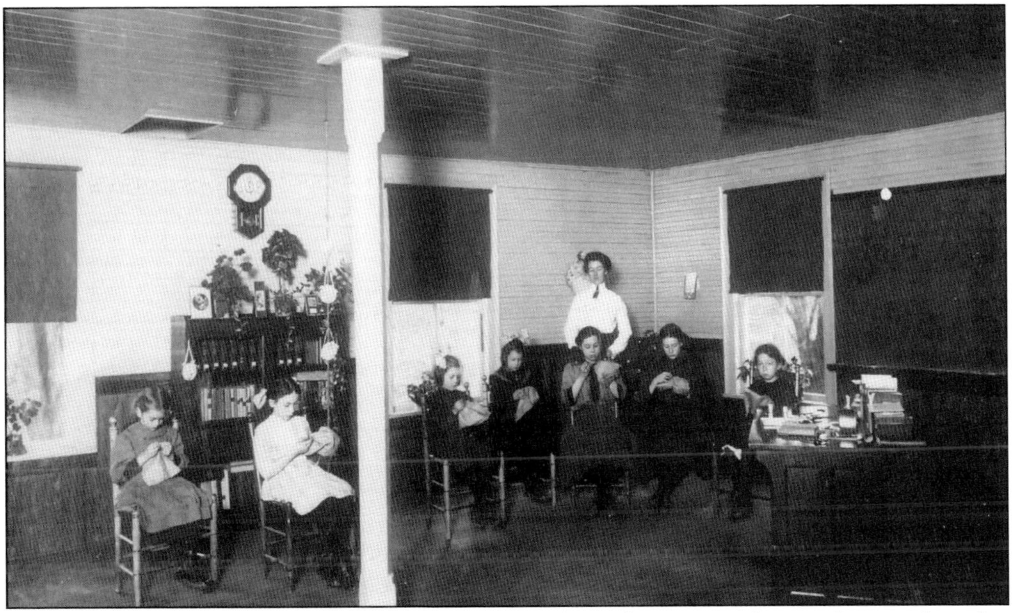

This is the Marcellus Falls School District No. 1. The girls were on the top floor, and in this photograph, one can see they are working on their needlepoint skills. The teacher is Bridget Kelley and the girls from left to right are Helen Webster, Fannie Kelley, Marguerite Kelley, Amelia Steele, Winifred Kelley, Mary Waters, and Aileen Smith.

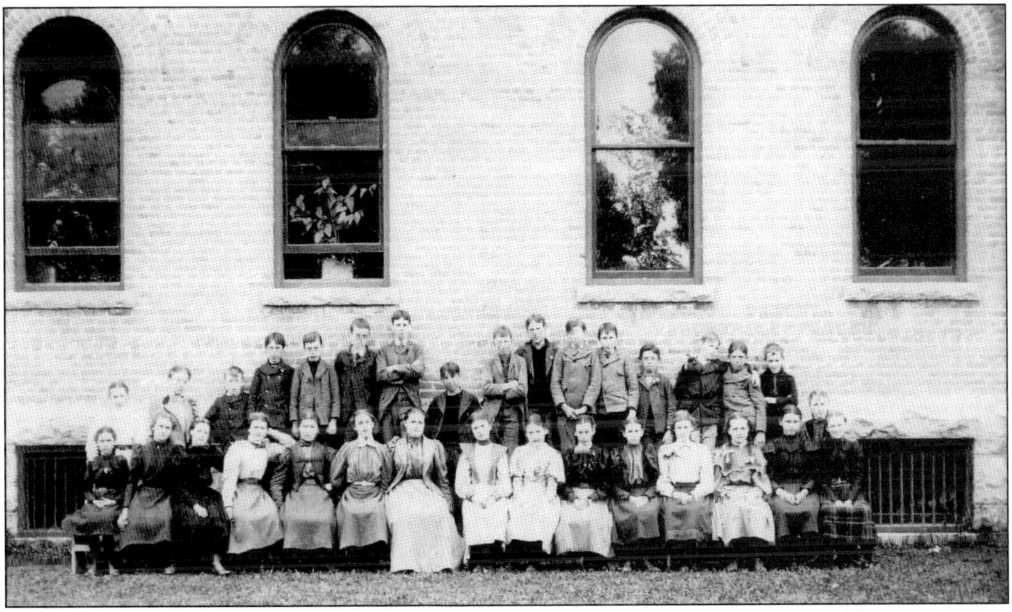

These children were attending the Union School in 1898. Those pictured are (first row) Lizzie Haster, Margaret Conley, Jessie Stearns, Mayme Murphy, Katie Callahan, May Hunt, Inez Austin, Nellie McHale, Anna Curtin, Alice Sarr, Lucy Amidon, Katie Weidman, Nellie Curtin, Sara Mulroy, and Sadie Connell; (second row) Ruth Phillips Griffing, Miss Rogers (teacher), Art McKenzie, Allie Julia, unidentified, Tom Curtin, Cletus Duggan, Austin Rutherford, Phillip Amidon, George Scott, Berlin Smith, Eddie Dolan, Will Needham, George Helganz, Fred Woodbridge, and Emil Smith.

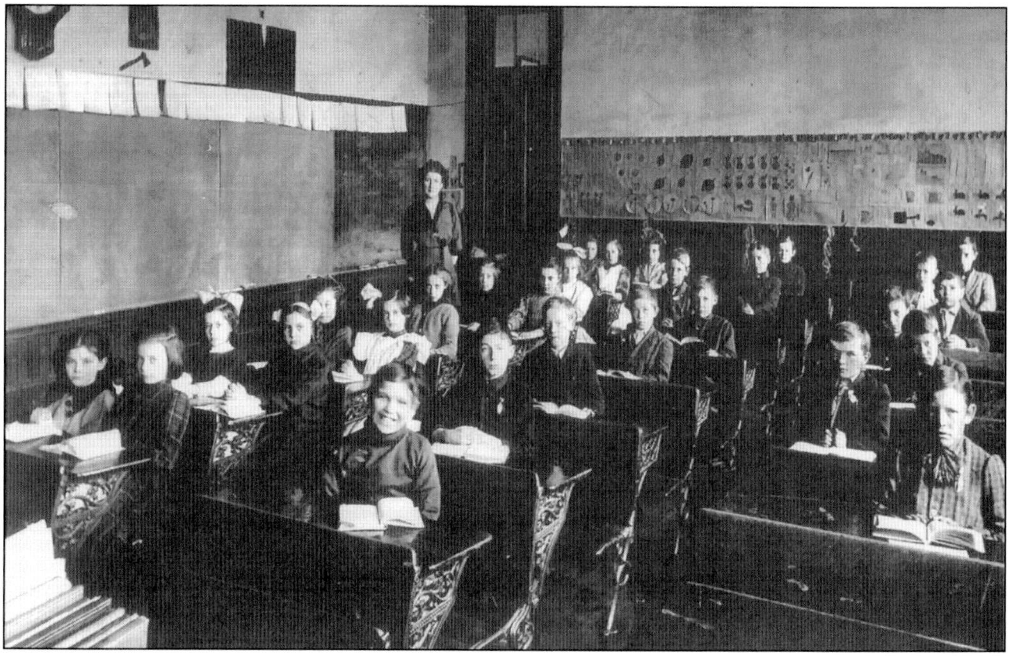

This photograph is of the third-grade class in 1910. The teacher is Winnifred Crowley. Students identified here are Bessie Weedon, Dorothy Stone, ? Hellganz, Ruth Darby, Ruth Walker, Alice Thornton ?, Florence Schanzle, Louise Wing, Emily Sauber, Mary Malcolm, Arthur W. Wilson, Dan McLaren, ? Wilson, Joe Bain, Douglas Scott, Earl Carter, Paul Curtin, Rollin Stone, Arthur Burnis, Bert Hertach, and ? Muldoon.

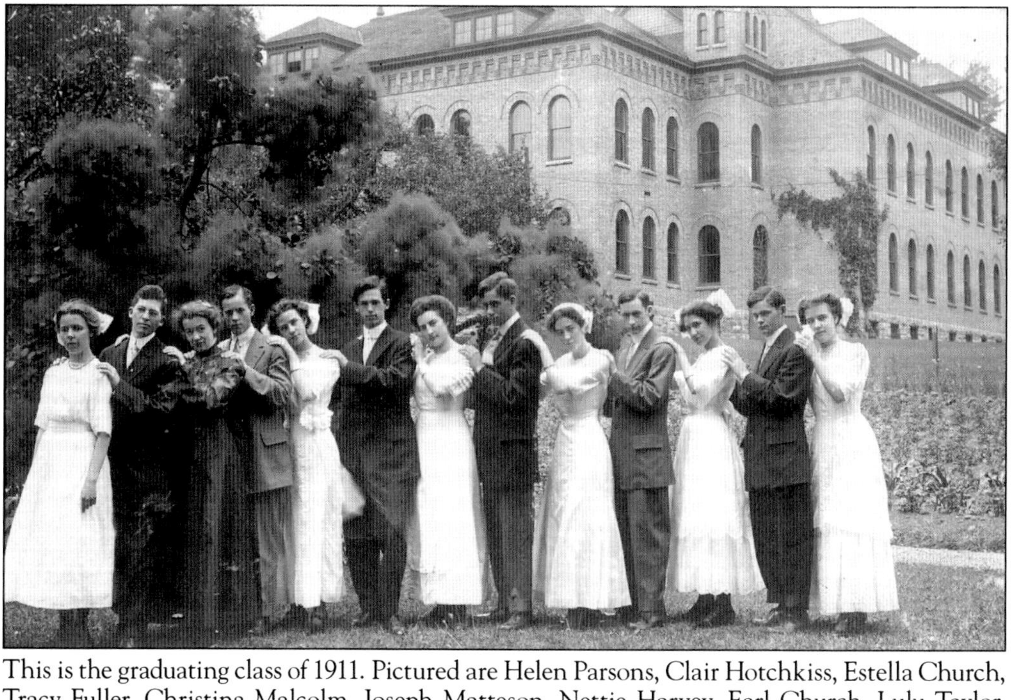

This is the graduating class of 1911. Pictured are Helen Parsons, Clair Hotchkiss, Estella Church, Tracy Fuller, Christina Malcolm, Joseph Matteson, Nettie Harvey, Earl Church, Lulu Taylor, Charles Dillon, Mable Hellganz, Leonard Wilson, and Mary Jackson.

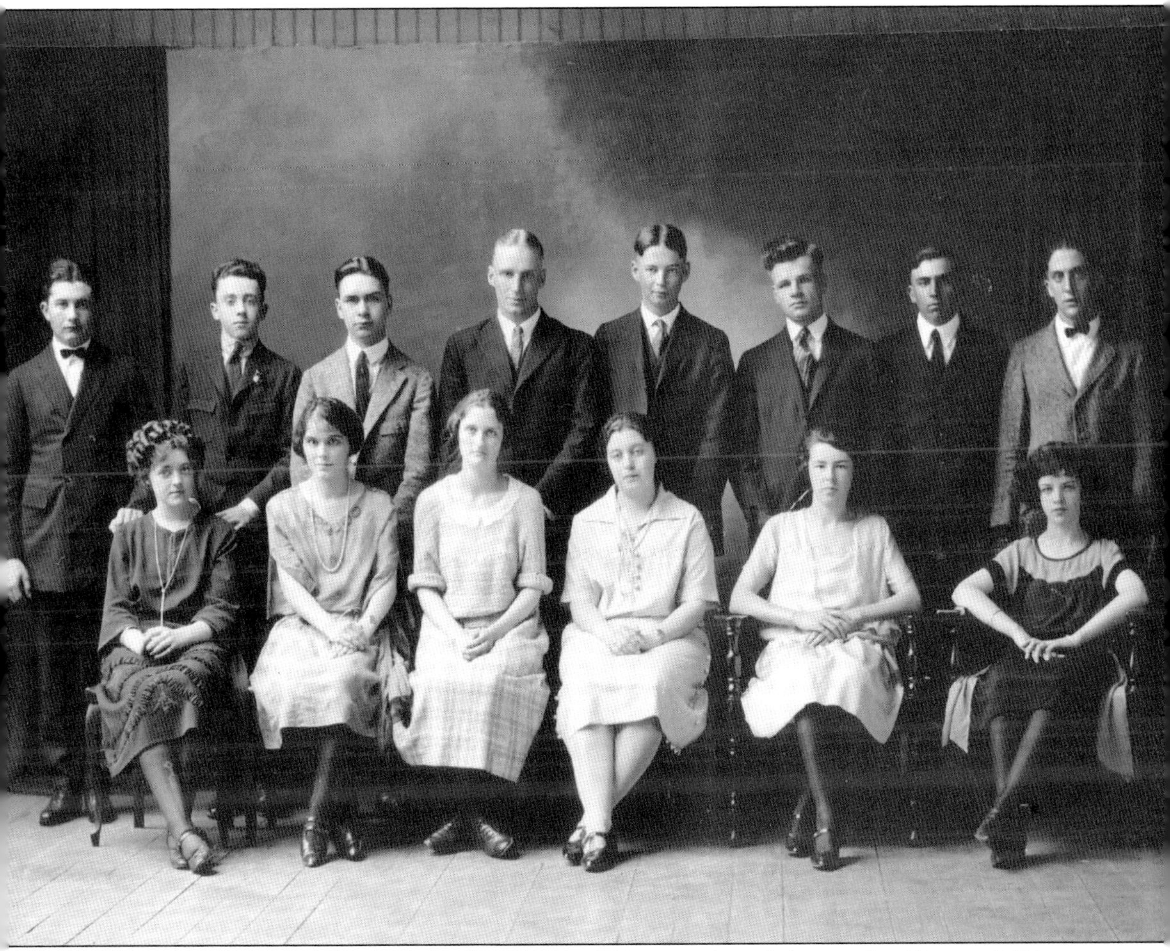

This is the class of 1922 Union school graduates. They are, from left to right, (first row) Edna Hogan, Louise Stone, Ina Black, Alice Thornton, Cornelia Parsons, and Gladys Hill; (second row) Joseph Thornton, Eddie Murphy, Clayton Pilot, John Davis, Seymour Parsons, Edward Seeley, Lester Marshfield, and Martin Helfer.

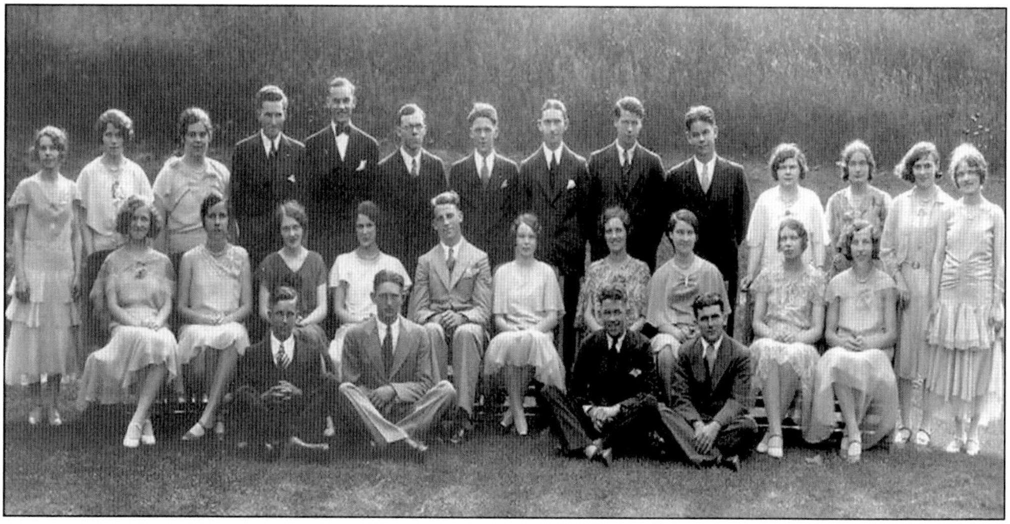

This photograph is the graduating class of 1930, from Marcellus Union High School. Pictured in alphabetic order are Doris Clarry, William Conley, Paul Cummings, Mary King Curtin, Edmund Dunfee, Clara Fenlon, Frances Gillett, Ronald Goodwin, Mary Rena Griffing, Mary Hadlock, George Harter, Catherine Hoffman, Grace Hoffman, Margaret Horne, Arlene Isgar, Donald Kilcoyne, Margaret Lavey, William Lavey, Marion Marquis, James Powell, Marie Sennett, Ruth Shay, William Shay, Virginia Showalter, Howard Smith, Winifred Jane Thornton, Charles Weeks, and Frank Wicks.

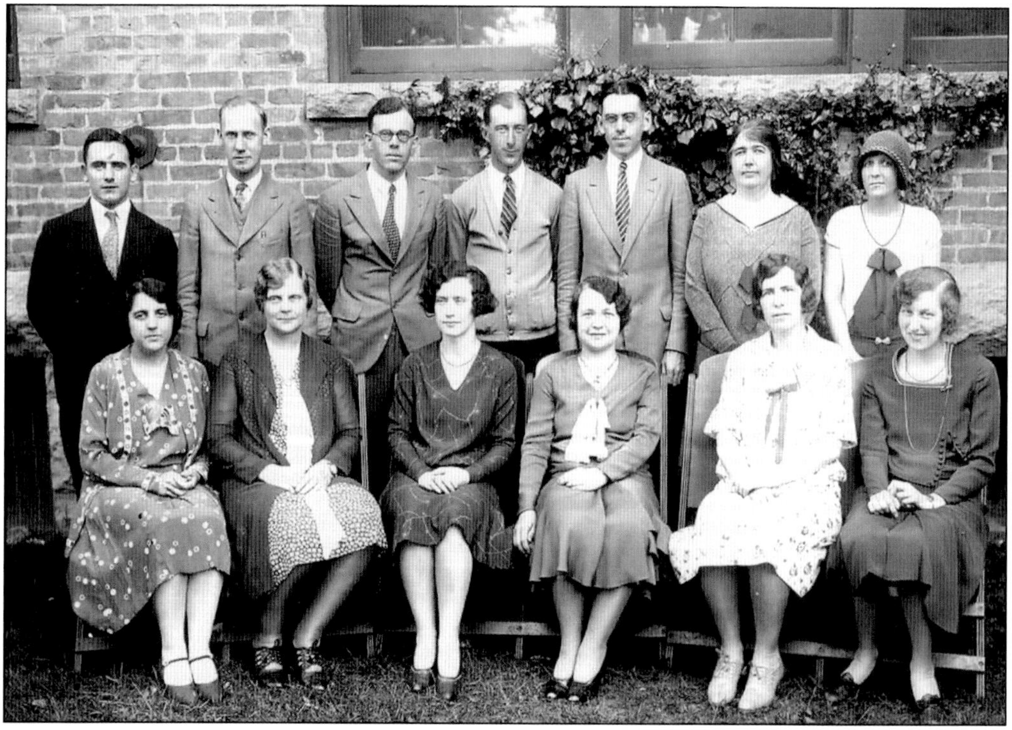

This 1930 photograph is of the Marcellus School Faculty. Shown are Betsy Gleason, Flora Smith, Elizabeth Slattery, Elizabeth Wicks, Emma Rena Avins, Janet Conklin, Wilfred Farrell, ? Salberg, Max Molyneaux, Arthur Hyatt, Francis Reynolds, Marguerite Pendergast, and Miss Bogardus.

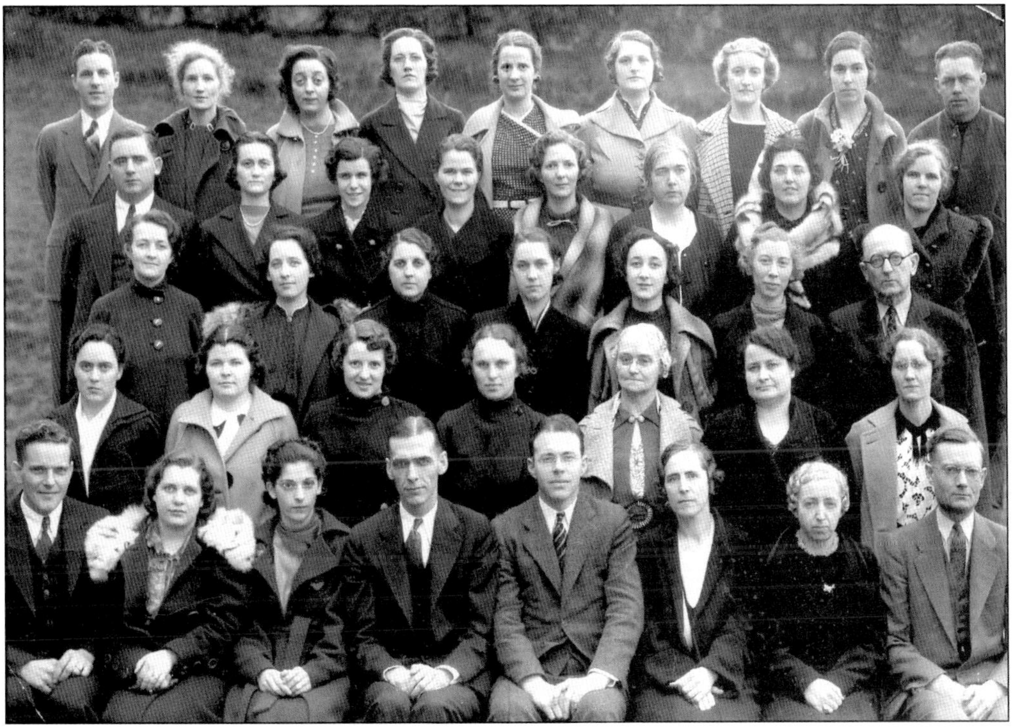

In this picture, the 1935 Marcellus faculty are (first row) Keith Burr, unidentified, Rose Rossi, Chester Driver, Max Molyneaux, Emma Rena Avins, Helen Heenan, and Raymond Jansen; (second row) unidentified, Clara Fenlon, Margaret Kavenaugh, unidentified, Hazel Hacket, Florence Donovan, and Mollie Reinmann; (third row) Mina Burns, Marion Crysler, Betsy Gleason, Dorothy Long, Florence Marmot, Kathryn Carr, and Mr. Patrillo; (fourth row) Wilfred Farrell, Marine Morehead, Gibbins Fitz, Janet Benedict, Florence Felton, Marguerite Pendergast, Lucinda Wright, and Lucy Sweet; (fifth row) Francis McLaughlin, Mary Seeley, Lillian Ducket, Marie Sennett, Ms. Harding, unidentified, Ms. Bradbent, Irene Morgan, and Carl Peterson.

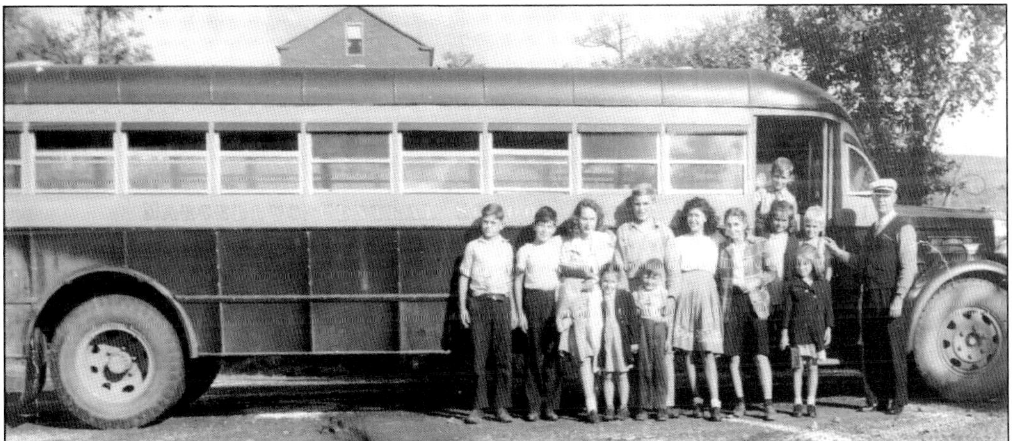

This 1944 photograph shows school children getting on the school bus. Seen here from left to right are (first row) Judy Stone, Thomas Lathrop, and unidentified; (second row) Arnold Rowe, Robert Gallinger, Peggy Ann Stone, William Riggall, Beverly Gallinger, Dorothy Rowe, unidentified, Ronald Rowe, and Reverend Fryer (driver); (third row) Eugene Knickerbacker.

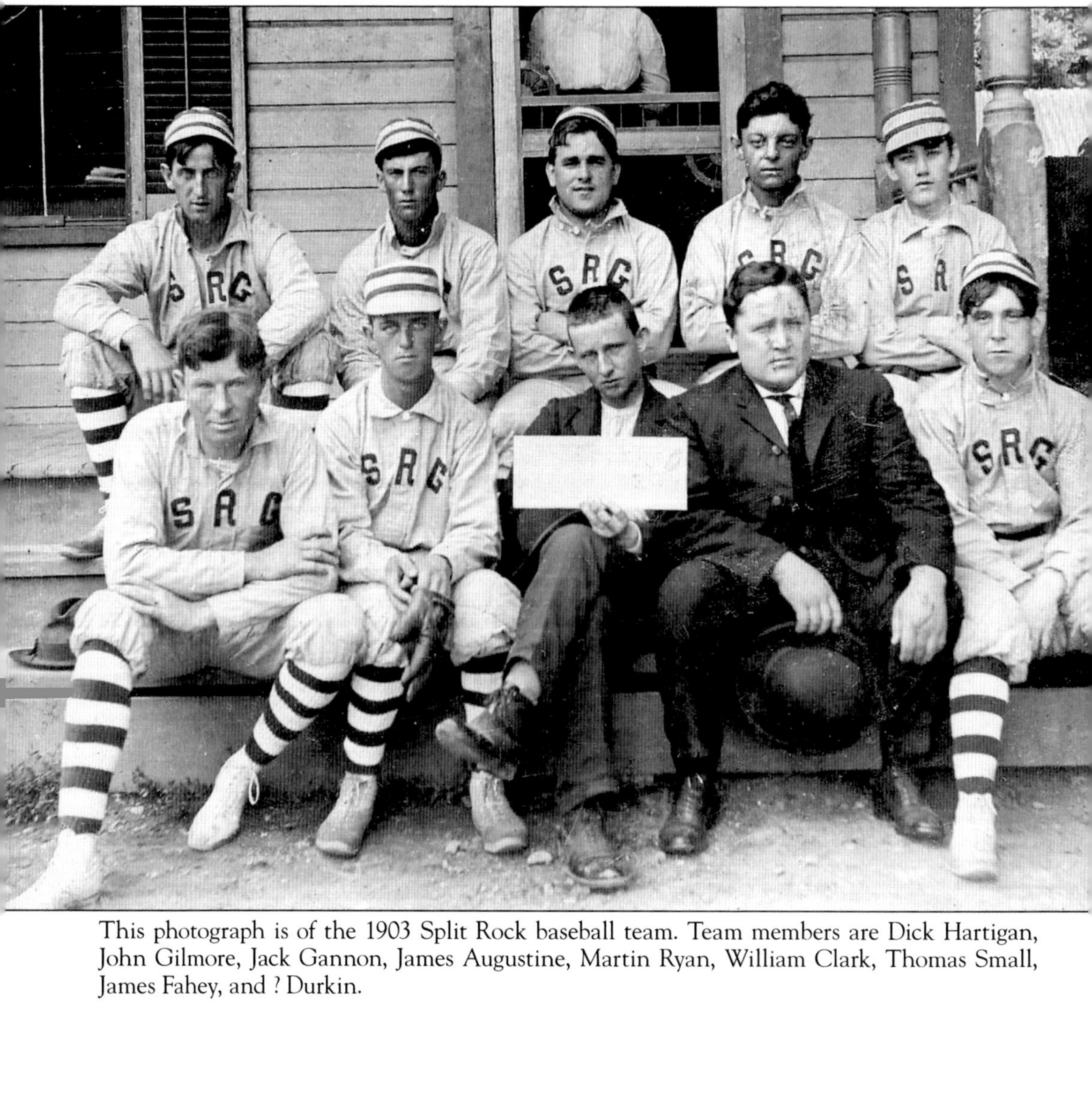

This photograph is of the 1903 Split Rock baseball team. Team members are Dick Hartigan, John Gilmore, Jack Gannon, James Augustine, Martin Ryan, William Clark, Thomas Small, James Fahey, and ? Durkin.

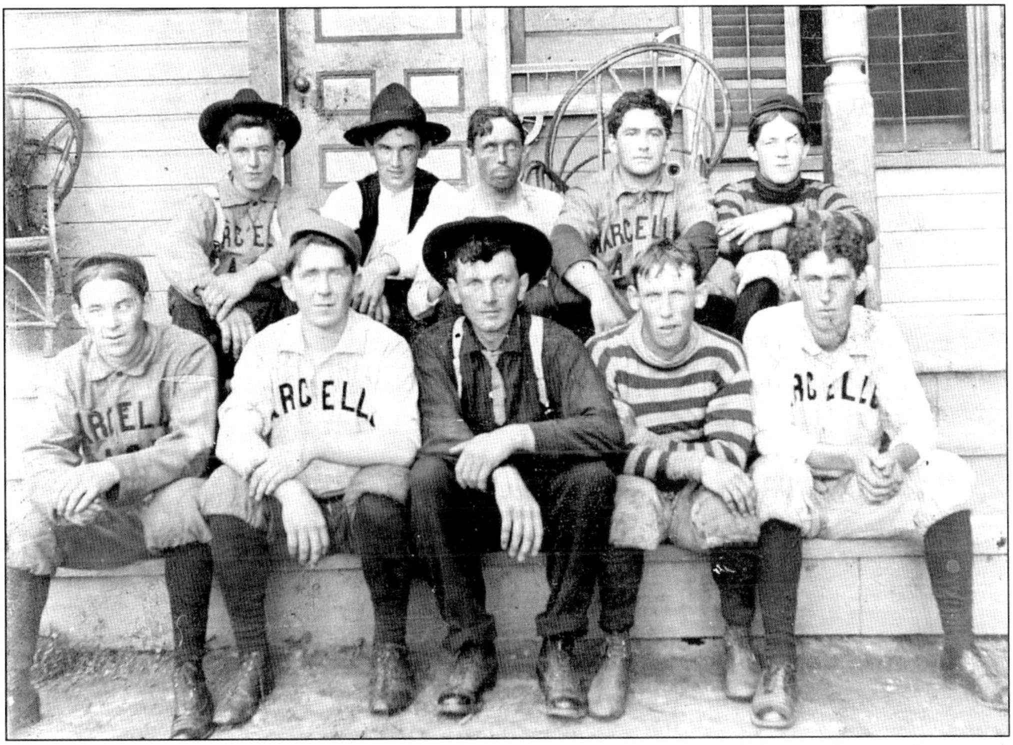

This is the 1903 Marcellus Falls baseball team. Team members, from left to right, are (first row) Ambrose Lawless, Eddie Kelly, Sport McAllister, Tim Coyne, and Jack Thornton; (second row) Tom Thornton, Bill Kennedy, Bill Everts, Jack Martin, and Charles Lawless.

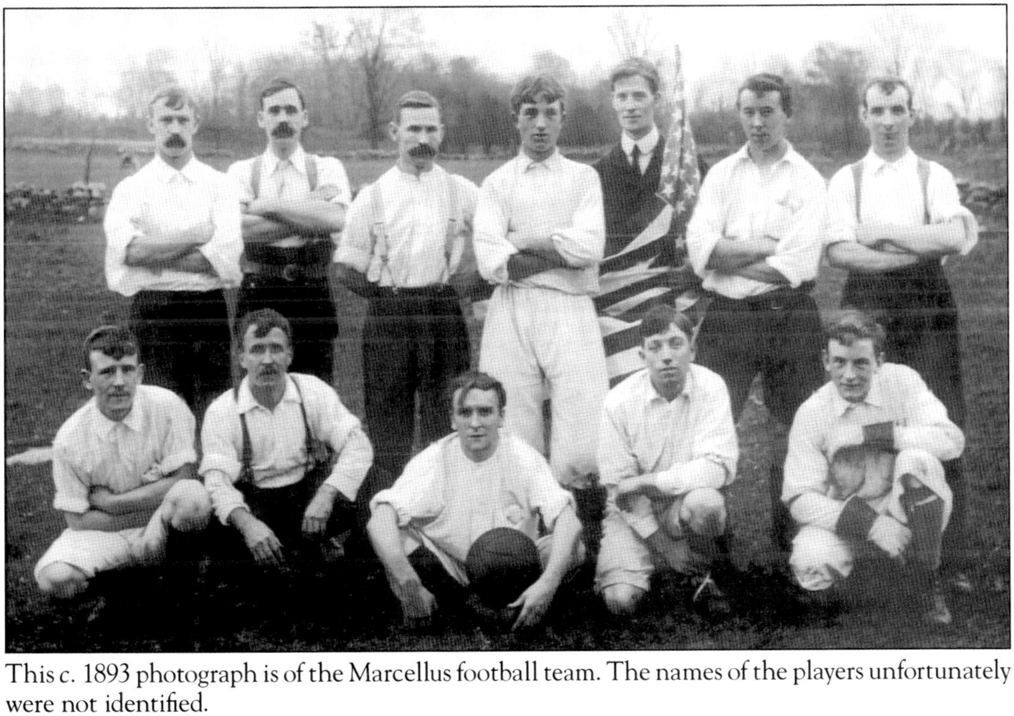

This c. 1893 photograph is of the Marcellus football team. The names of the players unfortunately were not identified.

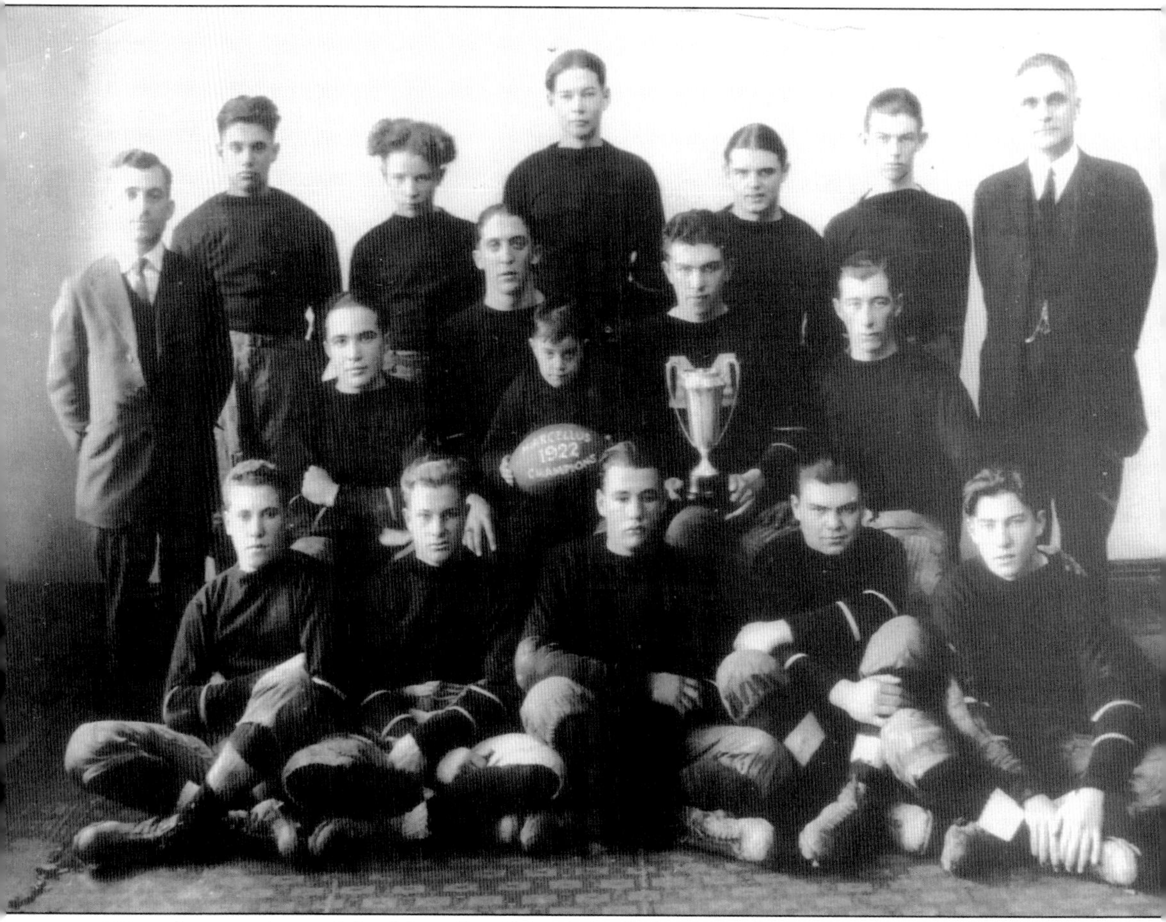

This photograph is of the Marcellus School football team, the winner of the county football championship in 1922. Pictured are (first row) Ken Spaulding, Henry Phillips, Rollo Wicks, Robert Shaffer, and Austin Woodford; (second row) Leon Guston, Martin Helfer (co-captain), John Horsington (mascot, seven years old), Paul Clark (co-captain), and Art Hyatt; (third row) coach Noaks, Harold Spikes, Martin Welch, Seymour Parsons, Venor McLaren, Chuck Shea, and Professor Helfer.

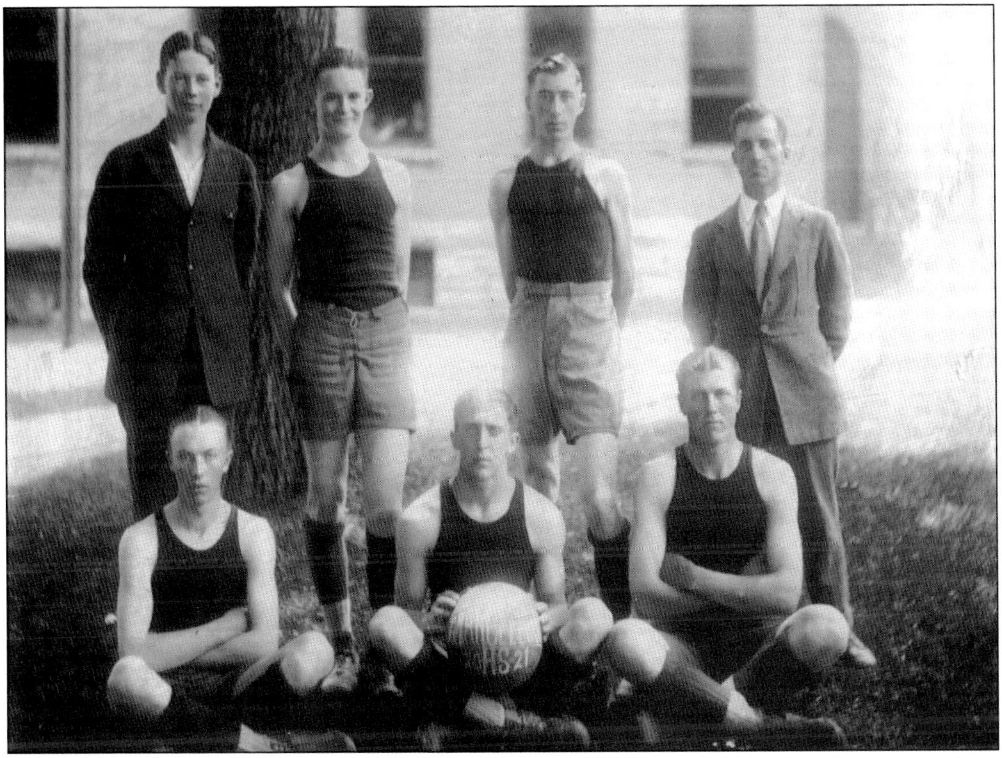

This picture is of the Marcellus High School basketball team in 1920. The players are, from left to right, (first row) Paul McAvoy, Martin Helfer, and Charles Black; (second row) Seymour Parsons, Arthur Wilson, Arthur Hyatt, and coach Irving Noaks.

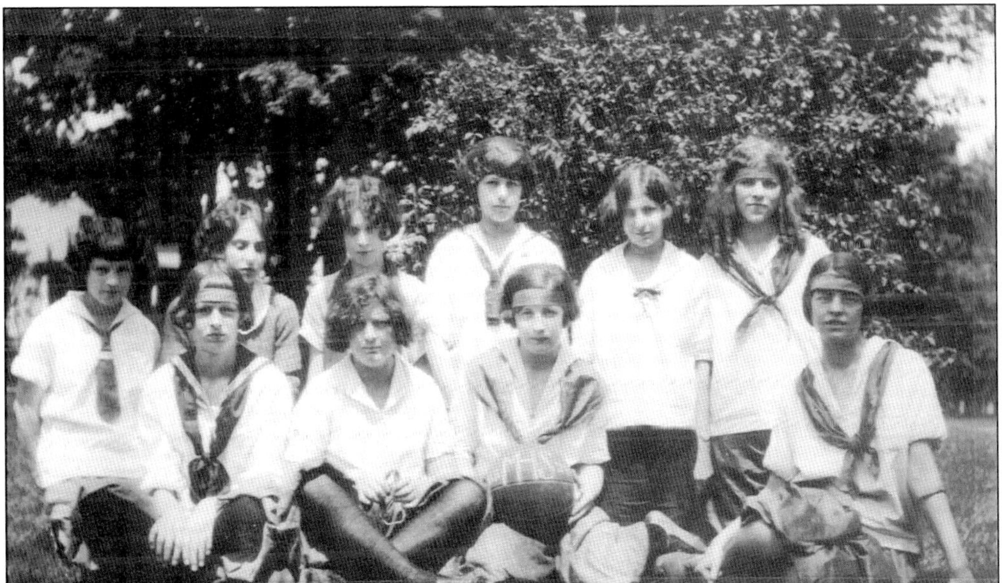

This is the girls basketball team in 1924. The girls are, from left to right, (first row) Dorothy Steele, Rosie Ward, Helen S., and May O'Shea; (second row) ? Spaulding, Louise Clark, Diana Weedon, Louise Bartlett, Emily Weidman, and Lucy Sweet.

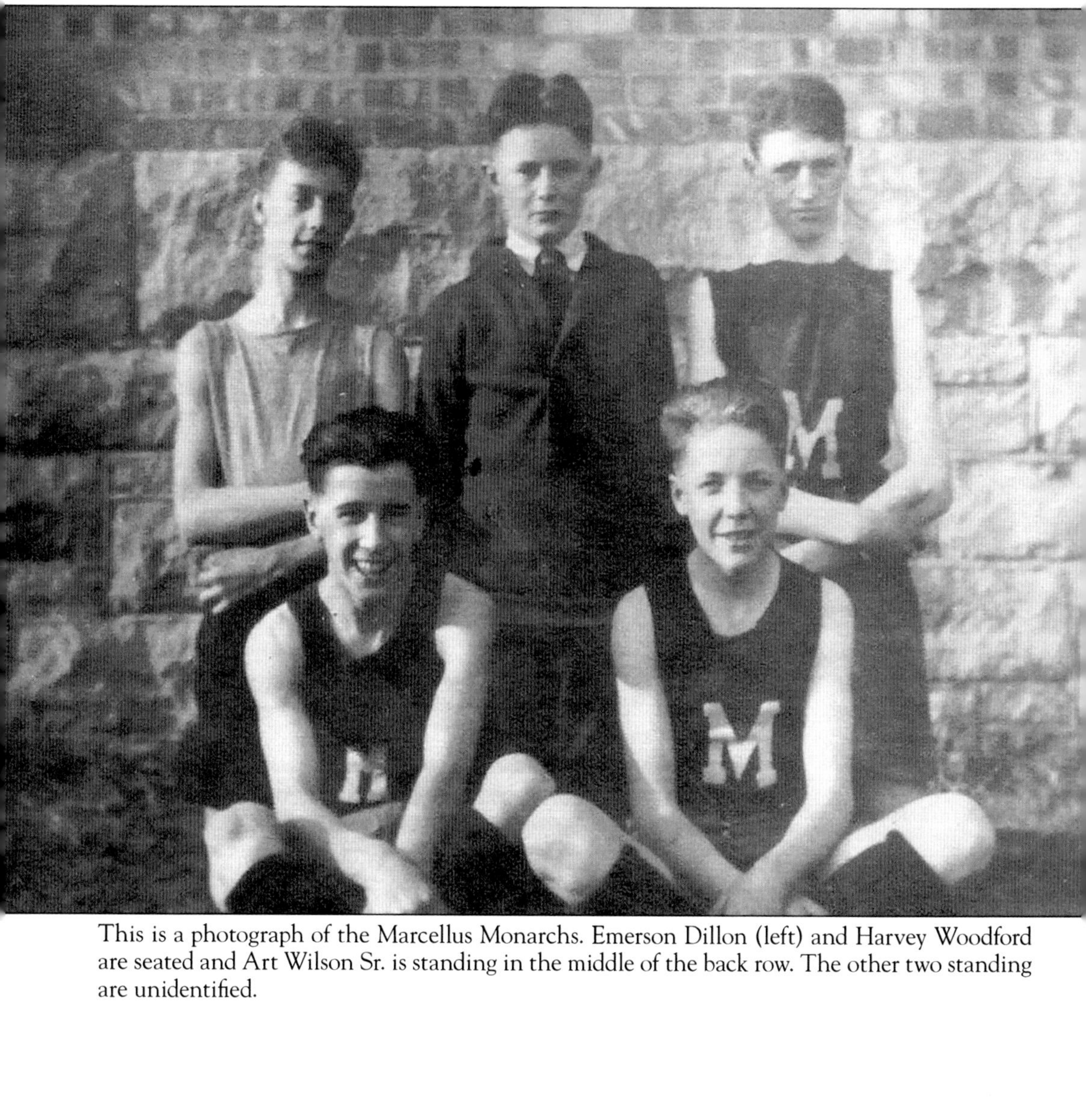

This is a photograph of the Marcellus Monarchs. Emerson Dillon (left) and Harvey Woodford are seated and Art Wilson Sr. is standing in the middle of the back row. The other two standing are unidentified.

Seven

Parades and Celebrations

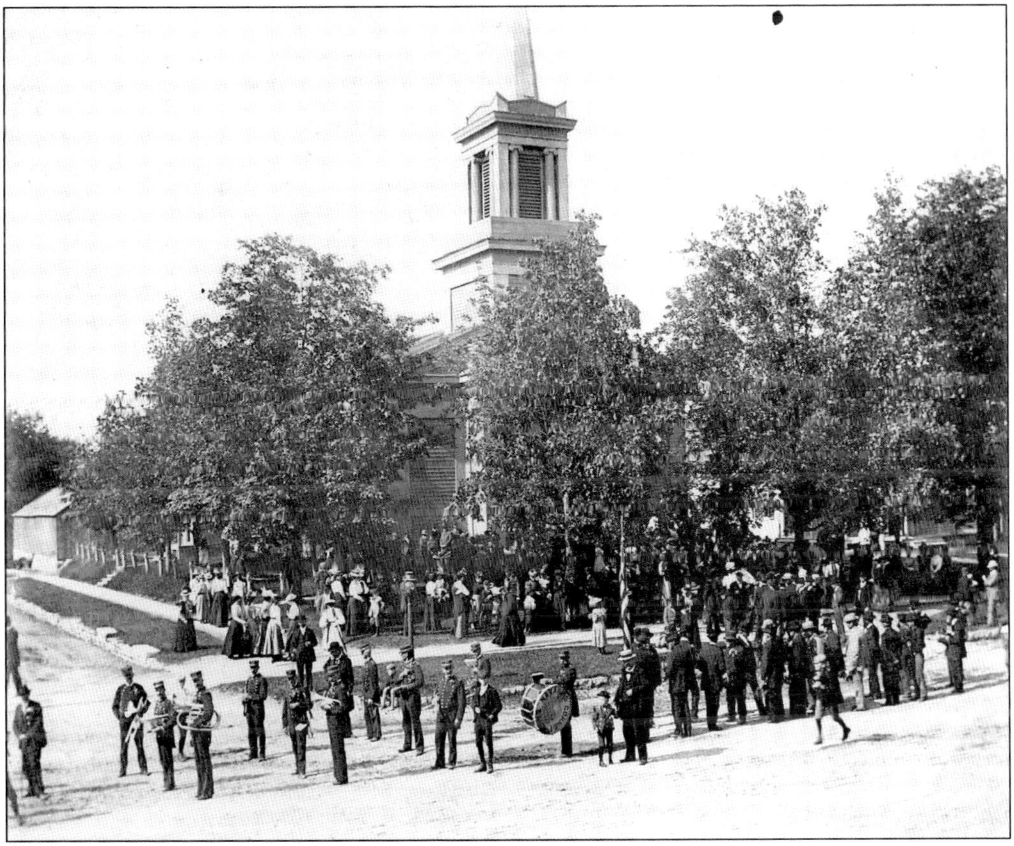

This parade down Main Street, around 1900, is halted in front of the Presbyterian church.

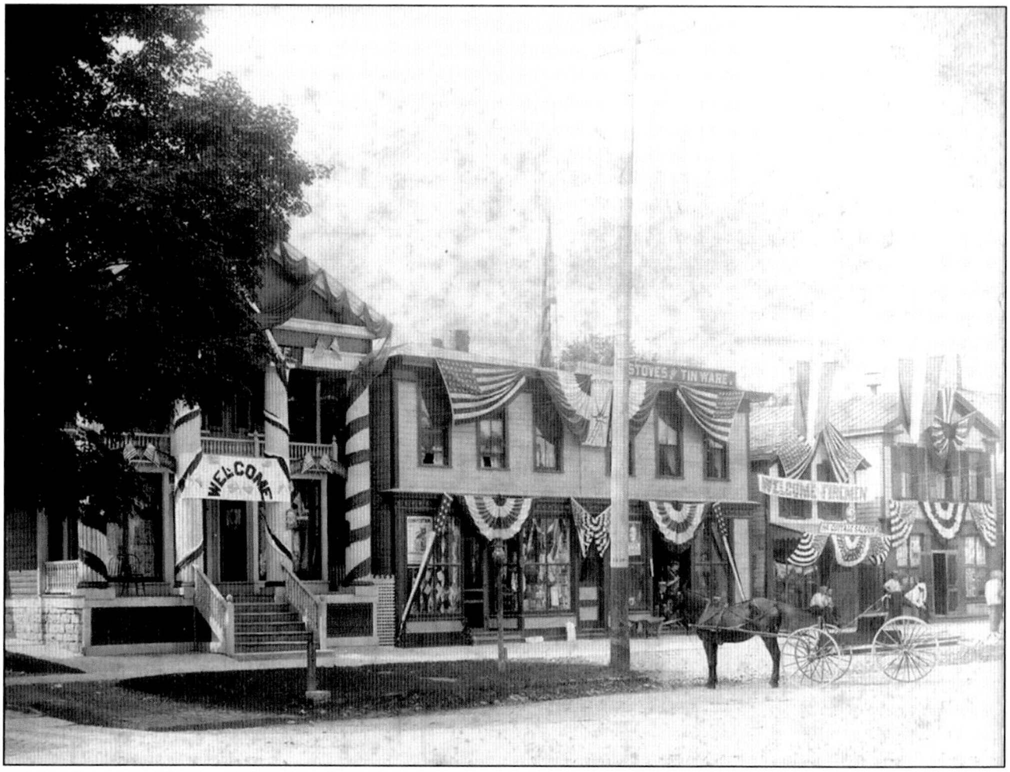

This photograph is of the south side of Main Street in 1914. The banners are welcoming the firemen for the firemen's convention.

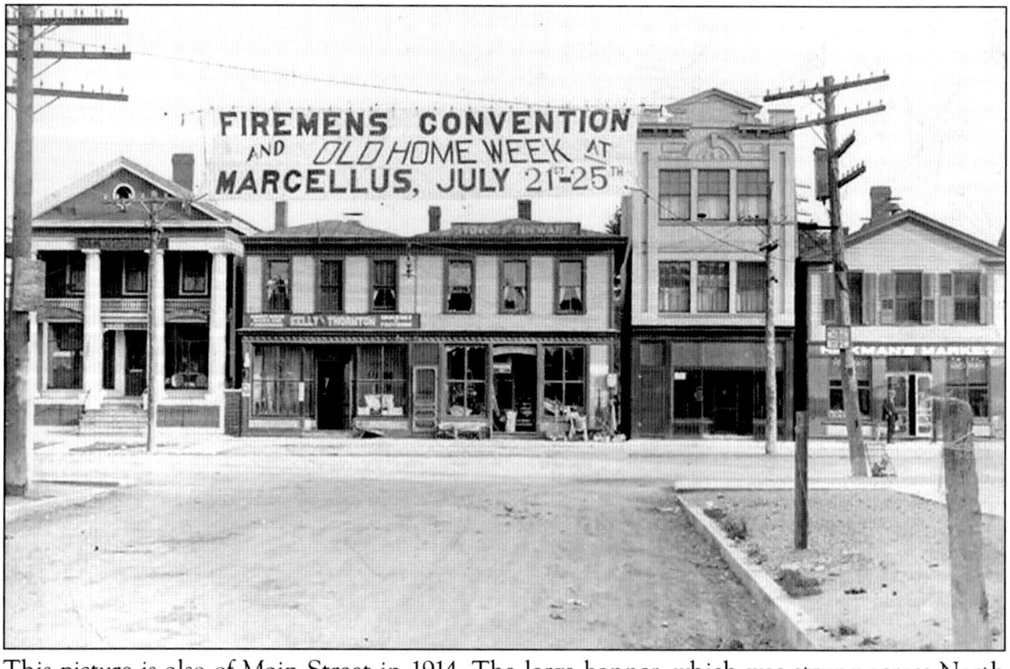

This picture is also of Main Street in 1914. The large banner, which was strung across North Street, welcomes the firemen and other visitors to old home week.

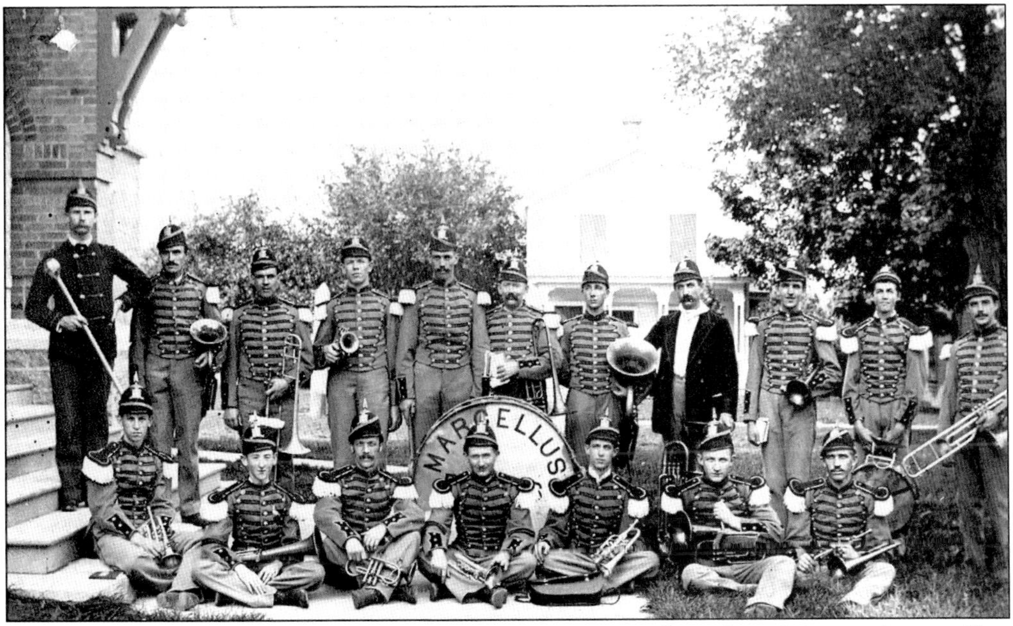

This is a picture of the Marcellus Brass Band in 1900. Members, from left to right, are (first row) unidentified, Charles Dugan, James Bishop, Herbert Newell, Harry Ridell, Lee Schultz, and unidentified; (second row) band leader Watson Matteson, Louis Avery, Will Griffin, James Pilot, Jack Hart, Greg Burlington, Nelson Gaunt, Irving Beach, Frank Gallup, Arthur Arnold, and Nealy Sheehan.

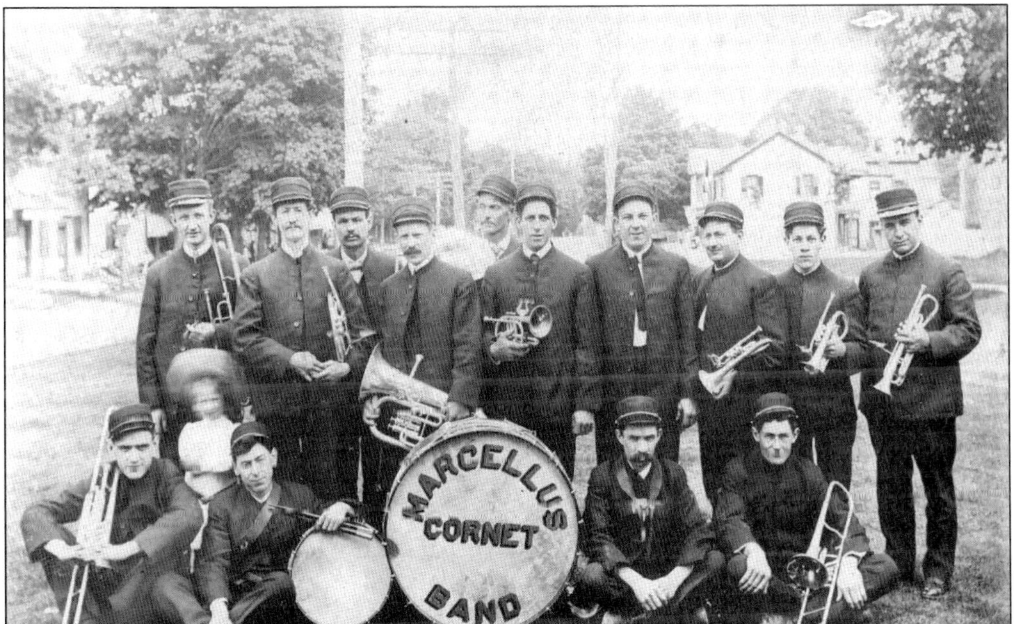

The band director of this 1905 Coronet Band was Charles Jones. Seen from left to right are (first row) Louis Scott, Lee Schultz's daughter Hazel, Philip Reynolds, John Coakley, and Ed Bartlett; (second row) Lee Shultz, Louis Blass, James Pilot, Peter Dunlap, Eugene Springstead, Charles Baker, Albert Taylor, Herbert Newell, Fred Woodbridge, and Charles Jones.

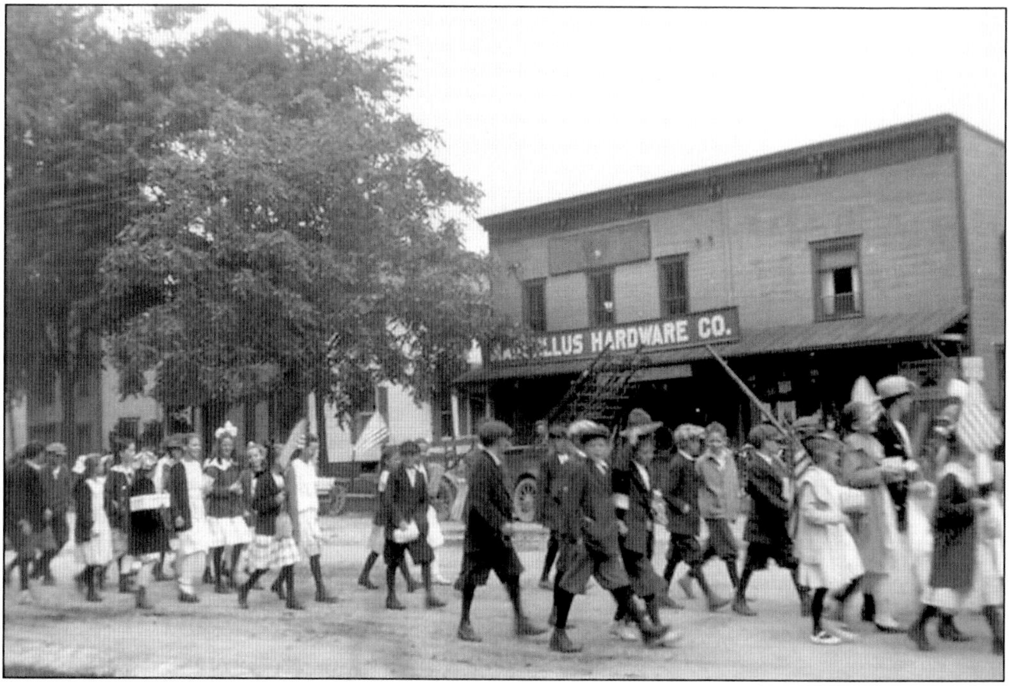

Seen here are children marching in the Fourth of July parade down Main Street in 1910. Behind them is Slocombe hardware store next to what is now the library, the police station, and historical society building.

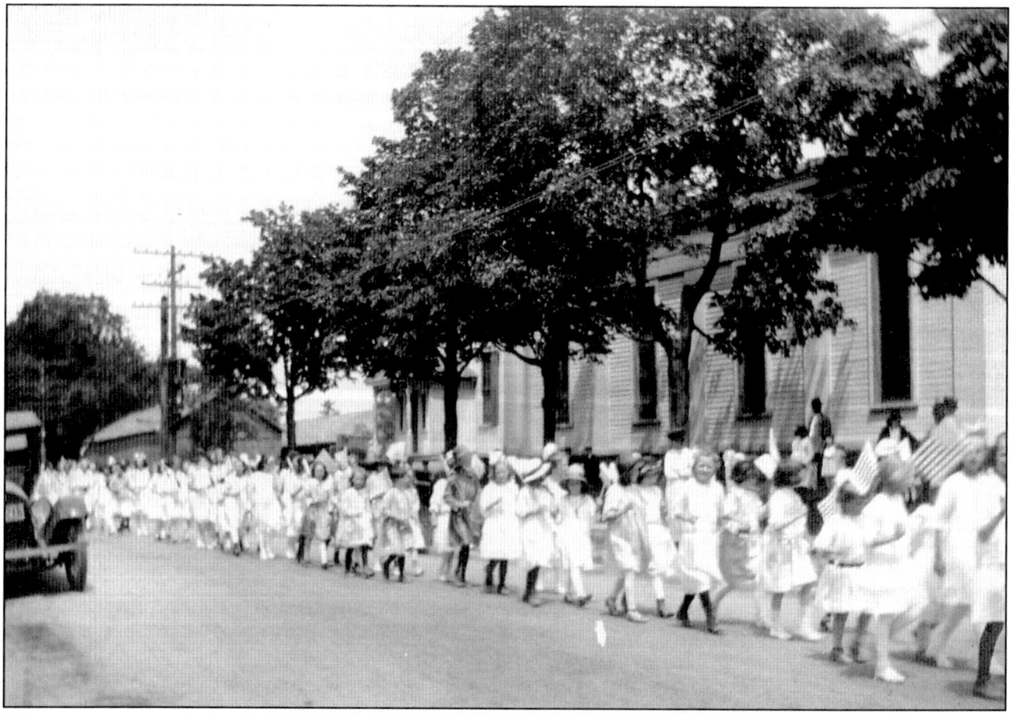

This picture is of the young girls marching in the Fourth of July parade in 1914. They are marching up North Street. The Presbyterian church can be seen on the right.

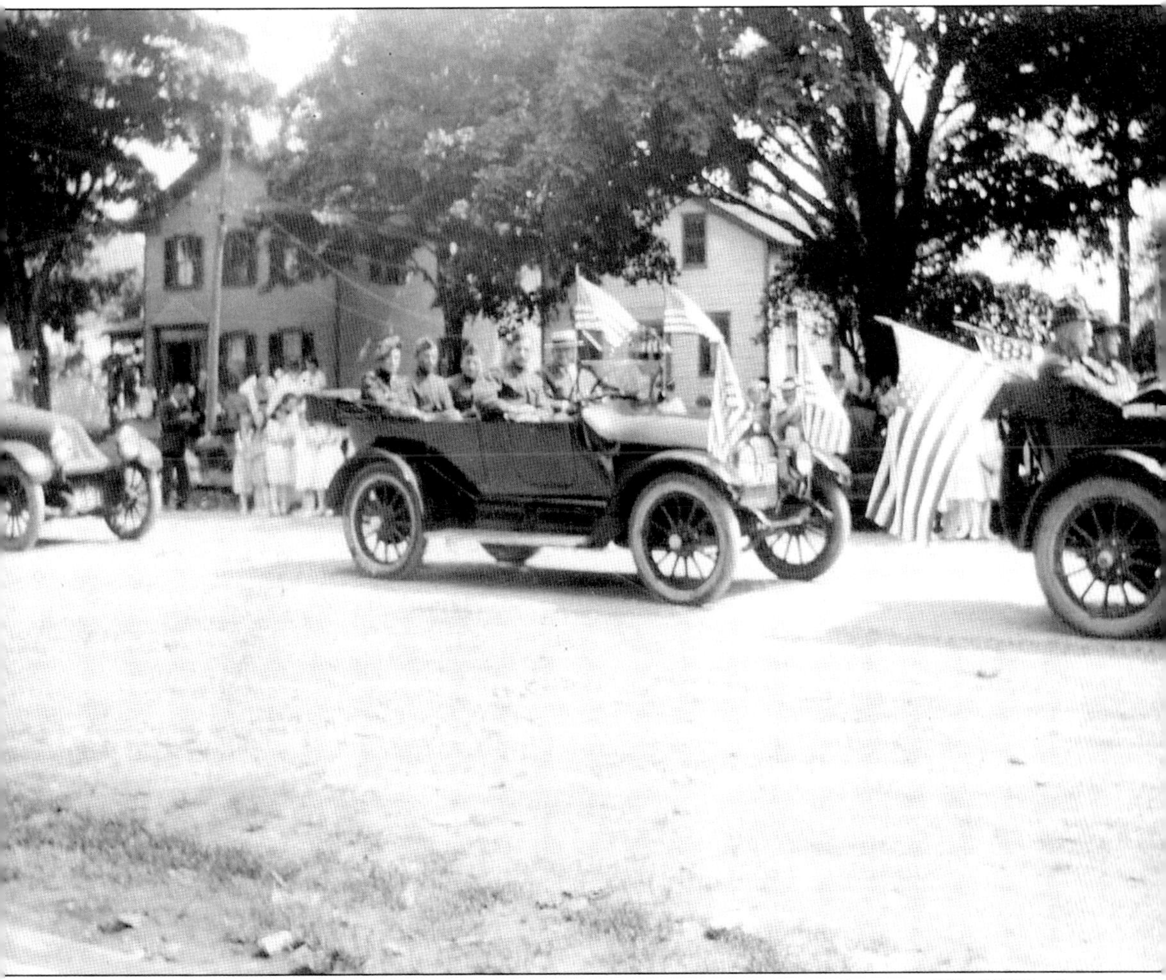

On July 19, 1919, Marcellus was the scene of a huge celebration welcoming home its World War I veterans in which the entire day was devoted to the servicemen. The celebration included this parade along with a banquet and other festivities.

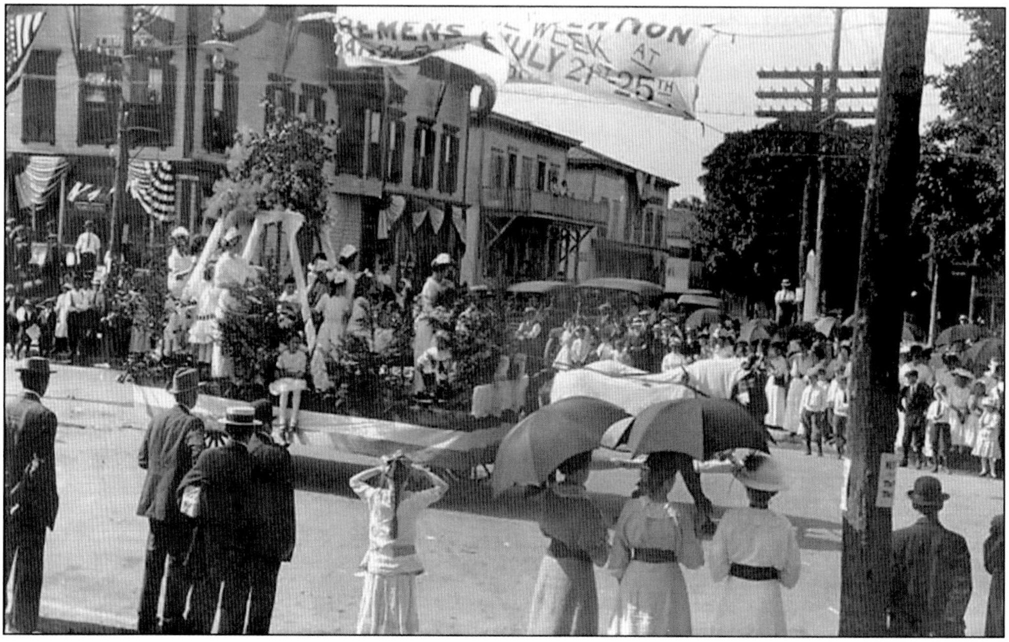

The Fire Days Parade in 1914 heads east down Main Street. Also visible is North Street as the float goes by.

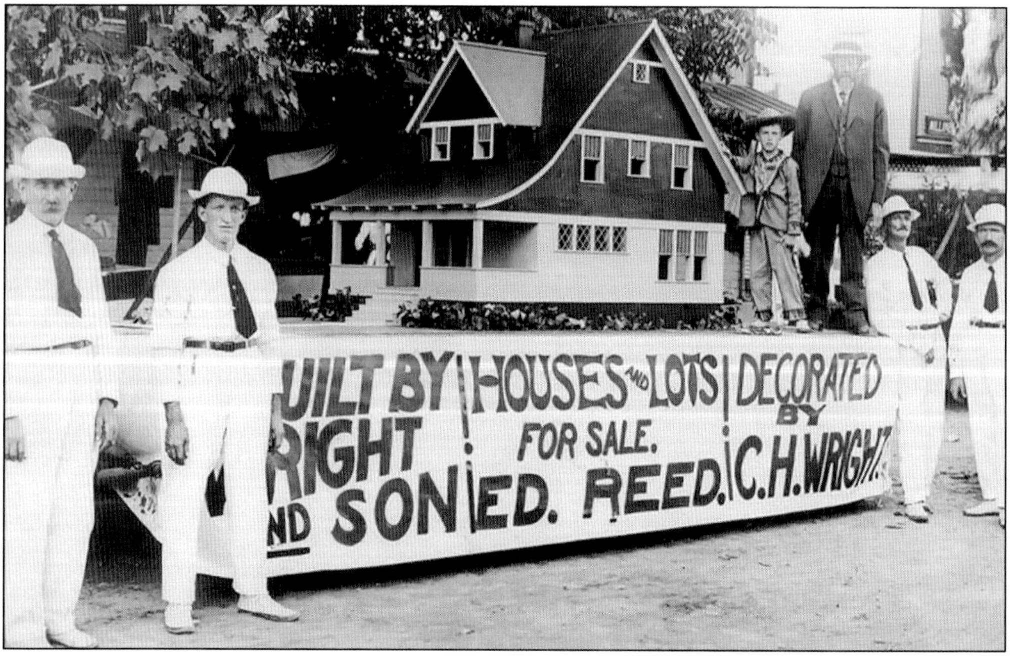

Edmund Reed's float, in 1914, carried a replica of a semi-bungalow, "price $3,000, ready to occupy; with electricity, water, walks, lawn, flower beds and shrubs." The replica is of a house he possibly built, which stands at 17 Reed Street today.

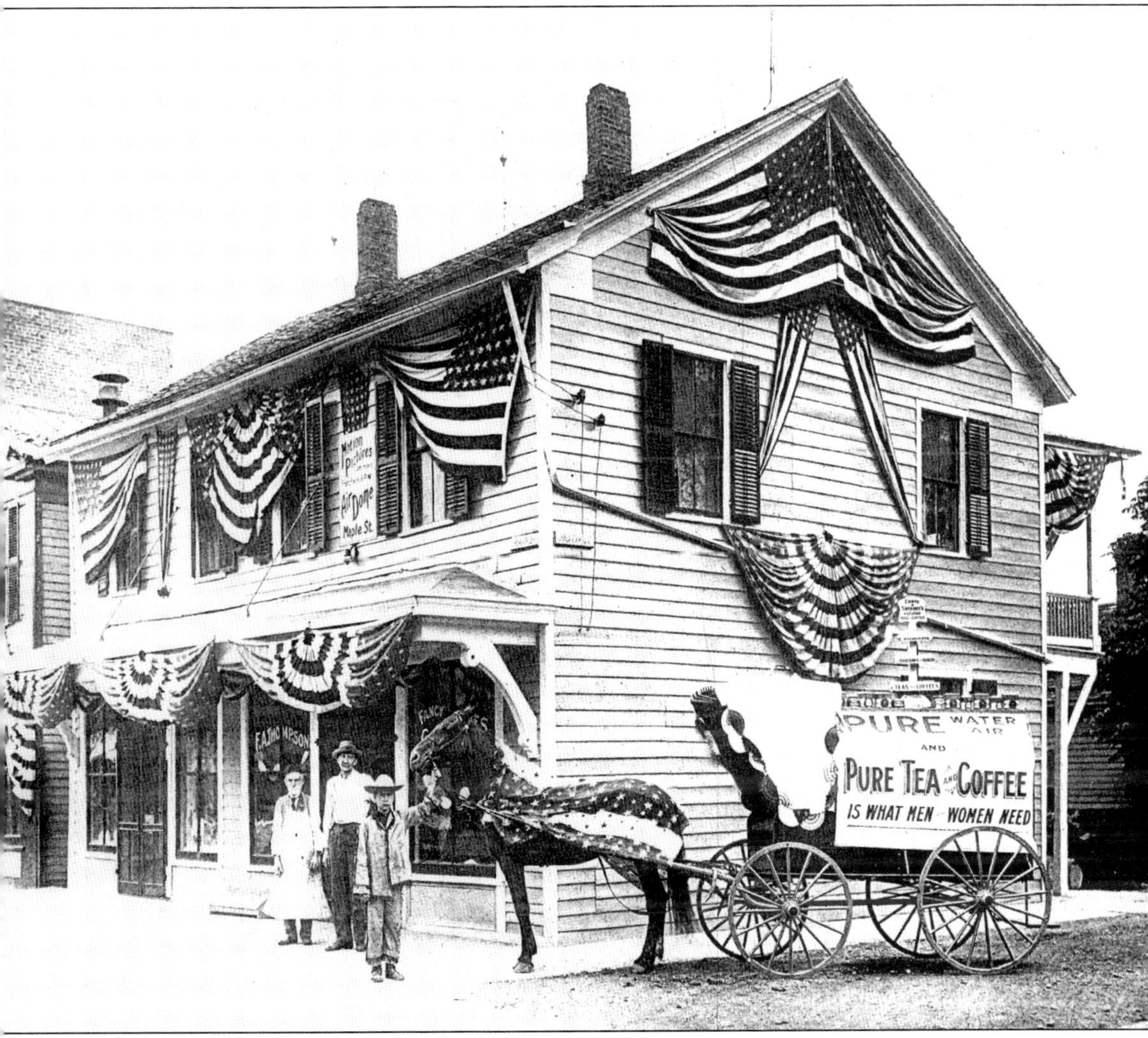

This photograph is of the corner store all decked out in flags and buntings. Even the horse is decorated as it pulls the wagon advertising "Pure Tea and Coffee."

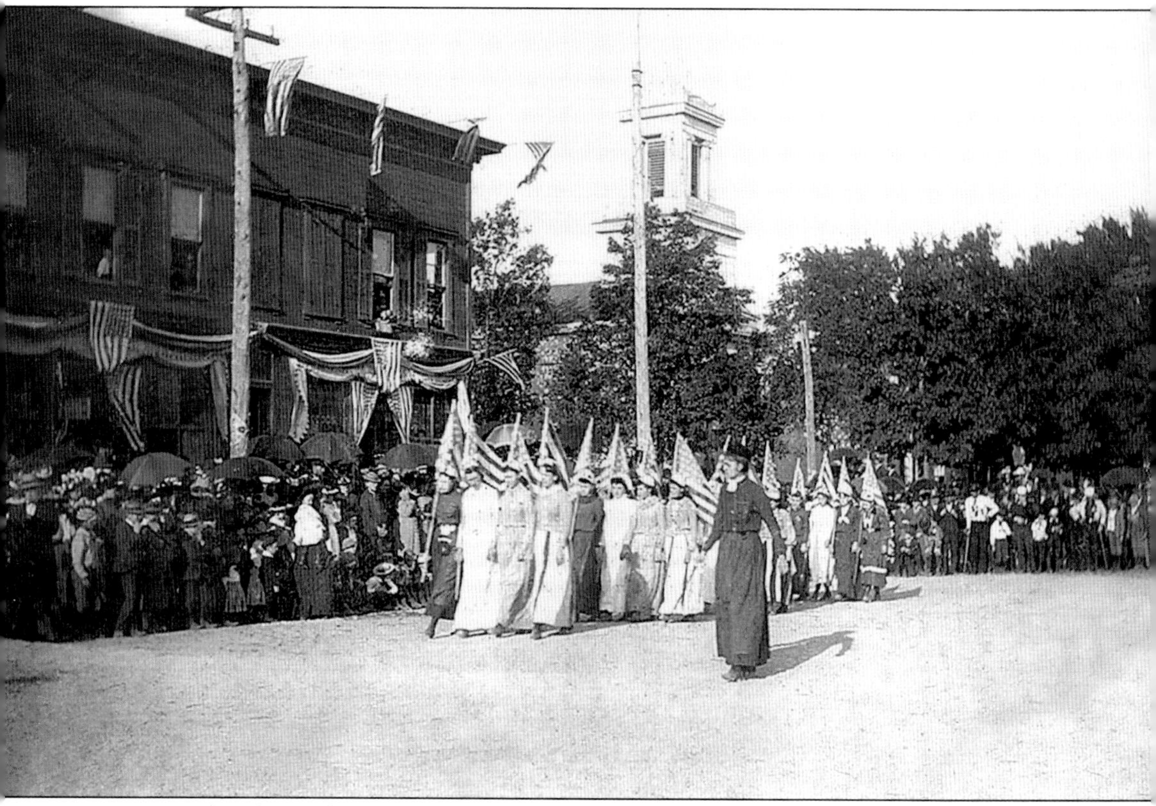

Young Lady's Flag Drill members are marching in formation down Main Street in 1917. The ladies are identified as Hattie Quick, Mary Cobb, Lizzie Waldron, Matie Monney, Maud DeCoudres, Maud Clements, Lou Wilbert, Emma Sherman, Libbie Richards, Addie Jones, Flo Anderson, Gertie Morton, Carrie Spinks, Claudia Everets, and Carrie Everets. Lillian Osmond was the captain.

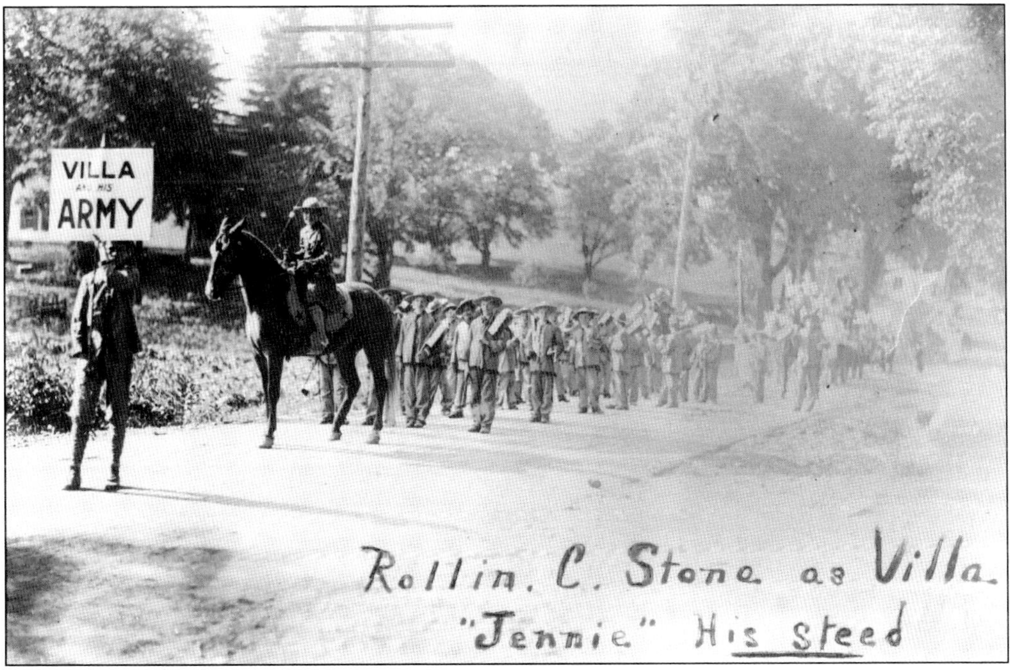

This photograph is of Rollin C. Stone as "Villa and his army." Stone is mounted on his steed Jennie.

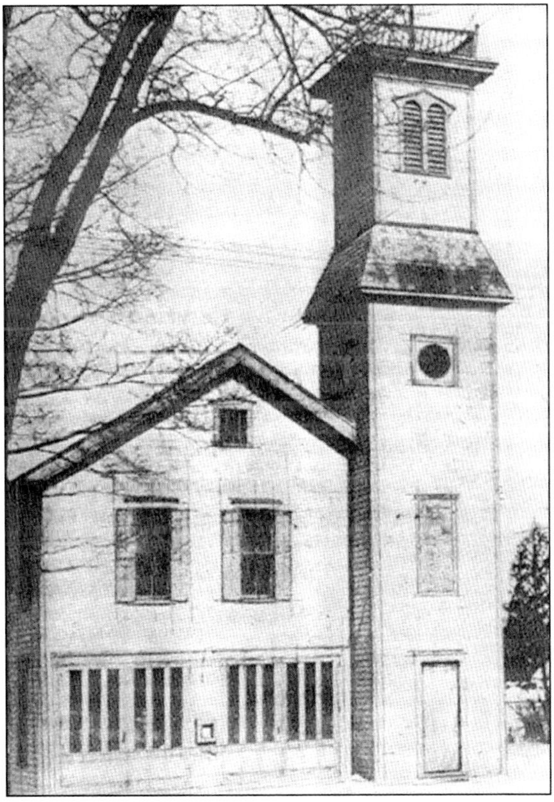

In the summer of 1884, the village voted to purchase firefighting equipment and the first volunteer fire company was organized. Four years later, the village voted to purchase land and erect an engine house. The old firehouse and village hall are pictured 1889.

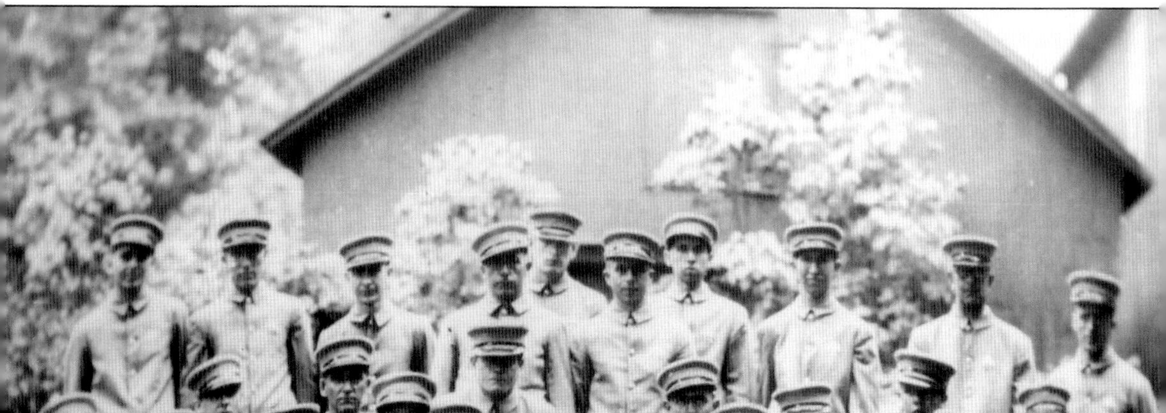

This photograph is of the Marcellus Union Fire Department. Members are identified as Thomas Sullivan, John Shay, Jack Alman, Mel Corp, Eddie LaRose, Paul Morgan, Eddie Williams, Clarence Wickman, Kenneth King, Giles Case, ? Corp, Steve Hunt, Joe Malcomb, Jake Snyder, Floyd Niggins, Ralph McManus, F. Bishop, Eddie Burke, George May, Richard May, Paul McAvoy, Clayton Pilot, Leonard Annable, Bill O'Hara, George Morgan, Earl Seymour, George Seymour, Bert Griffin, and Enrick Hackford.

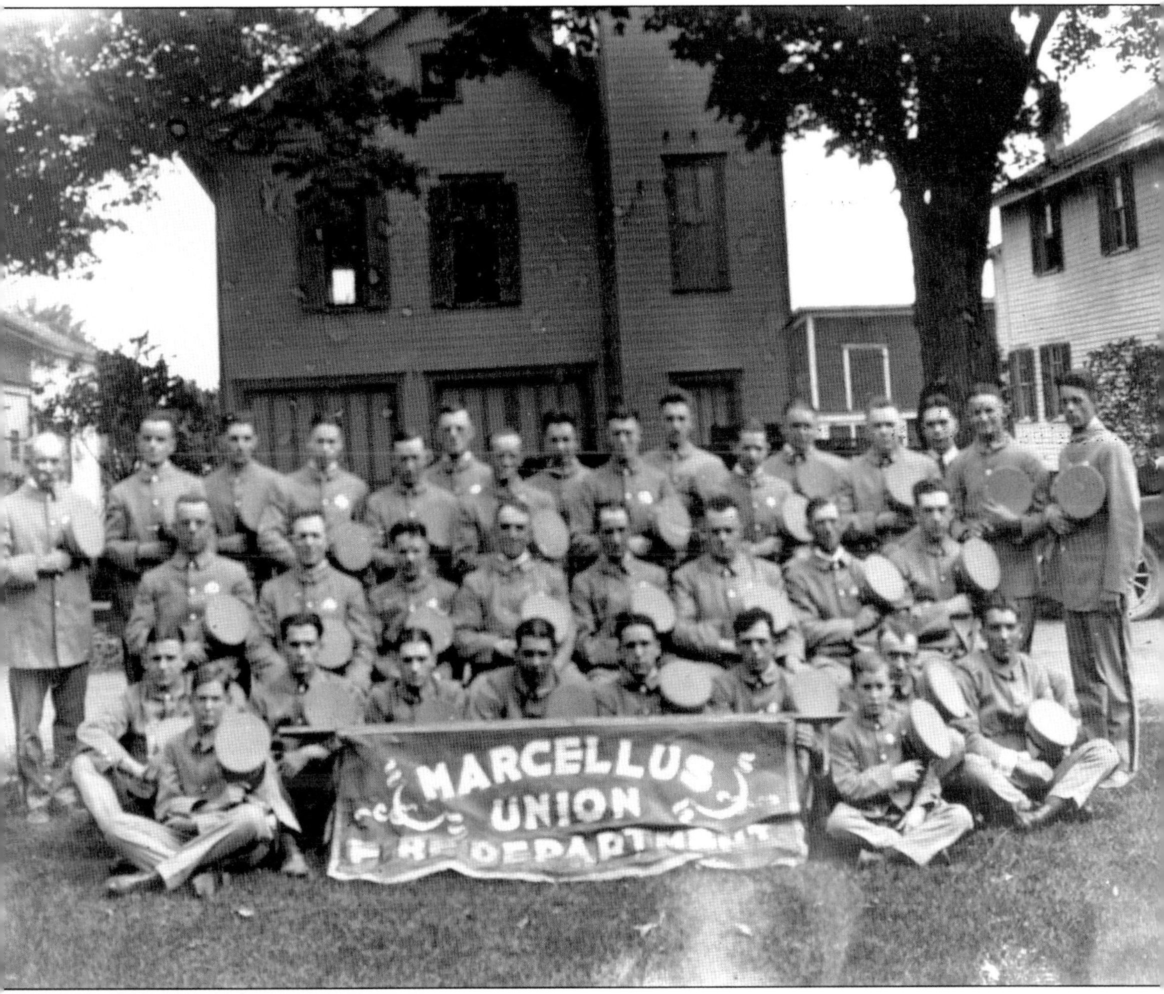

This is the Marcellus Union Fire Department in 1920. Seen here, from left to right, are (first row) banner boys Billie Rhodes and Mulvey Spaulding; (second row) Bill Rumsey, James Boone, Clem Armstrong, P. J. Kelly, Bert Spaulding, Jordan Hickman, Maurie Dunn, and Wilson Knapp; (third row) Giles Case, Victor Sheehan, Don Dillon, Jim Bishop, two unidentified, Harry Griffin, and Harold Powell; (fourth row) James Powell, Frank Anderson, Charles Wilson, Bryden Daye, Enrick Hackford, John Shay, Mert Wright, unidentified, Paul McAnay, Art Schanzle, John Armstrong, Horton Pilot, Fred Owens, Clayton Pilot, Art Wilson, and James Hogan Jr.

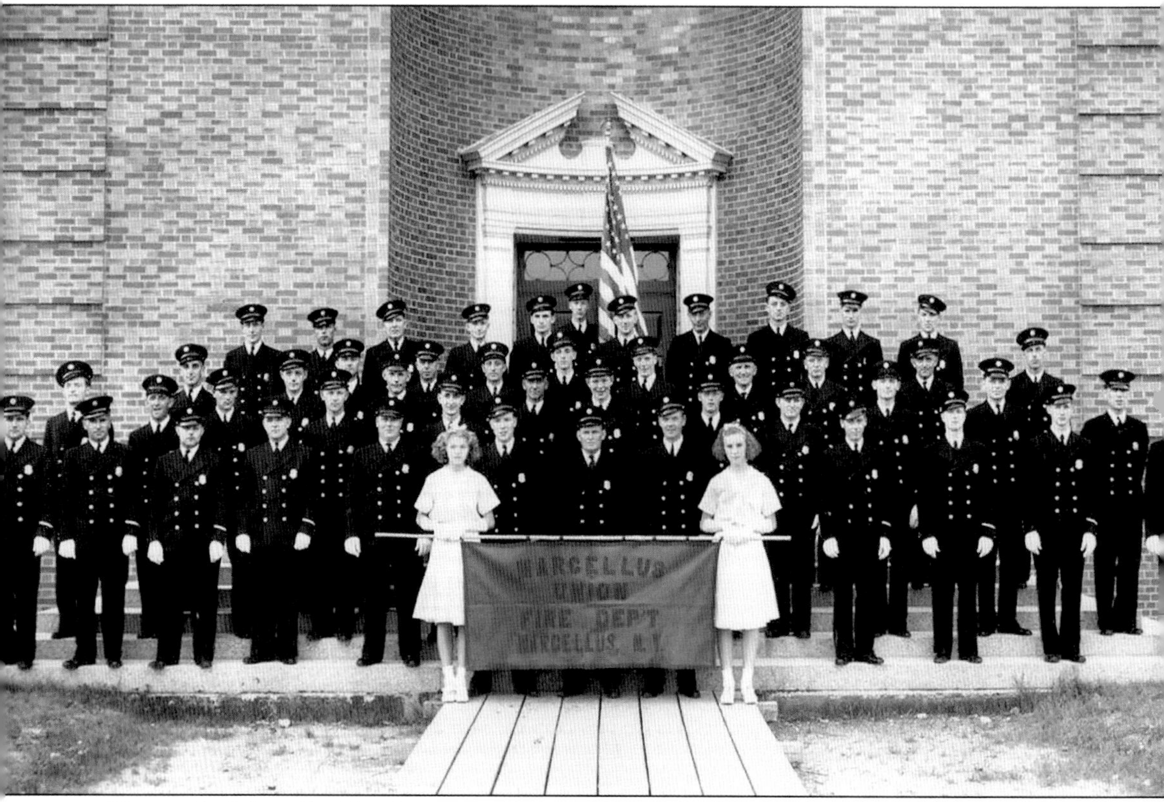

This is the Marcellus Fire Department in 1938 in their dress blues. The fire department was organized in 1884, and Dr. Henry Post was appointed chief of the fire department and Myron Whiting was appointed assistant chief.

Eight

Buggies and Cars, Trains and Trolleys

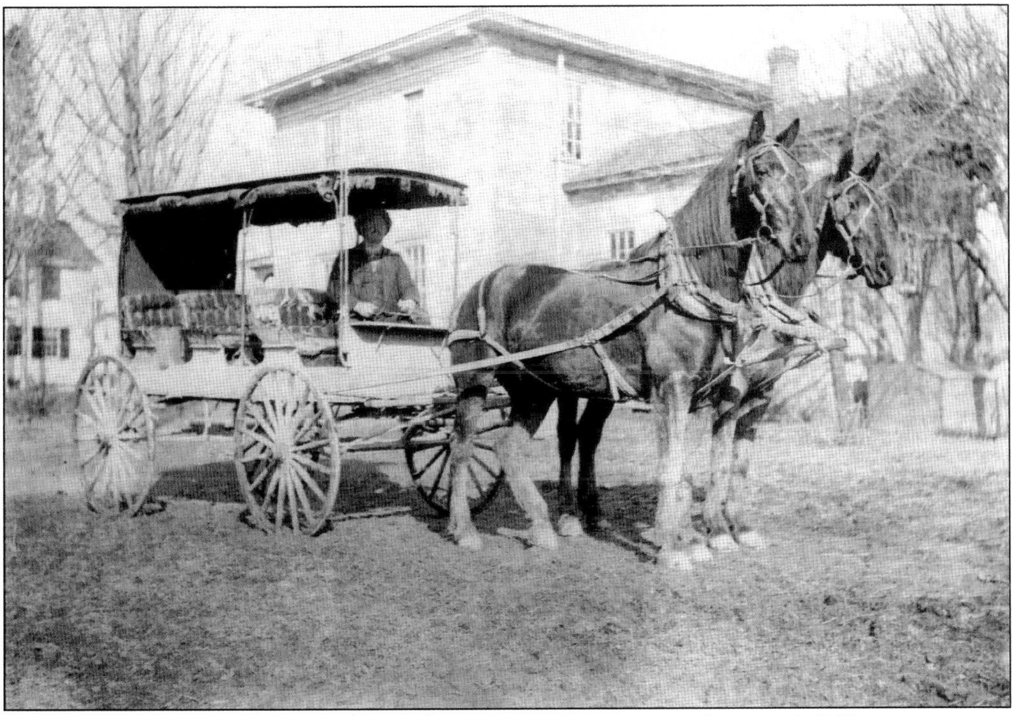

This photograph is of the Marcellus and Otisco summer stagecoach around 1888.

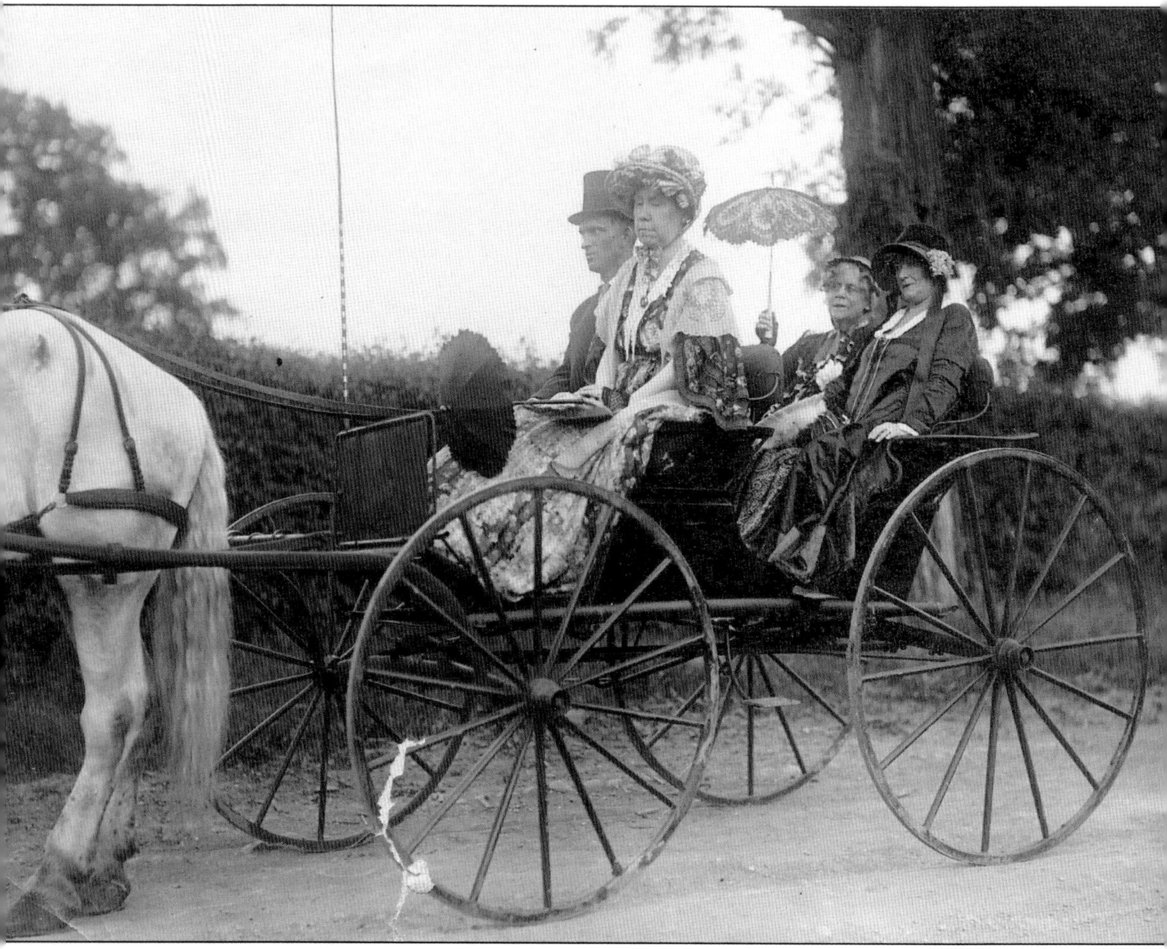

In this picture, the women are out for a carriage ride. They are Mrs. Fryer, Mrs. Merrill, and Mrs. Fellows. The driver is unidentified.

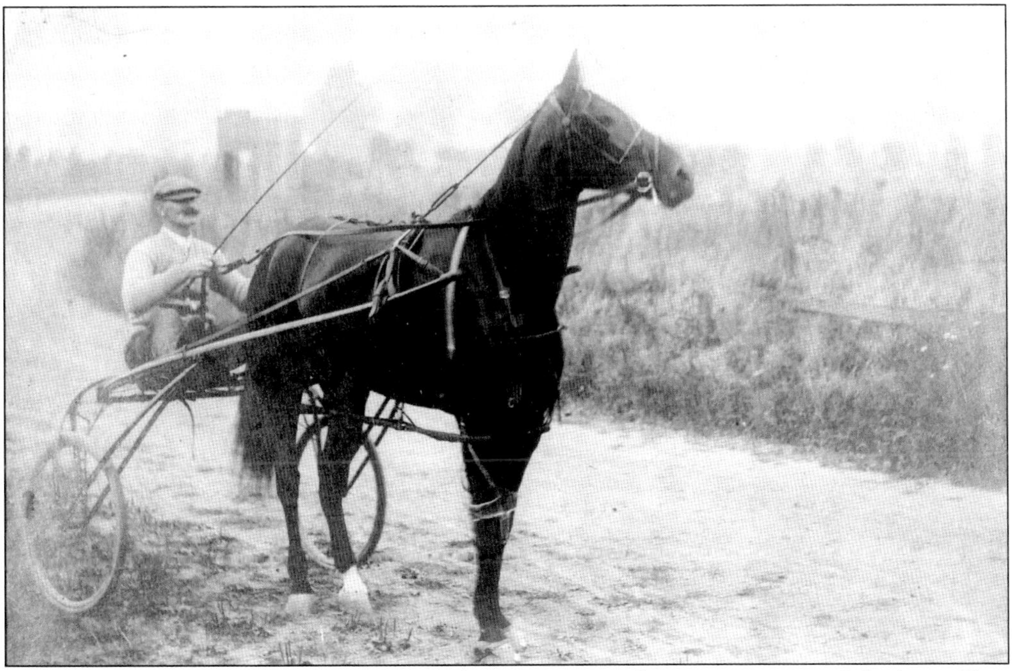

This is a picture of Fred Schoonmaker in his racing gig. There was a racetrack built on Slate Hill Road by Cheney Amidon. Many men of the early 1900s were excellent horsemen and many horsemen enjoyed "pulling the reins over the backs of the trotters." It was also open for bicycles.

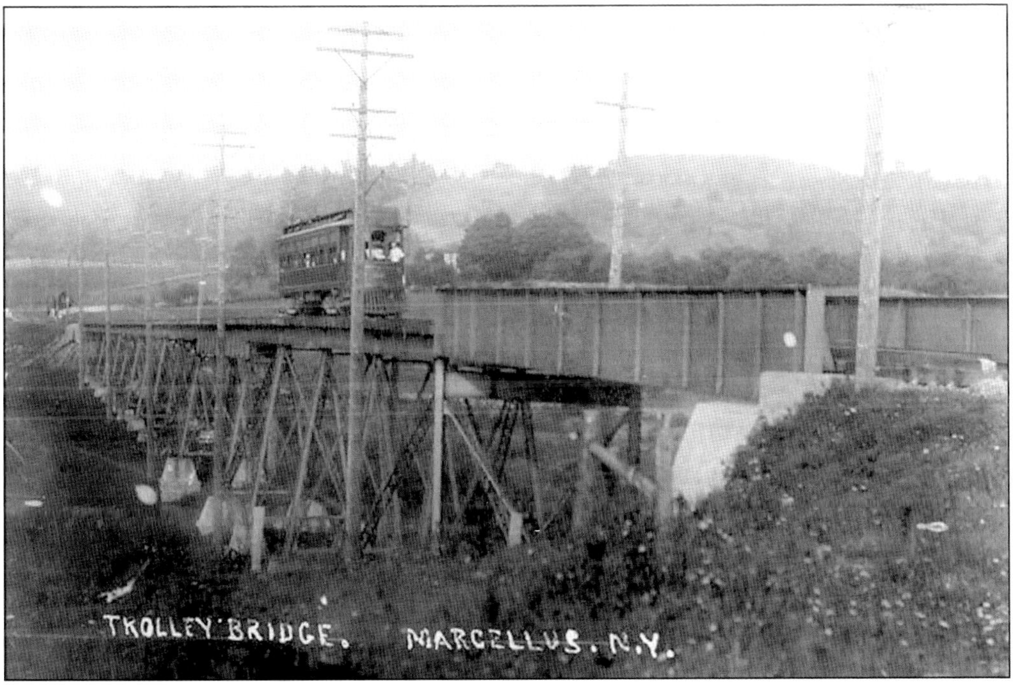

In 1904, the Auburn and Syracuse Electric Railway was constructed. The trolley line appearing in this 1909 photograph operated until April 15, 1930. The trolley bridge is now the site of Lee Mulroy Highway between Marcellus and Skaneateles.

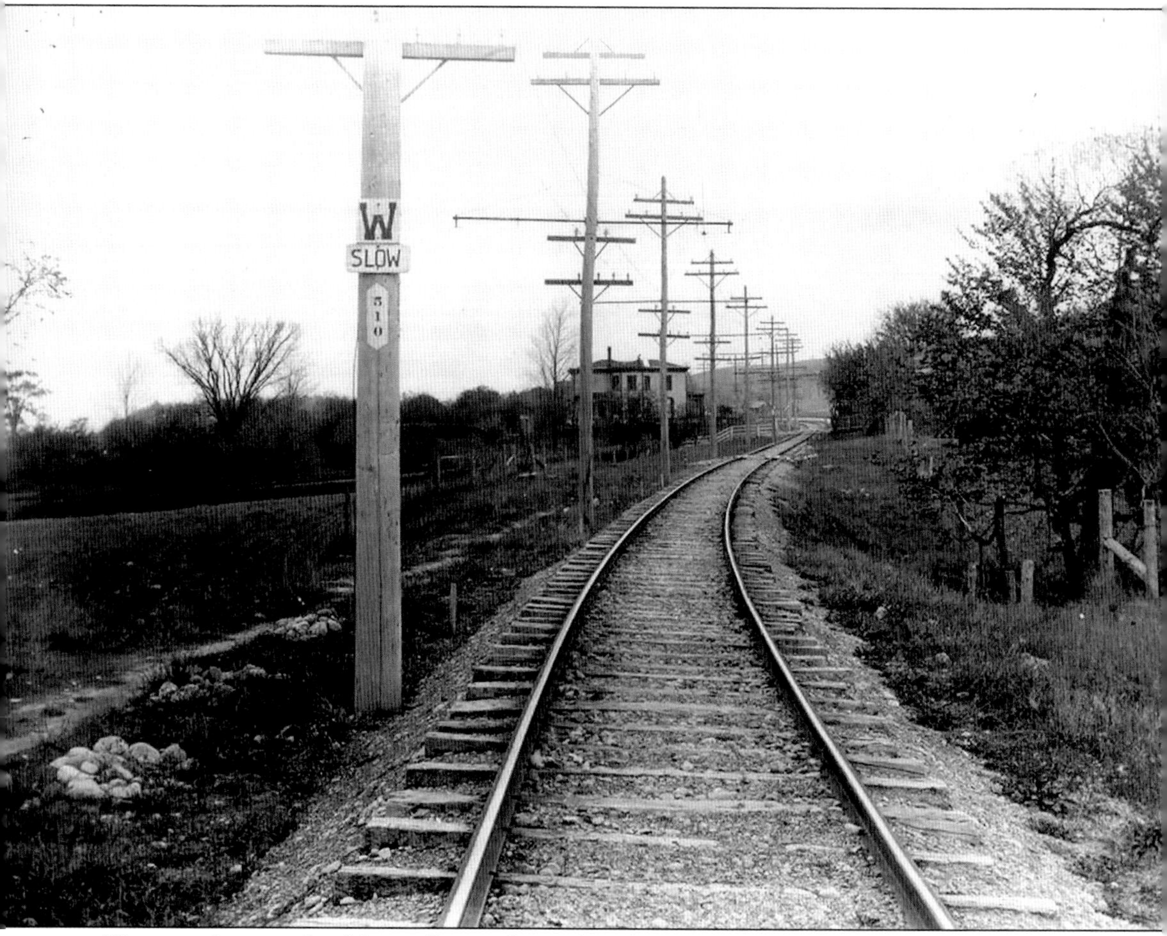

This is a photograph of the trolley tracks, and in the distance is the Sheehans' house.

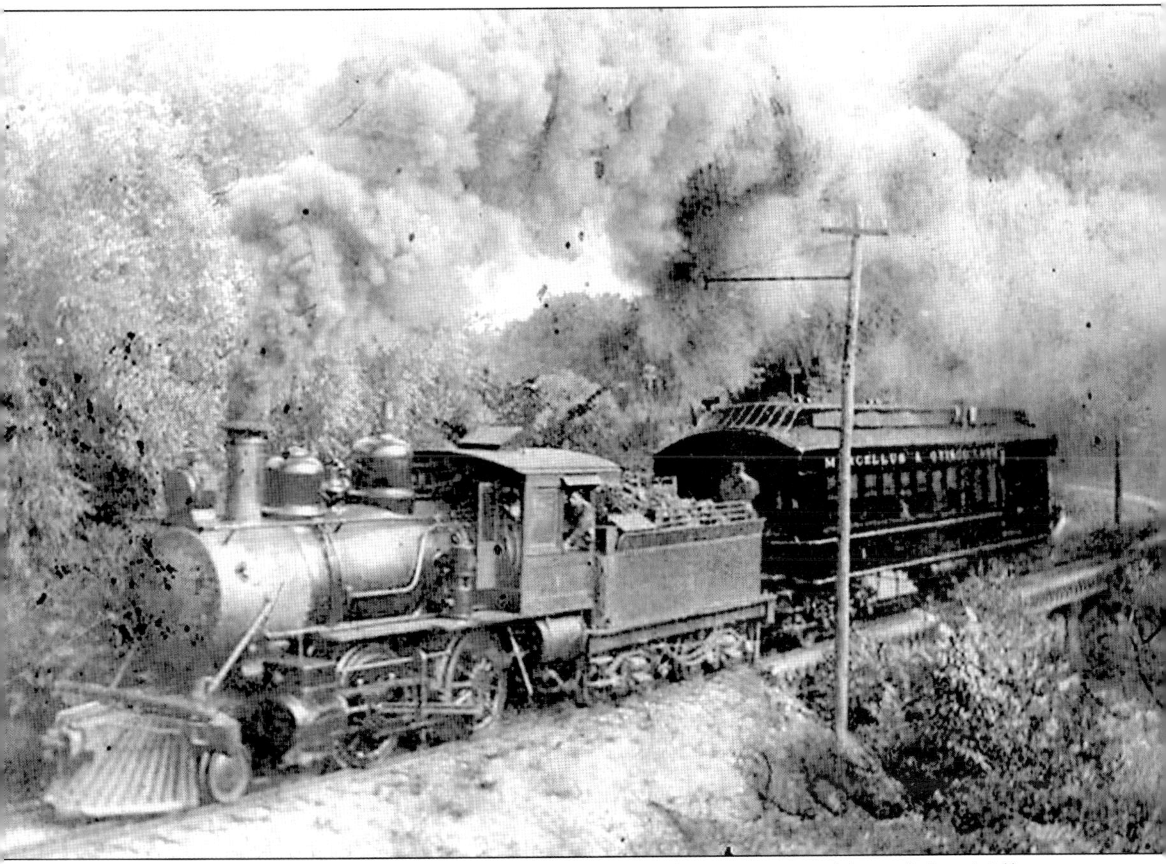

The Marcellus and Otisco Lake Railroad train is pictured in 1907, possibly with Jim Miller in the cab. The line ran from the Martisco Central Station all the way to Otisco Lake. The train made three round trips a day, and along with transporting passengers, the trains also carried the U.S. mail.

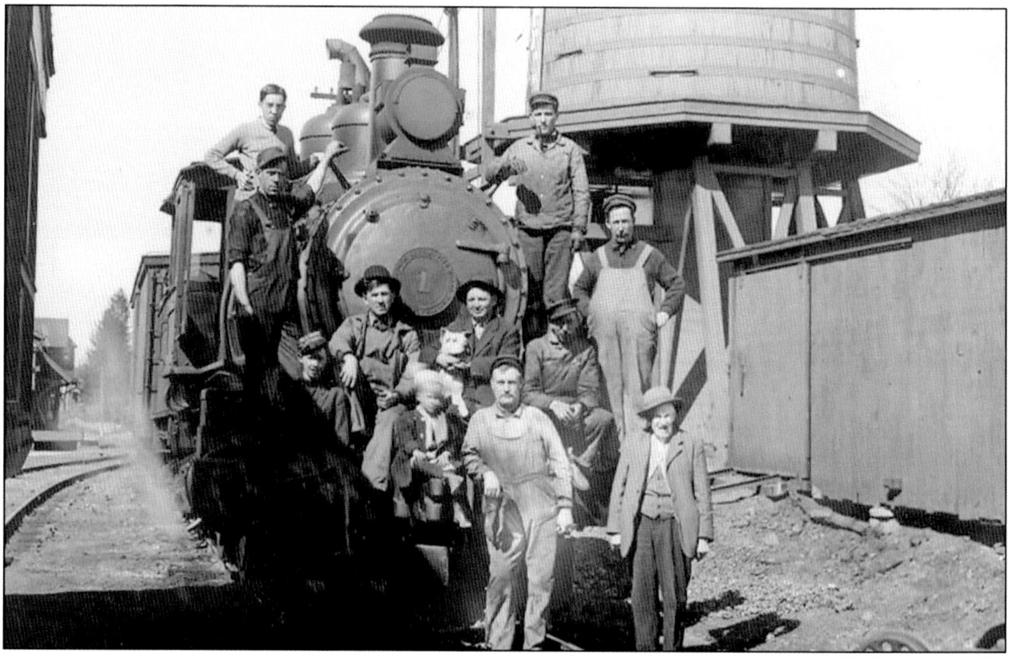

This photograph was taken in 1915 of the engine and workers of the Marcellus and Otisco Lake Railroad. This railroad began service as a passenger rail on July 1, 1905. The railroad's last run was on July 18, 1959.

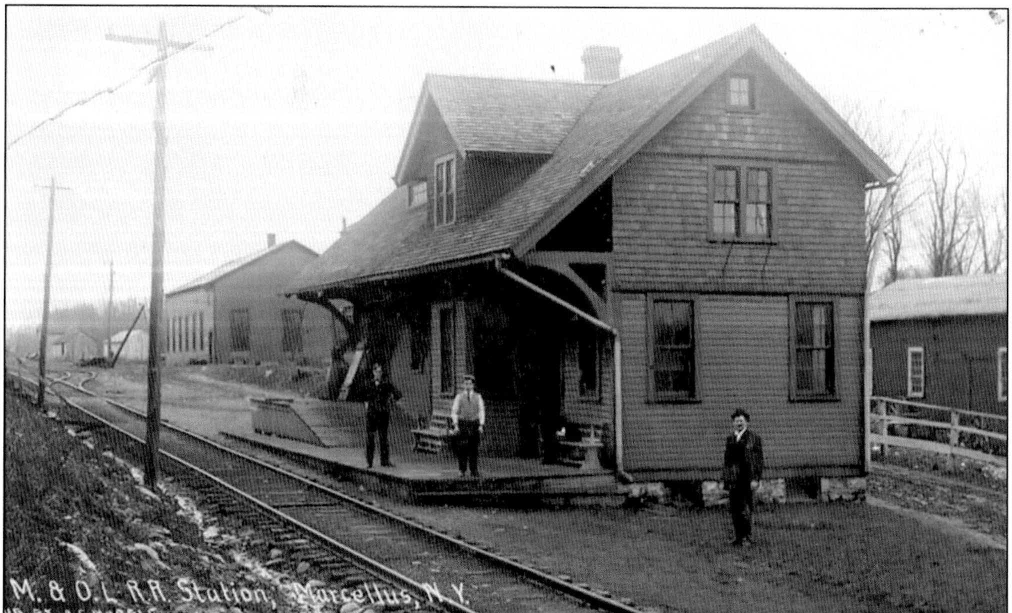

This train station was located on Station Lane, bordering Nine Mile Creek at the base of East Hill. It was part of the Marcellus and Otisco Lake Railroad system.

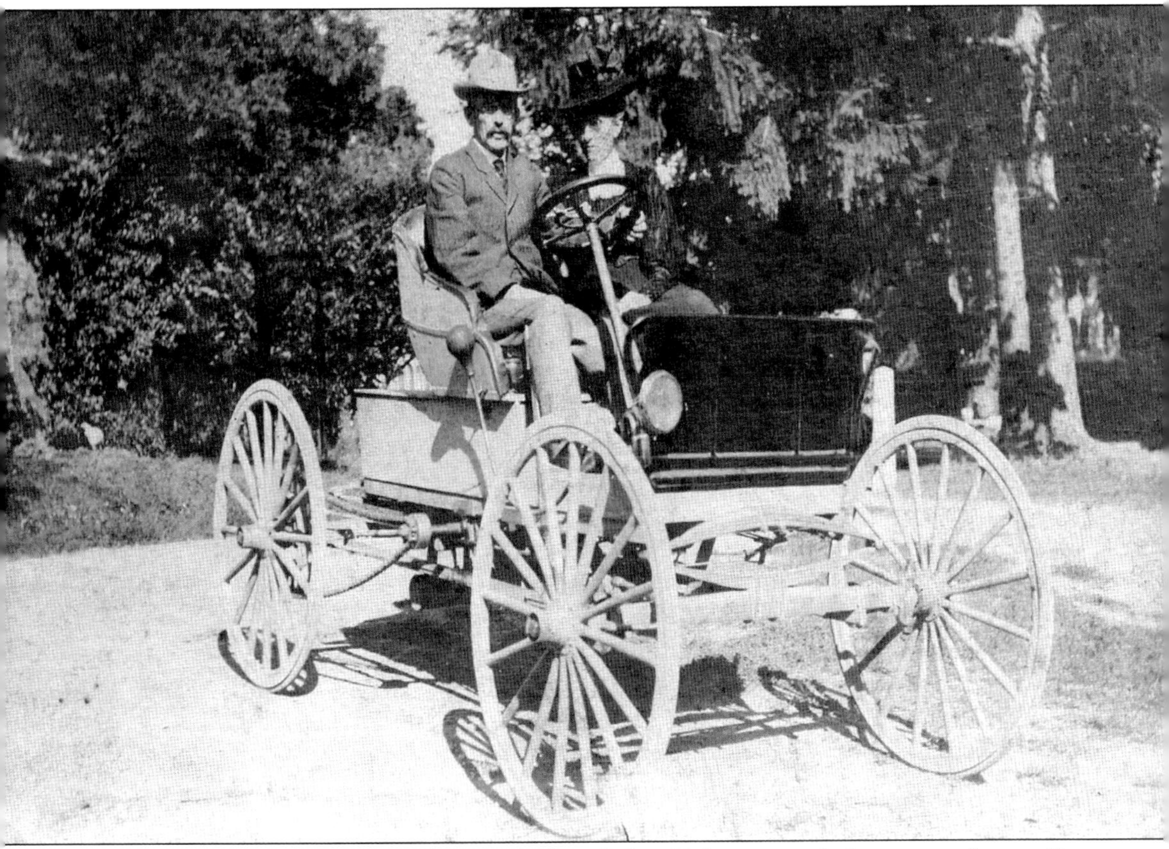

This photograph was taken of Robert and Clara Baker. Robert owned the grist and sawmill in Marcellus. His dam, which powered his mill, later furnished electrical power for the first telephone and the first electric lights in Marcellus. He was described as a man who could make anything. He built his own automobile, which he steered with a tiller, by installing a one cylinder motor in the front of a buggy. His invention, which would run but had little power, is now in the Hershey Museum in Pennsylvania. He also built a gasoline-powered two-seater, which ran on the railroad tracks and was used by the superintendent of the Marcellus and Otisco Lake Railroad to inspect the tracks.

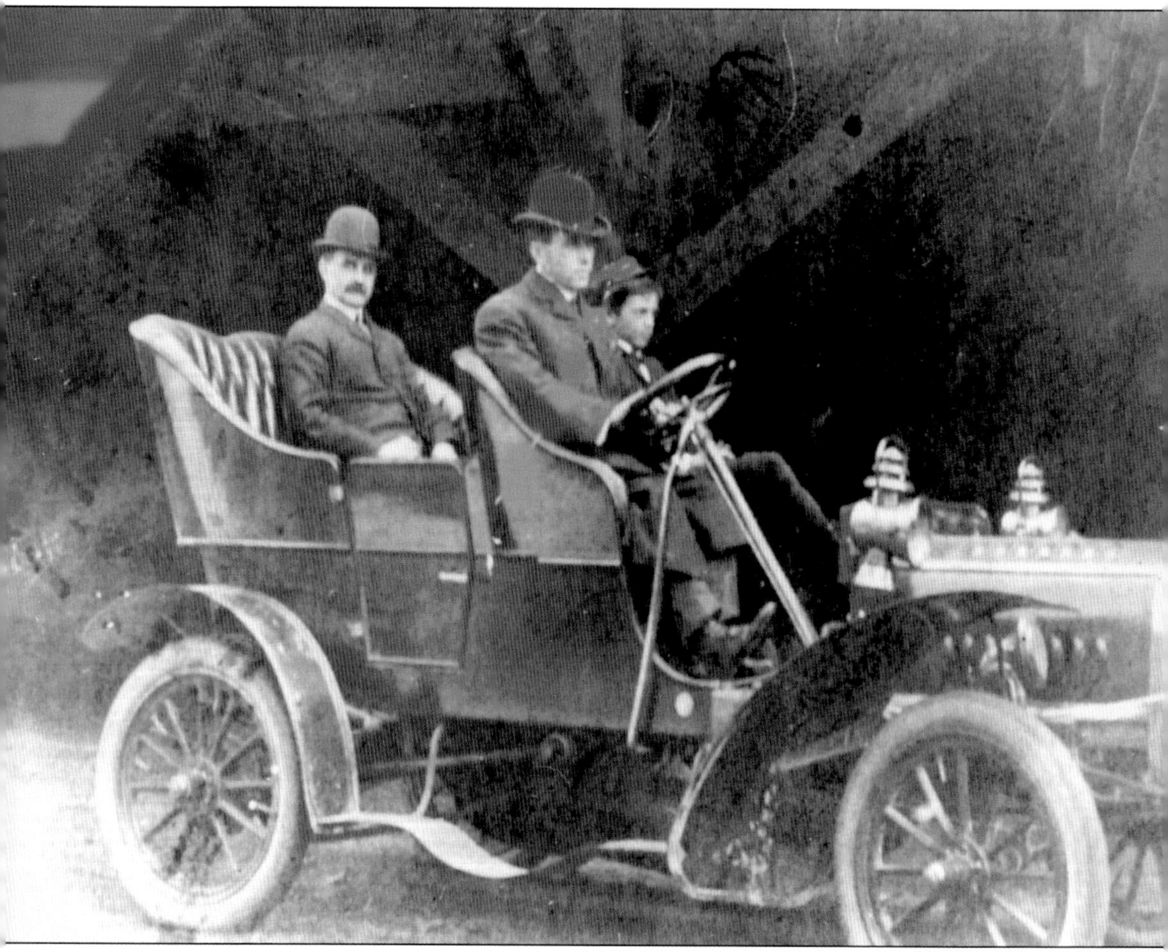

This was Edward Moir's car, driven by John Chapman with young Joseph Matteson by his side. Edward Moir is in the back seat. It is said to have been one of the first cars in Marcellus.

BIBLIOGRAPHY

Bruce, Dwight H. *Onondaga's Centennial.* Boston, MA: Boston History Co., 1896.
Clayton, W. W. *History of Marcellus, New York.* Syracuse, NY: D. Mason and Co., 1878.
Campbell, Wallace Hamilton. *Historic Marcellus and Vicinity.* Marcellus, NY: Finger Lakes Telephone Company, 1963.
Curtin, John P. *Pucker Street, the First 100 Years.* Victoria, Canada: Trafford Publishing, 2003.
Heffernan, Kathryn C. *Nine Mile Country.* Visual Artis Publications, Inc, 1979.
http://home.earthlink.net/%7Eggghostie/nathan.html
http://mhs.marcellusny.com/MHS_Home/Street_Names.html
http://www.njcu.edu/Programs/jchistory/Pages/S_Pages/Smith_Erminnie.htm
http://www.rootsweb.com/%7Enyononda/WAR/marcellusveterans.html
http://www.sonrisecenter.org/m_dan.html